The Moving Universe

A Spiritual and Mundane
Perspective on the Transits

The Moving Universe

A Spiritual and Mundane
Perspective on the Transits

Joseph Polansky

Winchester, UK
Washington, USA

First published by Dodona Books, 2016
Dodona Books is an imprint of John Hunt Publishing Ltd., Laurel House, Station Approach,
Alresford, Hants, SO24 9JH, UK
office1@o-books.net
www.o-books.com

For distributor details and how to order please visit the 'Ordering' section on our website.

Text copyright: Joseph Polansky 2011

ISBN: 978 1 78099 195 5
978 1 78099 196 2 (ebook)
Library of Congress Control Number: 2016949859

A CIP catalogue record for this book is available from the British Library.

Design: Stuart Davies

Printed in the USA by Edwards Brothers Malloy

We operate a distinctive and ethical publishing philosophy in all
areas of our business, from our global network of authors to
production and worldwide distribution.

CONTENTS

Preface

This book is designed for the student of astrology. The author presumes that the reader can cast a Natal Horoscope - either personally or by computer and can calculate transits. This work will help in interpreting the transits. Every possible transit is given here. The interpretations are valid as written but will also spark the intuition to show other nuances in interpretation.

There are many fine books on the transits. Robert Hands's work[1] immediately comes to mind. But here we are giving two levels of interpretation - the mundane and the spiritual perspective. This I have never seen in print. The mundane (worldly) interpretation shows what is likely happening in the outer life. The spiritual perspective gives the interior lessons and challenges that the transits are bringing. Understanding these issues gives the student a deeper perspective on what's going on in the client's (or personal) life.

Many students of astrology are on a spiritual path, and understanding the spiritual perspective will help them on their path.

Since the internal is always causative to the external, ignoring the spiritual dimension is a serious handicap which the author wishes to rectify in this work.

These interpretations are valid as written. But transits tend to be complicated by the fact that we are often subjected to "multiple transits" at the same time. And sometimes, one transit is contradicting another. For example Jupiter might be making a beautiful transit to Venus - a positive for the love life. But at the same time, Uranus or Saturn might be afflicting Venus - a negative for the love life. Here is where the intuition of the student must come into play. Which transit is stronger? Which transit shows a trend, which shows only a "bump on the road"? Are there more transits supporting the love life than afflicting it? All these factors must be taken into account. And, by their nature are beyond the scope of this work. One must be looking at the actual Horoscope to deal with these issues.

There are hosts of aspects that a transiting planet can make, but here we are dealing with the major aspects - the Conjunction (the planets more or less occupy the same space), Opposition (the planets are opposite each other), Square (the planets are 90 degrees apart), Trine (the planets are 120 degrees apart) and Sextile (the planets are 60 degrees apart). This is enough to keep us busy for a long time. These are the most powerful and important aspects. Eventually it is good for the student to study the minor aspects - the [2]Sesquisquare (the square and a half - 135 degrees apart), the Quincunx (150 degrees apart), the Semisextile (30 degrees apart) and the Semisquare (45 degrees apart). These aspects are like condiments in a meal - they add flavor and nuance, but are not the meal itself. The meat and potatoes are the major aspects.

The interpretation given here are valid for both the Natal chart and for the Solar Return of a given year. This gives the work more usefulness. Once you've learned the meaning of the transits in your birth chart (or client's birth chart) you can still use them year after year - when you study your Solar Return. Our readers surely know that we get a new Solar Return every year.

There is another dimension to transits which must be understood. Every planet has its universal rulership - its generic meaning - and these are being used in this book. But the serious student needs to keep in mind that every planet has "subsidiary" meanings depending on the Houses that it rules in the actual Horoscope. For example, Venus in her universal rulership rules love, partnerships and the social life in general. However, in a given Horoscope she can rule the 3rd House of communication. Thus she can behave like Mercury in that given Horoscope. Her transits would affect the mentality as well as the love life. If this is the case, read the Venus transit and also read the Mercury transit. This will give a deeper insight to the transit.

I was contemplating including the consideration of each planet as a "Lord of a House". It soon became apparent that the book would have tripled or quadrupled in length. It seemed more appropriate to do this in a companion volume. This will come out in the future.

Joseph Polansky

THE MOVING UNIVERSE

In observing life, I have found that it is the simple, the natural, things that are always the most powerful. Humans will celebrate a Michaelangelo or Picasso (and they rightly deserve celebration) yet, with all their artistry they cannot create anything as beautiful as the natural flower, or tree, or humdrum, everyday bird that camps out in our backyard. With all the awesome technological might of humans, they cannot create a living, breathing child - the ultimate in creativity. With all their technological prowess they cannot duplicate the nerve impulses of even the humble fly. They are getting better at their creations, but always it is a "copy cat" kind of process. The most gifted writer can write reams of poetic words about a tree, but never will his verbiage equal the actual tree.

We have all seen the most beautiful photographs and paintings of sunsets. Yet great though they are, they never equal the power and majesty of an actual sunset.

Science is a wonderful thing. It has improved life for millions. Yet, the most unlearned person - who never studied chemistry - will initiate in himself and his partner complex, advanced chemical trans-formations that will result in a fetus and then a living child.

Yes, science is wonderful, but we need to get back to basics. We need to look at the miracle of the everyday in another way - at the basic natural things - day and night, winter and summer, the changes of the seasons, the new and the full moon. Traditionally this has been the province of the poet and the mystic. But it is also indispensable for the Astrologer. The good Astrologer needs to be little bit of a poet.

We live in a moving universe. This is indisputable. Never does it stop for even a second. Every 4 minutes the Earth turns 1 degree on its axis. Not only is the Earth spinning on its axis - which is the cause of the daily cycle of sunrise, noon, sunset and midnight - but it is also moving around the Sun, one degree per day (approx). The Sun in turn is orbiting around a galactic center. And the galaxy is orbiting around a Universal Center. We are on a "cruise through space" as many have pointed out. We are spiraling through space. Yet, because we don't feel these movements on a "sensual" basis, we tend to ignore them.

But there are even more movements going on. As we are spiraling through space (we are never in the same segment of space from one moment to the next) the planets of our Solar System are also moving. The Moon will orbit the Earth every 28 days or so. All the other planets are constantly changing their relationship to the Earth as they make their orbit around the Sun. We are traveling through space, but we are not alone, we have an entourage of planetary companions.

All of this is actually happening, whether you are a believer or non-believer. It is happening while you are at your computer, or driving your car, or cooking dinner or at the nightclub. Ceaseless and eternal.

And these movements - this moving universe - is the basis of the science of Astrology.

Astronomers also study the movements of the universe. An astronomer can also tell you when the New and Full Moons will occur and in what signs they will occur. They can tell you the position of any planet at any given time. They can tell you the physical compositions of the planets and many interesting "outer details" - their size, shape and volume. All of this is good, but this is not Astrology and is of almost little concern to an Astrologer.

For the Astrologer, the important thing is "meaning" - this is basically what separates us from astronomers. The Astronomer can tell you the planet's position, but the Astrologer wants to know "what does this mean to me - to my client - to the world - that Mars is at 15 degrees of Sagittarius, or that the Moon is in Pisces today".

Both the Astronomer and the Astrologer will tell you when an eclipse will occur - and where. But the Astronomer leaves it at that. It will occur on such and such a date and such and such a time, and that's the end. The good Astrologer will not leave it at that. He or she will look for the meaning behind this given eclipse - for its impact on both the personal and collective level. Eclipses are powerful events for the world - especially when seen through an Astrologer's eyes.

A good definition of Astrology would be - the study of the movements of the universe and their impact on the earth.

THE STUDY OF TRANSITS

The word transits is just an astrological term to describe what we have been talking about - the moving universe. A planet in motion is called a transit.

A Natal chart (Natal means birth) is like a photograph of a moving universe at a given time and place. It is as if we photographed runners during a marathon. We catch them at a certain time - but they keep moving. So it is with the universe and the planets in our solar system.

The birth chart (and here is where the analogy with runners breaks down) is more than just photographing runners at random. It has a special significance. For anything born on the Earth partakes of - is an actual incarnation of - the total cosmic atmosphere of that time. Something is born, it will grow and develop according to its nature. It will have a certain destiny, mission and purpose.

"The Heavens declare the Glory of God and the firmament shows forth the work that his hands are doing". Psalm 19

In the heavens we read what the Divine is about to create on the Earth - and those who are born are part and parcel of this new creation and this new "declaration of glory".

So, a person has his own birth chart - uniquely his own. Like his fingerprints. So far (I'm practicing over 30 years) I haven't seen two identical charts. I've seen charts that were very similar (cases of identical twins born only minutes apart) - but never identical. Who knows perhaps I will come across it. This chart shows the person's internal nature - the character, talents, abilities, urges and desires.

But the transits (the planetary movements that have never stopped moving) are showing how the universe is impacting on him or her at a given time. Sometimes these movements are helpful, sometimes obstructive, most of the time, it is a mixture - some planets are helping, some are obstructing. Some are helping in a given area of life, but are obstructing in another area of life. Thus a person may be having a banner career year, but a stressful love life (or vice versa). Sometimes love and career are good, but health issues are stressful. Many, many scenarios are always occurring

Understanding the different impacts that the transits (the ever moving universe) has on our lives, is at the heart of the study of transits.

THE MULTI-DIMENSIONALITY OF TRANSITS

Transits are read on many levels. The first level of interpretation (and this is what we read in most of the literature on transits) involves the universal or generic rulerships of the planets. Every planet has its natural rulership. The Sun rules children, creativity, life force, love affairs, and the joy of life. The Moon, generically, rules our moods, emotional life, home and family situation. Mercury rules the mind, communication and intellectual faculties and interests. Venus rules the love life and is a factor in finances too. Mars rules sex (along with Pluto), independence, physical strength, the use of force (which is sometimes necessary) to either solve disputes or gain ones ends. Jupiter rules expansion and abundance - also philosophy, religion and metaphysics. Saturn rules limits, discipline and order. Uranus rules changes, the breaking of barriers, the new, a person's originality and innovativeness. Neptune rules a person's highest spiritual ideals, the urge to transcend, to unite with the Divine. Pluto rules a person's urge to transform him or herself and others, also sex, birth and death and occult interests.

Reading on this level is very useful and accurate. But in a given chart, it might leave out many nuances. For example, Venus, which generically rules love and marriage - the urge to beauty and harmony - might be the Ruler of the 8th House of sex. Thus a transit of Venus (or to that particular person's Venus) will impact on the sex life, sexual expression as well as love.

This level of reading is beyond our scope in this work. But it is important to understand it when reading your own or another person's horoscope.

In a given chart, the planets never lose their "generic" nature, but take on many different roles. The depths of a Horoscope have never been completely plumbed - nor will they ever be. Since every person is in essence infinite, so is the Horoscope.

Planets can not only take on different roles in life - in a given Horoscope - but can also represent specific people in the life - a mother, mother in law, spouse, sibling, grandchild etc. Every person who is in your life is in your Horoscope, and is represented by a certain planet. Thus if we know which planet represents who - it will give us still another level of transit interpretation. This too is beyond our scope here, but is important for understanding.

ALL ASTROLOGY IS SPIRITUAL

In our compartmentalized society it is common to create boundaries where none really exist. Thus in the astrological world, we talk of mundane astrology (how astrology affects our worldly life and affairs), medical astrology, esoteric or spiritual astrology, electional astrology ad infinitum.

But these definitions are arbitrary. They have some practical use of course, but the truth is that all astrology is essentially spiritual astrology - esoteric astrology.

Since the planets exert a "metaphysical"[3] influence in the world and are really spiritual forces interacting with each other and with the world - all of astrology is basically the study of these spiritual forces. Even if we are reading the most mundane "materialistic" area - such as a person's finances or sex life - we are only looking at how "spiritual" forces are impacting in these mundane areas. Whatever happens in these mundane areas - all the physical phenomena - are only side effects of these spiritual forces.

Since the Divine is always bringing about good - though it is difficult for humans to see this sometimes - when we view the transits from a spiritual perspective, they are never negative. Some are more pleasant than others, but each is bringing some spiritual lesson for the native. This is why it is good to read the "spiritual perspective" on the transits as well as the mundane perspective.

Astrology is under attack from two basic fronts. One is the secular scientific community, the other is the religious (and parts of the spiritual community). The one, the scientific community, cannot grasp how the planetary energies work. For, basically they are dealing with a strictly mechanical, material universe. They have the same problems with spirituality, religion and metaphysics that they have with Astrology. An atheistic scientist with a secular world view will never grasp astrology - and many other things as well. Energies that are not registered by the 5 senses (and the extension of the 5 senses that one gets from mechanical instruments) simply don't exist for them. But, as science develops better instrumentation - and it is happening - these issues will be settled in a scientific way. The truths of astrology, or religion and spirituality, will become clearly demonstrable - and we are getting closer to this every day.

The attacks from the religious community also stem from basic misconceptions. There is one form of attack, usually from the fundamentalist sector (of any religion) that rejects astrology outright as the "work of the devil". But if astrology is simply natural law - the way the universe was created by the Great Creator - this attack falls under deeper analysis. Astrology could no more be the work of the Devil, than electricity, chemistry, or physics. It is part of the creation. In essence Divine.

Now it is true that if these things are abused, they can become the "work of the Devil" - no question about it - but in essence they are pure. It is pretty commonplace to see the Holy Laws of

Mathematics used to cheat, defraud and cause harm to people - all we need to do is look at the recent spate of corporate scandals that occurred from 2001 to 2005. The Holy Laws of Electricity are often abused - used by thieves and murderers to achieve some dastardly aim. Cell Phones are used by terrorists to make bombs. Religion, which in essence is something very beautiful has also been abused. And when this happens there is great harm done. But is it the mathematics, the electricity, the cell phone, the religion that is at fault - or man's misuse of these things?

There is a more serious attack that comes from the spiritual community. This needs to be taken more seriously as there is something to what they say. Some of these people are spiritual giants - masters of the invisible forces - and we cannot simply ignore them.

Here is their position as I understand it. A person's focus needs to be totally on the Divine - one pointed, unobstructed. Anything that distracts a person from this focus is evil - not because it is innately evil - but because it distracts the person from the goal. Thus a focus on the Horoscope is just another distraction from essence and should be avoided by spiritual aspirants.

Now **this** is a powerful argument. It should be taken to heart by every spiritual aspirant.

But it seems to me, that this argument was valid only because of the way that astrology was presented in the Western world, for the past few hundred years - since the age of the enlightenment.

The attack is not on Astrology per se, but on the way that Astrology was practiced and presented to the people. And we, the astrologers of the West bear the blame for this[4]. Astrology was taught and practiced as a form of "secular science" - like mathematics or astronomy. The Divine was not in the picture at all. It had nothing to do with spirit. If this planet does this, X happens. If another planet does Y, Z will happen. The whole heart, soul and essence of what astrology is, was lost.

Yes, this kind of astrology will certainly distract a person from essence. It is much like studying mathematics so that one can outsmart or cheat another. Or, like studying physics so that one can make a more powerful gun or bomb with which to destroy one's enemies. This is not what mathematics or physics is about - in a sense it is an abuse of these things.

And so it is with Astrology.

But if we understand (as the Hindus do) that the planetary powers, the zodiacal forces are not independent or arbitrary powers, but "executors and agents" of a Higher Power, subject totally to this Higher Power, never acting on their own, but only "announcing and bringing to pass what this Higher Power is doing" we will have another perspective on things. Such an approach is not a distraction from essence, but takes us deeper and deeper into essence.

As we study the planetary movements we are studying the "movements of the Divine" - of the Mind of God. We are seeing what this Mind wants to bring forth on both a personal level and on a collective world level.

This approach to Astrology is more than just "not a distraction". It seems to me that it is essential - a must study - for anyone on the spiritual path. For, it answers questions that no other study answers. Why was this prayer answered instantly and the other only after 5 years? Why was yesterday's meditation so powerful and uplifting, and today it feels "blah"? Why am I having trouble getting into my meditation today? Yesterday the Presence of God was so strong and today it has left - why? Has God forsaken me? Have I sinned? Last month my ESP and intuition was right on target - this month it is awry - why? Why are my moods the way they are? What makes them shift from hour to hour and day to day? Why are there so many religions in the world? So many spiritual paths? Why do I gravitate to one path, while my best friend prefers another? Why are people the way they are? Why do Libras have tantrums if someone is not color co-ordinated? Why are Virgos so distressed if something is not perfect? Why does so and so analyze love so much? Why is Miss X so reckless in love and Miss Y so cautious?

Anyone with a true and authentic inner life will soon be led to the truths of Astrology - to the understanding of the Astrological influences always at work. It is inevitable.

THE SUBTLE BODIES

Though modern science doesn't yet acknowledge their existence (to their pain and the pain of the multitudes), humans have more bodies than just the physical one.

This is an accepted fact - universally acknowledged - in esoteric circles. I have read different descriptions of them, and some are called by different names - but in essence everyone agrees that we have many bodies - many modes of expression.

We are more than what is "beneath our hats" as Whitman says.

Understanding the subtle bodies is very important in spiritual healing. Diseases wind up in the physical body, but never begin there. Their origin is always in one of the subtle bodies - either the mental, upper mental, astral or etheric bodies. (There are more bodies than the one's mentioned, but since these are immune to any pathology, they are not mentioned here.)

A disease that is diagnosed in the physical body - even though it seems to have been just recently - actually has a long, long history on the other dimensions of existence. This history can even date back thousands and even millions of years.

The pathologies of mental or upper mental are mainly involved with "error" - erroneous thoughts, or erroneous beliefs or philosophies. These not only cause errors in judgement, bad decisions and the resultant pain, loss and suffering that come from this, but if held long enough, will actually manifest in the physical body as some form of disease.

Pathologies of the astral body tend to come from emotional traumas. These are wounds in this body, often only partially healed - and sometimes still open and bleeding.

Pathologies of the Etheric body have to do with blockages of energy - electronic energy. This is the body where the arts of acupuncture, reflexology, homeopathy, polarity healing (and hosts of other therapies too numerous to mention) are applied. Energy is either blocked or unbalanced. These are energetic pathologies.

There is another pathology of the mental bodies - a form of malnutrition. We experience this as a "gap of knowledge" - something is missing in our knowledge and understanding and this "gap" causes a subtle form of mental distress and unease. In my experience, no one is immune from this. Everyone has it in some form or another - some more than others. The only solution to this is "full and complete knowledge" - which is the destiny of every human being. No matter how long it takes, it will eventually happen for the species. Humans were intended to arrive at "omniscience" eventually.

So, Astrology, by giving us the answers to so many questions, is a healing for the mental bodies. It fills the gaps in our knowledge.

Oh, it still might be uncomfortable to deal with the rashness of your Aries friend or the sensitivities of your Pisces spouse - but at least we can understand why they are the way they are. Our mental bodies are not impacted. We can smile and be philosophical. It is just "natural behavior" and will soon pass. When our phone calls don't go through on a Mercury Retrograde, or the bank makes an error in our statement - we can smile. When Saturn is making a stressful transit - we don't need to feel that we are sinners and being punished by Divinity - we know that there is some other agenda at work. It is difficult, yes, but we can smile. At least the mental trauma is gone.

When there is understanding - which is really the main gift of Astrology - even more important than its "practical" applications - even emotional traumas are easier to heal. I have found, on a personal level, that forgiveness was very difficult when I didn't understand the reasons for the other person's behavior. Through spiritual practice one can sort of "force" forgiveness - but it's a struggle. But once the cause of the hurtful behavior was understood - once understanding dawned on me - forgiveness came very easily.

Almost automatically.

Astrology supplies the understanding, and thus forgiveness comes that much easier.

TRANSITS OF THE SUN

The Sun is the source of light and life in our solar system. It is the focus - the lens - through which a Higher Power - lights and powers our world - our solar system - our Earth. His nature is to shine - to give light and life.

Thus when the Sun makes a transit over any planet, that planet is going to get stronger - more alive. Its innate nature is going to blossom - much in the way that a plant blossoms when exposed to the Sun. The emotional energy of the Moon becomes more emotional, more sensitive when the Sun contacts it by transit. The intellectual prowess of Mercury also get sharpened and more illuminated. Any planet contacted by the Sun becomes more of itself. The planet in question becomes like a star - it shines. There will be more light and life in any of the affairs governed by the planet. But the experience will be brief.

The Sun, while not the actual creator of the solar system in absolute terms - is the creator in a relative way. He is the delegate of an even Higher Power in the creative process. He does the actual physical work of creation, based on a plan that comes from above. Thus, there will be more creativity in any planet - and the affairs that it governs - when the Sun comes in contact with it.

The Sun is considered a "joy bringer" - light tends to banish sadness, fear and depression. Thus a solar contact with any planet will tend to bring joy - happiness - to the affairs governed by the planet. (The urge to joy will be there, but whether it gets expressed properly or not depends on whether this aspect is being reinforced or denied - but all things being equal, it will tend to bring joy.)

From a spiritual perspective, the solar transit can be likened to a contact with the Christos[5] power - which is what the Sun represents on a spiritual level. This power is going to heal anything it contacts - going to make it right. Even if we touch the "hem of its garment" we are healed. But, if there are things in the planetary power that

15

don't belong there - misqualifications of the natural energy - miscreations of wrongly used planetary force - they get consumed. Only what belongs there remains. Thus among the Hindus, the Sun is considered a "malefic" planet - no doubt they are focusing on this "consuming" destructive side. But here in the West, the Sun is considered "benefic" - light and life are unquestionably benefic forces.

When the Sun contacts a planet, the affairs of life ruled by that planet get illuminated. Where there is light there is clarity and right decision making. The affairs of the House in question should prosper because of this.

The Sun will always bring good - but the question is will the good come in a pleasant, easy way, or in a stressful way. These kinds of issues are shown by the kind of contact that the Sun is making with the other planet - if the contact is harmonious, such as a trine or sextile, the good promised by the Sun will manifest easily with little struggle (provided no other planetary aspects are contradicting). If the aspect is a stressful one - such as a Square or Opposition - the good will come, but perhaps through effort or conflict or re-arranging of present reality.

In Kabbalah the Sun is associated with Beauty and Harmony. It is the harmonious center of the Tree of Life, just as it is the harmonious center of our solar system. So transits of the Sun are also going to harmonize and beautify any planet that it contacts. I remember once, driving though one of the so-called "worst" neighborhoods in Brooklyn - inner city - site of slums - high crime rates - drive by shootings occurring daily. A very notorious kind of neighborhood. But, the Sun was setting as I drove through, and to my vision he was touching the tops of the houses - the so-called slums. Just his light, his presence, transformed this so-called slum into a picture of beauty. One moment, it was a place of slums, the next, as the Sun touched it, it was resplendent with glory. One could see that the Divine did not consider the neighborhood as "bad" or "ugly" - its presence made it a thing of transcendent beauty. In fact (perhaps because the neighborhood was considered so ugly, and the transformation was so dramatic) I still remember this vision as one of the most beautiful I have ever seen - it rivals the beauties of Waikiki and Maui.

This is an illustration of what happens when the Sun contacts a planet. Though the affairs of the house that it rules be "slumlike" - while the Sun is contacting it, these affairs will be beautiful and harmonious.

Now the beauty of the Sun is a bit different than the beauty that we associate with the planet Venus. The beauty of the Sun is the beauty of light and color. It is an energetic kind of beauty. It is a beauty of Force. The beauty of Venus is more of a beauty of Form and Shape. The beauty of the Sun is on a level that is above our psychological consciousness - we can perceive it psychologically - but it resides more in our awareness - it is not usually a sensual kind of beauty that we can touch, taste and feel. We are aware of it, but we cannot grasp it. The Beauty of Venus is more sensual and tangible. It is Beauty on the feeling level of life. We eat something sweet and it tastes "beautiful". This is something tangible. We see a beautiful person - the person is well formed, symmetrical, and proportional. And if we are lucky we can interact in a physical way with this person. The dress in the store is beautiful in a very tangible way - and one can wear this dress - one can own it. One can enjoy the person wearing the dress. The Sun transforming a slum into a thing of beauty is a solar beauty. Now, if an artist were to paint a picture of this scene - and somehow caught it - the painting would perhaps be a Venus kind of beauty. Now it is something tangible - something that can be owned - something that can be "handled".

It is important to understand these distinctions for later on when we deal with Venus transits - and she too is associated with beauty and harmony.

Transiting Sun Conjunction Moon

A happy, but short term transit. It brings sunny, optimistic moods and emotions. It is good for meditation or self programming as your subconscious is more receptive to your dictates. There is harmony (if nothing else denies) with the opposite sex. A feel good day.

The Spiritual Perspective. The spiritual message here is that while it is normal for the different genders to have different perspectives and different natures, this need not lead to conflict. Harmony and unity is possible without one gender trying to be the other. Real gender harmony arises when the differences are accepted, understood, and each is allowed to be who it is.

Transiting Sun Conjunction Sun

A happy, but short term transit. Today is your birthday - the beginning of your Solar Return. The cycle of the year ahead is being set now. Good to meditate on future goals, review the past year, and make corrections where appropriate. You get your way today. You shine. Your will is stronger than usual. Libido is stronger.

The Spiritual Perspective. Again, as with the Lunar Return, we have the symbolism of the "end of the old and the beginning of the new". A new cycle is being born today. The past year is over with. Its lessons should be digested and absorbed and now we are to move on to a whole new experience, with new vistas of expression opening up to us. Things that were impossible last year can be very possible this year. Things you needed last year might not be needed now. Take only the wisdom of the past with you as you enter this new cycle.

Transiting Sun Conjunction Mercury

A happy, but short term transit. Your mind is energized. New ideas come. You receive illumination on various problems. You have more communication and intellectual power which you should use constructively. Good for learning, teaching, writing, sales or marketing.

The Spiritual Perspective. Spirit presents you with a choice today. You have greater mental power and ability. How will you use it? Will this mental power be used for constructive and happy purposes, or wasted in idle speech or negative gossip? Your choices matter.

Transiting Sun Conjunction Venus

A happy, but short term transit. A wonderful love transit. Romance is in the air. Romantic opportunities come. Your personal sense of beauty and aesthetic sense is stronger than usual. You are more creative as well. Good for buying works of art or things of beauty. Social grace is stronger and you are probably being invited to parties or social gatherings.

The Spiritual Perspective. Gender harmony is possible and can be cultivated. Today it is easier to attain. Spirit gives you the taste of it. Remember for the future.

Transiting Sun Conjunction Mars

A happy, but short term transit. Overall energy and libido is much stronger. If nothing else denies, exercise and sports regimes go well. A day when you achieve your personal bests athletically or physically. You get things done in a hurry. Actions are decisive. You are fearless and bold - and perhaps considered a "risk taker" by others.

The Spiritual Perspective. Spirit presents you with a choice. Your physical energy is very much enhanced. How will you use it?

Transiting Sun Conjunction Jupiter

A happy, but short term transit. A wonderful financial transit. A lucky day. Dame fortune is with you. Financial windfalls or opportunities come. There is great philosophical and religious clarity as well. You are jovial and living "affluently" today. Speculations are more favorable (though other things could deny here).

The Spiritual Perspective. Its as if the heavens open up today and pour down their blessings. Each comes away with their personal capacity. Those who have the capacity of a tea cup, will take that. Those with larger capacities will come away with more. The riches of heaven - both material and mental - are revealed.

Transiting Sun Conjunction Saturn

A happy, but short term transit. Your ability to organize and order your life and environment is greatly strengthened. Good to do those tasks that you don't enjoy but that MUST be done.

The Spiritual Perspective. Spiritually the message is that Joy and Duty need not be antagonistic. Duties should be performed joyously, and joyous activities often go better when there is planning and forethought. Spiritual rapture includes our duties and responsibilities - it is not a negation of them.

Transiting Sun Conjunction Uranus

A happy, but short term transit. Your originality and inventiveness is greatly increased. New and unique solutions come to you - suddenly and unexpectedly. You are in the mood for freedom - to be footloose and fancy free. This is a wonderful social transit as well and you should accept invitations to seminars, group activities and social gatherings.

The Spiritual Perspective. Spirit is ever new and ever renewing. Every moment is something new and different. And this perception is being shown to you today.

Transiting Sun Conjunction Neptune

A happy, but short term transit. Your idealism is very strong today. Idealistic activities bring fulfilment. You are closer to the spiritual world. Intuition and psychic ability is very strong. Spiritual illumination is happening. You are very inspired and creative. You rise above all circumstances.

The Spiritual Perspective. For those on a spiritual path this is an especially happy transit as you are more in tune with the Will of Spirit, and there is great joy in this. You are in the flow of life. Joy and Bliss guide you to the spirit and to its ends. The Will of Spirit is not some onerous duty today - what you most want to do, is what spirit wants for you.

Transiting Sun Conjunction Pluto

A happy, but short term transit. Libido is magnified a thousandfold. Hormones are roaring. You have unusual ability to focus on what you want and thus to attain it. Your ability to transform yourself and your circumstances is strengthened. Prosper others today and your own prosperity will come very naturally.

The Spiritual Perspective. This is another one of those transits where Spirit presents you with a choice. It has given its gift - enhanced libido, power to transform and to eliminate negativity - how will you use it?

Transiting Sun Conjunction Ascendant

A happy, but short term transit. You are in a yearly "personal pleasure peak". Sensual desires are gratified. You look wonderful. You have more energy. You are a star. You attract positive attention. People notice you. There is more self confidence and self esteem.

The Spiritual Perspective. Spiritually, the heavenly forces are giving you a glimpse of what the body can and should feel like when energy is flowing properly and one is in tune. Some will realize it more than others. One sees, under this transit that spirit cares for things of the body as well as the spirit.

Transiting Sun Conjunction Midheaven

A happy transit. You are in one of the most powerful career periods of your year. Career is boosted - there is good progress. Perhaps honors and recognition come to you (unless other things deny.) Perhaps there is a raise or promotion at work (unless other things deny). Career opportunities are coming. Push forward with your career goals.

The Spiritual Perspective. Spiritually, the spirit gives you a glimpse of your true place in temporal society.

Transiting Sun Square Moon

A difficult but short term transit. Libido is weaker than usual. You have to work harder to get in synch with the opposite sex. Men and authority figures are not thrilled with your moods and sentiments. You'll have to work harder to create domestic and emotional harmony. Your urge for fun and creativity conflicts with family duties and obligations. A lover could be out of synch with family members.

The Spiritual Perspective. Spiritually, you are challenged to keep the faith, do what is right, regardless of your mood and feeling. There is a place in us that is above mere mood or emotion - this is the place you need to come from today.

Transiting Sun Square Sun

A difficult but short term transit. Energy and overall libido are not up to their usual standards. Rest and relax more today. Your will meets with conflict from outside - it seems out of synch with the public will or with authority figures. Though you are still a star and always will be, you might not be feeling that way today.

The Spiritual Perspective. Spiritually, you are learning the impor- tance of energy and overall vitality in your life. So many problems are not objective things per se, but are problems of lack of energy. Learning not to fritter energy away on non-essentials is an important lesson.

Transiting Sun Square Mercury

A difficult but short term transit. Authority figures are not thrilled with your ideas or thought processes. Do more homework before presenting them. Intellectual energy is not up to its usual standards. Double check all calculations and written material.

The Spiritual Perspective. Sometimes a challenge to our thought process or ideas is a constructive thing. It enables us to refine and improve them. This is the purpose of this transit.

Transiting Sun Square Venus

A difficult but short term transit. There could be conflicts with the beloved today. But don't over-react, this transit will pass. There are more difficulties in expressing love feelings than usual. Your friendships might not be appreciated by authority figures or the men in your life.

The Spiritual Perspective. There is a love that is above the heart, above the normal feelings that we call love. It is unconditional and always available in spite of any material condition. The challenge is to find this place today.

Transiting Sun Square Mars

A difficult but short term transit. There could be tendencies to rush, haste, argument. Energy and libido are not up to their usual standards. Try to slow down today in everything you do.

The Spiritual Perspective. Action is not always the answer to every situation. Sometimes non action will be better as, at least, you don't make matters worse. This might be a time for non-action - or at least action that is more thought out.

Transiting Sun Square Jupiter

A difficult but short term transit. Speculations are not favorable. The speculative judgement could be awry. Financial judgment could be better as well. Your code of ethics, religion or personal philosophy is out of synch with men and authority figures. It might be a good idea to review them. Beware of overspending or over indulgence.

The Spiritual Perspective. Spiritually, our faith needs testing every now and then, so that it can be made stronger. Faith is like muscle that gets stronger with use. Challenges to our faith often help us to clarify and refine it.

Transiting Sun Square Saturn

A difficult but short term transit. The way you manage and organize things might not find favor with bosses, men or authority figures. Your overall ability to take charge of your life seems temporarily weakened. The need for fun and the need to be responsible and dutiful conflict with each other and a compromise is called for. Your sense of time and scheduling is hampered.

The Spiritual Perspective. Spiritually this transit produces an apparent conflict between love and duty - but this conflict is only apparent and not real. Spirit challenges you to make your duties fun, and to put some structure into your leisure activities.

Transiting Sun Square Uranus

A difficult but short term transit. Your originality and inventiveness doesn't find favor with superiors, men or authority figures. Do some more homework or tone things down. There will be tendencies to more rebelliousness. Your urges for freedom don't sit well with authority figures.

The Spiritual Perspective. Originality is a wonderful thing. All progress depends on it. But it can be presented in a less strident and more harmonious way. Change can be made less threatening and this is the challenge that spirit presents you with today.

Transiting Sun Square Neptune

A difficult but short term transit. Intuitions and inspirations need more verification. They don't sit well with authority figures or the men in your life. There is conflict between what you want to do and what spirit is urging on you - but really you must find the middle way.

The Spiritual Perspective. We grow through dealing with contradictions, opposites and paradoxes. From a higher level these are not paradoxes. Today you are faced with the ultimate apparent paradox - your I Am seems out of synch with the Divine Will. A total impossibility of course. Yet, this is how it seems. Your job is to seek higher ground and see the deeper agenda that is unfolding. A good meditation today - Thy will, not my will, be done.

Transiting Sun Square Pluto

A difficult but short term transit. Libido is not up to its usual standard. Either you overdo it or under do it. Your urge to transform yourself or conditions finds resistance from men or authority figures. There is a tendency to a power struggle.

The Spiritual Perspective. The transformation process will always bring up the resistance to the process and this is one of those days. But this resistance will ultimately refine and perfect your process and give you more understanding.

Transiting Sun Square Ascendant

A difficult but short term transit. Issues of personal pleasure or sensual delight might have to be delayed for a while. Overall energy is not up to par. You will have to work harder to present your desired image.

The Spiritual Perspective. Our happiness should not be dependent on sensual pleasures. Though these should be enjoyed to the full, we should be happy when they don't come too. Sometimes we need to thank the Spirit for what it has NOT given us.

Transiting Sun Square Midheaven

A difficult but short term transit. Urges to fun, creativity and joy conflict with your career duties and responsibilities. You are torn between the two urges - after all isn't success supposed to lead us to fun? But sometimes fun has to be delayed or toned down. Authority figures can be out of synch with your career aspirations - try again another time.

The Spiritual Perspective. Any life work worth doing involves challenges and today is one of them. The joy of overcoming is yours today.

Transiting Sun Opposition Moon

A difficult but short term transit. There is a huge gulf between what you feel like doing and what you are urged to do. The men and women in your life are not in synch and hold opposite positions and perspectives on things. Family duties and obligations pull you one way, while joy, creative pursuits and perhaps love affairs pull you in another. Your moods could be down today. The way you feel seems out of synch with what your conscious mind knows.

The Spiritual Perspective. This is a day to "rise above" differences and see the synthetic position. As you hold to the idea of unity, the differences will be seen as a part of it. The differences highlight the richness and diversity of the overall unity.

Transiting Sun Opposition Sun

A difficult but short term transit. You are called upon to shine in ways that are alien to your nature. The normally shy person may be asked to take the spotlight; the natural ham may have to be more discreet and shine in silence; the activist may be called upon to be patient; the thinker may have to act etc. Your personal sense of self worth seems out of synch with what the public values as self worth. There could be conflicts with authority and prominent men today. Know that regardless of what is happening out there, you are still a star - still someone worthwhile. Libido and overall energy is not up to its usual standard. Many will feel out of touch with their own spiritual selves - their true I Ams.

The Spiritual Perspective. Opposition should always make you think of unity. The play of opposites in the world, in manifestation, is merely the Divine Play - the Leila. At the root all is oneness. Also keep in mind that the Sun is now in its "full Moon" stage of your solar cycle. It is at the height of its power, and thus, because you are exerting more power - shining very brightly - you could be attracting more opposition.

Transiting Sun Opposition Mercury

A difficult but short term transit. Men and authority figures (perhaps children) are not in synch with your logic, ideas or thought processes. Communication with them is much more difficult and you will have to work harder to get your ideas across. The intellectual faculties are not at their strongest and you might want to reschedule communication projects for another day.

The Spiritual Perspective. Differences of opinion can widen the mental and intellectual perspective. Try to see things from the perspective of other people. Though you might not change your position (you might be right) at least you will gain a tolerance and understanding of them. Perhaps you may see that you too would think like them if you were in their shoes and had their experiences. This widening of perspective will enhance future thinking and communication.

Transiting Sun Opposition Venus

A difficult but short term transit. Not an especially good day for romance, parties or social gatherings (but other things in the chart could deny this.) There is a tendency to love disputes. There is more difficulty in expressing feelings of love and perhaps there is rejection. Because of the difficulty in expressing love feelings, some people over-compensate and this could cause even more rejection. Try your romantic overtures on another day.

The Spiritual Perspective. If love is true, the challenges to love will only strengthen and purify it. This is a time to "step back" in your relationships and see the good in others and to remember why you were friends or lovers in the first place. Too much resistance to social challenges will probably make matters worse. Let the passions of the moment die down.

Transiting Sun Opposition Mars

A difficult but short term transit. Libido is not up to par or may be over-expressed in an unbalanced way. Your actions are out of synch with authority figures, children and men in general. You don't especially feel like exercising or indulging in sports today (though other things in the chart could deny this.) In a woman's chart this could show short term conflicts between the men in her life. In a man's chart it could show conflict with other men - arguments etc. Mars is a passionate planet and he doesn't like to be thwarted thus there could be violent tendencies too.

The Spiritual Perspective. Sometimes, lack of drive or physical energy can be a good thing. It opens the doors to other possibilities. Perhaps there is a way to achieve the same goal without the physical effort that you thought was necessary.

Transiting Sun Opposition Jupiter

A difficult but short term transit. Creative and fun loving pursuits are not in synch with financial duties or with the financial situation. That junket to the Caribbean might be a good deal, but it might not be the right time for it. Your religious and ethical beliefs - your view of the world and life - is in conflict with authority figures, men and perhaps children - not a good day to try to teach them these things. There is a danger of over-spending or under-spending today. Neither is good. Your I AM self pulls you in one direction while your religious beliefs pull you in another - what is right ethical conduct today?

The Spiritual Perspective. The testing of our religious and philosophical beliefs, though not always pleasant, is usually a good thing. We have opportunity to refine and perfect these things. We have opportunity to refine the way we express it to others too. If you meet financial challenges with an optimistic attitude - with a consciousness of spiritual affluence - the challenge will be the actual doorway to greater wealth.

Transiting Sun Opposition Saturn

A difficult but short term transit. Your natural organizing ability is weakened today. You are in conflict between "duty" and the need to "enjoy life" - both are valid perspectives. You need to do a little of both. If your legitimate duties are not done, it will detract from the joy of life. And, if you have some fun, you will be more able to bear the burdens of duty. Authorities in your life are in conflict with each other. Children seem more rebellious. Your sense of order is not in favor with men, children or authority figures. Try again another time.

The Spiritual Perspective. Though joy and duty are really not separate things - they are merely two sides of a coin - today, you feel that they are separate. You need to make a special spiritual effort to see the unity of these two things. Dereliction of your legitimate duty, will not bring you the joy that you envision. But neither will neglecting your self. Stand in the middle. Do a little of both.

Transiting Sun Opposition Uranus

A difficult but short term transit. Your sense of originality and inventiveness is opposed by men, children and authority figures. Perhaps this makes you even more rebellious. You want to fight the establishment. But rather than fight, try proposing or implementing this originality at another time when they are more receptive. The men in your life - and the authority figures - are facing more rebellion - not necessarily from you.

The Spiritual Perspective. The spiritual message here is that opposition to what you think is an original idea or invention can serve a good purpose. Look at the nature of the criticism or opposition and see if there is something in it that can make you improve your idea. Opposition used creatively will only enhance originality.

Transiting Sun Opposition Neptune

A difficult but short term transit. Difficult to discern the spiritual guidance today. Intuition seems clouded. Hard to separate what is coming from Spirit, what is coming from your own personal desires and what is coming from outside authority figures. Intuition needs confirmation. Dreams will probably involve men and authority figures - perhaps children.

The Spiritual Perspective. Spirit could be calling you to transcend your own ego and take actions that seem to go against it. Inspired ideas might not go over well with men, children or authority figures today - try again at another time when they are more receptive.

Transiting Sun Opposition Pluto

A difficult but short term transit. Libido is either over expressed or under expressed. Is sex about pleasure or it is about power? Your efforts at transformation are in conflict with men, children and authority figures. More difficult to borrow money today or to increase your line of credit. Try again at another time. There could be violent tendencies with the men in your life - or with children. Stay cool.

The Spiritual Perspective. Sometimes transformation requires resistance. A certain power is needed to transform a given area of life or thing - the resistance builds your muscles. Hold firmly to your will.

Transiting Sun Opposition Ascendant

Usually this occurs with the Sun in your 6th or 7th Houses. If the Sun is in the 6th House, dietary or health concerns conflict with your desires for personal and sensual pleasure. If the Sun is in the 7th House, social concerns - the desires of others - the need to please others - obstruct your desires for personal pleasure. Not an especially great day for self esteem. Personal confidence is weakened. However it is a good social day and good for dealing with health concerns. Your appearance and sense of style might not meet with the approval of men, authority figures or children.

The Spiritual Perspective. Spiritually speaking there is a need to balance your personal desires with those of other people. Give each their due. Don't go too far either way.

Transiting Sun Opposition Midheaven

A good day and period in general for finding your point or emotional harmony, for dealing with family and domestic issues and for inner work on your career and aspirations. Actual career work is not that interesting - though other things in the Horoscope could nullify this.

The Spiritual Perspective. Spiritually speaking, the Sun is in the "night side" of your Horoscope. Night is for dreaming. The night is mother to the day. This is a time for pursuing the career through "night" methods rather than day methods - through dreaming and living in your dream. Outer (day) action will come in its own good time very naturally and spontaneously.

Transiting Sun Trine Moon

A happy but short term transit. Moods are good today. Your moods are in synch with what you want to do and should do. There is more harmony with the opposite sex and with the family. Men, authority figures or children are doing things to bolster your moods. You have more capacity to give emotional support today.

The Spiritual Perspective. Your overall good mood is no doubt a reward for past things done right - and the strength of the good will be in exact measure.

Transiting Sun Trine Sun

A happy but short term transit. You shine. Libido is stronger than usual. Self esteem and self confidence are strong. You get your way, because your way is in synch with the Cosmos. Personal creativity is very strong and is appreciated by authority figures, men and children. A day for fun and personal pleasure. Overall energy is enhanced.

The Spiritual Perspective. Sometimes we shine in spite of difficulties and sometimes because there are none - this is a case of the latter. (Though other things in the Horoscope could deny this, even so you will shine more than usual.)

Transiting Sun Trine Mercury

A happy but short term transit. Intellectual power and communication ability is enhanced. This is the time to present new ideas to men, authority figures and children. They appreciate your logic, ideas and thought process. You communicate with confidence and with harmony. The mind is illuminated. There is mental clarity.

The Spiritual Perspective. Spiritually speaking you must think of how you will use this intellectual capital in the most wise way.

Transiting Sun Trine Venus

A happy but short term transit. A wonderful transit for love, romance and social activities. Your ability to express feelings of love is strong. Your social grace and magnetism is enhanced. You have a more refined sense of beauty too.

The Spiritual Perspective. Whether you are involved with someone or not, stay in the vibrations of love - it is good in its own right even if there is no apparent object.

Transiting Sun Trine Mars

A happy but short term transit. Libido roars(more than usual) but is not overdone. Overall energy is enhanced. You excel at sports and exercise regimes. You achieve more in less time. You are more coura-geous and bold. Men, authority figures and children appreciate your actions and boldness.

The Spiritual Perspective. Bold actions are sometimes called for in life and this is one of those times - and where it is likely to succeed. Sometimes we can achieve our ends through grace and sometimes through power, if power is needed, it is there for you.

Transiting Sun Trine Jupiter

A happy but short term transit. A lucky day. Overall Horizons are expanded. There is financial increase and opportunity. Speculations are favorable. You are jovial and optimistic. The good life calls to you. Many receive religious or philosophical illumination today.

Your religious beliefs and ethical code are favorably received by men, authority figures and children. A fun kind of day. Educational and travel opportunities come today.

The Spiritual Perspective. The storehouses of heaven are open and you can perceive that there is no lack of any kind.

Transiting Sun Trine Saturn

A happy but short term transit. Your need to organize and order your life - to take charge of it - is greatly strengthened. Your sense of organization and discipline is supported by men, authority figures and children. If nothing else denies, it is a good time for dealing with the government and with authority figures. Managerial judgement is excellent. Duty can be fun today.

The Spiritual Perspective. Duty, discipline and limits are not necessarily onerous things, as you are learning today - when used properly, they bring you to your heart's desire.

Transiting Sun Trine Uranus

A happy but short term transit. Your inventiveness and originality is unusually strong. New solutions and insights come to you like flashes of lightning. Your originality and inventiveness finds favor with men, authority figures and children. You know how to rebel in a positive way - through the creation of systems that are truly superior to the old ways. A good day for friendships and group activities. New insights on science, technology and astrology come to you.

The Spiritual Perspective. Being original has its up and down side. Original people are often out of synch with the people around them who seem to demand conformity above all else. But today you are seeing the upside of it.

Transiting Sun Trine Neptune

A happy but short term transit. This is a transit that brings spiritual illumination. Your spiritual unfoldment continues apace. Men. Authority figures and perhaps children support your spiritual urges. Your idealism and spirituality finds favor with men, authority figures and children. Intuition and psychic abilities are stronger than usual. Meditation goes better.

The Spiritual Perspective. A good glimpse into the spiritual world can change a person's life - in one fell swoop - this is one of the things that can happen today.

Transiting Sun Trine Pluto

A happy but short term transit. Libido roars. Your ability to focus and concentrate is much stronger and thus you achieve more. Your "focus" gets respect from men, authority figures and children. Efforts at self transformation go well. A good day to borrow or pay down debt - or to negotiate re-financing. (If nothing else in the Horoscope denies.)

The Spiritual Perspective. Personal transformation can often be a messy business - but today you are seeing the positive side of it.

Transiting Sun Trine Ascendant

A happy but short term transit. Self esteem and confidence are strong. You believe in yourself. You look great and your appearance draws compliments from men, authority figures and children. There is more fun and sensual pleasure today.

The Spiritual Perspective. Though your body is not you, you can see that spirit cares about it and its welfare. It supplies everything that the body needs in harmonious ways.

Transiting Sun Trine Midheaven

A happy but short term transit. Career goals and aspirations are boosted. Perhaps you get some recognition from authority figures.

The Spiritual Perspective. On a spiritual level, the Midheaven shows your mission in life (not just your worldly career) and today you have opportunity to get closer to that mission - this is the most important thing in life.

Transiting Sun Sextile Moon

A happy but short term transit. Moods will tend to be good - unless other things in the chart deny. There will be opportunities to create domestic and family harmony and to create harmony with the opposite sex. Your subconscious is more receptive to your conscious mind today.

The Spiritual Perspective. You will receive encouragement today and it is good to pass this on to others. You will be shown, perhaps by revelation, how to harmonize the male and female principles within you.

Transiting Sun Sextile Sun

A happy but short term transit. You will have opportunities to shine today. Self confidence and self esteem should be good. Libido is stronger. A day for fun, pleasure and creativity - and the opportunities will come.

The Spiritual Perspective. Your career and creativity will receive encouragement, note how good it makes you feel. In the future you will have opportunity to do this for others.

Transiting Sun Sextile Mercury

A happy but short term transit. You will have opportunities to strengthen the mind and to communicate your ideas to men, authority figures and children. Educational opportunities will come. Sales and marketing activities should go well - if nothing else in the Horoscope denies. Intellectual pursuits receive encouragement from others.

The Spiritual Perspective. Ideas come to us from all kinds of places - some of them from the mass mind and some even from the underworld. But today you will have opportunity to receive ideas that come from your "Immortal Nature", and these ideas are precious.

Transiting Sun Sextile Venus

A happy but short term transit. A happy love aspect. Love and social opportunities will come. You will have opportunities to create harmony with the opposite sex. Your social urges receive encouragement from others - especially men.

The Spiritual Perspective. Since you are better able to harmonize the masculine and feminine principles within yourself, outer experiences will merely reflect that.

Transiting Sun Sextile Mars

A happy but short term transit. Opportunities for exercise and sports will come. Libido is stronger and harmoniously expressed. Sexual opportunities come. Overall energy is enhanced.

The Spiritual Perspective. Your overall energy is much increased today. You have more voltage. If firmness or force is needed in a situation (and sometimes it is) you have it. You are more likely to use power in a correct way today and thus avoid the messy karmic kickbacks that come from its abuse. The question spiritually is - how will you make use of the extra energy (which is like money in the bank) today?

Transiting Sun Sextile Jupiter

A happy but short term transit. A lucky day. Financial and educational opportunities will come. Financial judgment is sound. You will have opportunities for religious and philosophical illumination. In general you are optimistic about the future - unless other things in the chart deny.

The Spiritual Perspective. Your consciousness of affluence is stronger today and so inevitably there will be more wealth opportunities. You also receive more moral and philosophical clarity, which leads to more powerful actions.

Transiting Sun Sextile Saturn

A happy but short term transit. You will have opportunities to bring order and organization into your life - and this will be supported by men, authority figures and children. Managerial judgement is good.

The Spiritual Perspective. Order is heaven's first law. Right order is a wonderful thing. It is every man's duty to create a good order in his or her life. And, today, it is easier to accomplish.

Transiting Sun Sextile Uranus

A happy but short term transit. There will be happy opportunities to make friends or to get involved in group activities. There will be opportunity to invent, innovate and express originality to men, authority figures and children - and these should be well received.

The Spiritual Perspective. Your own originality, uniqueness and innovativeness will get clarified today and this clarity will make these things stronger in you.

Transiting Sun Sextile Neptune

A happy but short term transit. Spiritual and meditative opportunities present themselves. There opportunities to expand the spiritual life. Intuition, psychic ability and inspiration is strong.

The Spiritual Perspective. The sun shines on your spiritual ideals and spiritual aspirations. You see them clearly in the light of day. This clarity makes them stronger and more "realizable".

Transiting Sun Sextile Pluto

A happy but short term transit. Libido is stronger than usual and you will have opportunities - happy ones - to express it. You will have opportunities to harmoniously transform yourself, your life, present conditions. You will have opportunities to borrow or lend money and to increase your line of credit.

The Spiritual Perspective. The light of day is being shed in the underworld of yourself - those areas of your mind and emotions that are normally hidden. This helps you to correct problems emanating from there.

Transiting Sun Sextile Ascendant

A happy but short term transit. You will have opportunities to improve your personal appearance and to get personal accessories or clothing that improve your appearance. Perhaps new ideas on this score come. Interesting opportunities for sensual indulgence come. In general, self esteem, self confidence and personal appearance are good - if nothing else in the Horoscope denies.

The Spiritual Perspective. The body and image has more light and energy today. How will you use it? The light of day shines on your body and you are more able to make corrections there.

Transiting Sun Sextile Midheaven

A happy but short term transit. Opportunities come to further the career and life work. You should take them.

The Spiritual Perspective. The light of day - of your conscious mind - shines on the career and spiritual mission enabling you to take the right steps or make important corrections. Those of you seeking your life's purpose and mission will get important messages today.

TRANSITS OF THE MOON

The Moon's nature is watery, reflective, emotional. Where the masculine Sun gives light, illumination (both physical and spiritual), life and energy, the Moon's energy brings a sensitivity and flexibility to any planet it contacts. It will soften the energy of the planet, but this will, in many cases, enhance the power of the planet in a different way. Too much radiance, glory, and power (such as the Sun gives) can make the energy of the planet too strong - too over powering - too dynamic - and in many cases unpleasant to others. It is wonderful to have a sharp mind, but when it gets overbearing (perhaps from too much solar contact) it is uncomfortable for others. Ideas are pushed with too much force. Whereas if the Moon contacts the mind (Mercury) the ideas will come out softer, more gracious, more easy for others to handle.

This is the Moon's role in our solar system. She modifies, softens, re-qualifies the solar energy in ways that we on earth can assimilate. Without her, the light and life of the Sun would consume us instantly. Her job is to distribute this light in safe and comfortable ways. And she does this when she transits any planet. She will modulate the energy, soften it, sensitize it, so that it goes forth in safe non-hurtful ways.

The Moon will bring that subtle quality of feeling to any planet that she contacts. When she contacts stern Saturn, he will be that much more in tune with feeling as he radiates his energy. Thus, the boss (Saturn) might be just as demanding a disciplinarian, but he will do it in less hurtful and more sensitive ways. He will still insist on order - but instead of barking orders - he might say "please" or "thank you".

But the feeling side of things which the Moon brings to any planetary contact has other functions. We can do an activity, just from sheer duty, will power, or high spirits. But if we feel what we are doing, if we are in the "mood" for doing a certain thing, the

41

process will go much easier and better. In the right mood, in the right state of feeling, there is no project that is difficult. But when the mood is not there, even the simplest of tasks, becomes a chore and a bore.

So the Moon, by putting us in the right mood for certain activities (depending on the Houses ruled by the planets she contacts) is performing a great and important function. The projects should go better. People who are in tune with the Moon - the feeling oriented types - are more cooperative in the project.

Mood has its right use, which we have just discussed, but also its wrong use. If moods go negative (and this can come from other factors in the Horoscope, personal or of a given time) then the energy the Moon will add to a project will be negative, and the project is not only doomed to failure, but will be joyless in the doing.

Also if the Moon is making a stressful aspect to a planet, the mood of the moment is not "in synch" with the affairs governed by the planet - and this creates a short term problem.

It is up to each individual to ensure that the Moon's great gift to us, is used properly as it was intended to be used.

Transiting Moon Conjunction Moon

A happy but short term transit. Today is your Monthly Birthday - your Lunar Return. You begin a new monthly cycle today. Good to meditate on personal goals. You can almost feel the change - the shift in gears today. The mood is good and you feel reborn. Emotional life is more harmonious. Your subconscious responds well to you.

The Spiritual Perspective. The Spiritual message here is a "new beginning". The past month with all its successes, failures, frustrations, pleasures, hopes, and wishes is gone. Its over. It exists only in memory. Now is a new beginning, with new possibilities and potentials. You are in a sense reborn. Nothing is exactly as it was. We are to look at the coming month as a "new born infant" with new eyes. On a deeper level, we can get an insight of what death is. Nothing to

42

be feared. Not as we imagined it to be. It is only a new beginning on another level. Life is endless and all that is. An old month "died" so to speak. And its death immediately gave birth to a new month.

Transiting Moon Conjunction Sun

A happy but short term transit. You have more energy today. You shine more. Women support your goals and appreciate you. Libido is strong. You tend to get your way today. Career is boosted. Life is more fun.

The Spiritual Perspective. The spiritual message here is that you are born to shine - born to be you - born to be who you are. At times, like today, this you, this light, will be appreciated. At other times, it might not meet with such appreciation or support (e.g. a week from now when the Moon will square your Sun or two weeks from now when it will be in Opposition). But no matter. Other's responses to you can be fleeting and temporary. The moods of the moment shift from day to day. But you are to shine - like the Sun that you are. Right now you experience the positive - enjoy it. But know that you can't hold on to it. When the disapproval comes, that too will be temporary. Only your light is eternal.

Transiting Moon Conjunction Mercury

A happy but short term transit. It lasts only a day. You tend to speak more forcefully. Your speech rings with conviction. You feel what you say. New, intuitive ideas come to you. Women disseminate your ideas or communication. If other transits are negative this can show too much "moodiness" in the thinking. Moods over-rule clear logic. You might be merely communicating a mood rather than a clear idea.

The Spiritual Perspective. The spiritual message here is to show you what is possible when logic and feeling are in agreement. Mind has its ways and purposes, and feeling has her ways. The best decisions, the best communications occur when they are both in agreement - in union - with each other. When the mind overrules the feelings, there are subtle dissatisfactions. When the feelings overpower the mind, dangerous things can happen. But when there is unity - harmony - agreement - such decisions will be powerful and successful.

Transiting Moon Conjunction Venus

Generally a happy transit. You are in the mood for romance. You express romantic feelings. Feelings tend to be harmonious. Gut feelings lead you to romantic opportunities. Generally this is a transit of domestic harmony. Good to make peace with the family and smooth over disputes. This is also a wonderful transit (if nothing else denies) for entertaining from home or for family type gatherings.

The Spiritual Perspective. The spiritual message here is to show you what is possible when the feelings are turned to love and good will - when they express in beauty and harmony. Everyday things become transformed - exalted - poetic - works of art. The ordinary becomes beauty and you see the omnipresence of beauty in everything. Slums, living conditions, material conditions of any sort, are no barriers to this great beauty. Remember this feeling - this truth - this revelation. It will help you later on when the aspects shift.

Transiting Moon Conjunction Mars

A Neutral and short term transit. Libido is increased. You are in the mood for vigorous exercise, sports and athletics and thus performance should be better. Beware of rush and hurry and watch the temper.

The Spiritual Perspective. Spiritually, the cosmos is giving you a choice today. How will you use your enhanced energies and dynamism? Will you put them to constructive use, or will you fritter them away in argument, anger or vain self assertion? A deposit has been made into your "energy" bank account. The deposit is given unconditionally. How you use this "extra deposit" is up to you.

Transiting Moon Conjunction Jupiter

A very happy transit. Generally it brings a short term financial good. You are more generous today and others are more generous with you. A good time of the month to ask for favors. You are luckier today than other days. You are more optimistic. Those who are on a spiritual path will receive spiritual or religious revelation.

The Spiritual Perspective. Spiritually, the cosmos is showing you the possibilities of enhanced emotional states - of what can happen when your mood, or the moods of others, support your financial and religious objectives. You can go very far and achieve much because of this. Though this condition is fleeting, it will nevertheless happen once a month. Eventually you will be able to maintain this state for ever longer periods - this is something to strive for.

Transiting Moon Conjunction Saturn

A Neutral and short term transit. It lasts but a day and returns every month. You are in the mood for discipline and doing the mundane things that you need to do. A wonderful day to do domestic chores, get the house in order, or set a righteous discipline for the family. Your sense of order is increased. Sometimes there is a tendency to get over-disciplined or over controlling. When the emotions are involved in anything there is a tendency to "disproportion" and this is the danger.

The Spiritual Perspective. Spiritually, the cosmos is showing you that there is no real conflict between "feelings" and a sense of duty and order. Duties - even apparently onerous ones - are best done with right feeling. The call to one's Duty often conjures up higher feelings than the merely sensuous ones. Doing one's duty regardless of how one feels is a great thing, but if we can enjoy our duties, it will be even a greater thing.

Transiting Moon Conjunction Uranus

You are in an experimental, rebellious mood today. You want change. You want a break from the routine. Your need for freedom is stronger. New, inventive and original ideas come to you - perhaps from women or mother figures. New astrological information will come. Science and technology issues will go easier (if nothing else denies).

The Spiritual Perspective. Spiritually, you are confronted with choice today. Will you channel your energy towards creativity, a new invention, a new way of doing things? Or will you merely be restless or rebellious?

Transiting Moon Conjunction Neptune

The spiritual urges are very strong today. Probably you will have vivid and prophetic dreams - in technicolor. The dream life could be more interesting than real life. Your intuition is much stronger.

The Spiritual Perspective. Spiritual revelation will come to those on a spiritual path. Psychic abilities are strong. A wonderful day for meditation. You are emotionally much closer to the spiritual world. Spiritual messages are coming - in a man's chart, it can come through the women in his life.

Transiting Moon Conjunction Pluto

Libido is increased. Psychic ability is also stronger. You are in the mood for focus and concentration. A good day to get rid of the excess in your life -whether it be possessions, character traits or effete material in the body. You can prosper by seeing value in what others consider to be "junk". Good to think about paying down debt.

The Spiritual Perspective. Spiritually, the cosmos is giving you opportunity to transform old emotional patterns. On a more mundane level this can manifest as the cleansing or transformation of part of your home.

Transiting Moon Conjunction Ascendant

A personal pleasure day. The good life calls to you. You express feelings easily. If nothing else denies this is a good health signal. Self esteem is stronger. Family members will probably contact you or perhaps even visit.

The Spiritual Perspective. Spiritually speaking the body is more sensitized today. Moods - whether positive or negative - have a more dramatic impact on the body and the personal appearance. You will register psychic vibrations right in the body.

Transiting Moon Conjunction Midheaven

A good career aspect. This represents a "monthly career high". Women are helping the career and boosting your status. Family cooperates with your career objectives. You are as ambitious for the family as you are for yourself. Family values are unusually important today as well.

The Spiritual Perspective. Spiritually, you get a chance to appreciate the importance of family in your own life and in the life of the human species. The mother aspect of spirit will be more appreciated.

Transiting Moon Square Moon

A difficult transit - but short term. Your personal mood and feeling is "out of synch" with the general mood and feeling. On an emotional level you are "out of synch" with the cosmic energy of the day, so this can lead to bad moods, emotional conflicts, irritability and conflicts with women. The way you normally feel is not "evil" and you are not a "bad person" but others can have different emotional positions because they see things differently. Don't make conflicts worse by dwelling on them. Let the dust settle and chances are the general mood will shift and things will work out.

The Spiritual Perspective. Spiritually, this is a good day to practice "emotional tranquillity" and equilibrium. To build inner power into the Astral body.

Transiting Moon Square Sun

A difficult transit but short term. The overall mood of people is not in synch with your urges to shine, your sense of self worth and your career aspiration. If there is too much personal ego you can expect an attack from others. The men and women in your life seem in conflict. The male perspective and the female perspective are out of synch. Both are correct but need some modification.

The Spiritual Perspective. The spiritual lesson here is to shine silently regardless of what others feel.

Transiting Moon Square Mercury

A difficult transit- but short term. Not a good day to schedule lectures to women or to try to communicate with masses of people (but other positive factors can modify this.) People are not in the mood or the right state to hear what you have to say. Though your logic be brilliant and true, the mood of the moment - the psychological atmosphere - is not conducive to reception. Try to establish the right emotional rapport (and it will require extra work) before you try reasoning with people.

The Spiritual Perspective. Spiritually, observe how emotions - especially those of others - affect your thought process and logic. A good day to "turn the mind off" and just observe things without judgement.

Transiting Moon Square Venus

A difficult transit but short term. Though you try to be loving and harmonious, the general mood of the day interferes with it. Romance is about mood and others might not be in the right mood today. It doesn't mean that they don't love you and you shouldn't take it to heart. Try again another day. Family members could temporarily be out of synch with your friends or lover. Domestic and family duties interfere with your social and love goals.

The Spiritual Perspective. Spiritual muscles can be developed by practicing love under difficult circumstances.

Transiting Moon Square Mars

A difficult transit but short term. This transit can lead to temper tantrums or conflict. The mood of the day - its tone and tenor is not conducive to your desires for exercise or sexual expression. Your physical energy and libido is not up to its usual standards. Family and domestic duties want your physical energy and there might not be enough left over for exercise or sexual expression.

The Spiritual Perspective. A good day to practice Karma Yoga - to do right regardless of how you feel or how it is received by others.

Transiting Moon Square Jupiter

A difficult transit but short term. Do you pursue financial goals or family duties? Do you pursue your spiritual life or deal with domestic issues? There is conflict here. Perhaps you need to do a little bit of both. Unexpected family or home expenses can temporarily crimp the bottom line or throw financial plans awry - but don't worry, things will straighten out tomorrow. These Moon transits seldom have any long term impact. The general mood could push you to make financial decisions that you will rue later on - you can be either too tight or too generous. Sleep on things before making a financial decision.

The Spiritual Perspective. The fact that your moral code and personal belief system is out of synch with the mood of the moment should not disturb you and this is the main spiritual lesson here. A true and correct belief system is above any temporary mood, feeling or psychological state. In fact, it can help you to deal with these things in a positive way.

Transiting Moon Square Saturn

A difficult transit but short term. More difficult to be organized, efficient and orderly today. The sense of discipline is weakened because the general mood of the day is against it. Your sense of duty and right order conflicts with the sentiments of those around you - perhaps they feel it is too cruel or too lax. If you insist on your way you run the risk of depressing others - making them sad. This is especially so with women or family members.

The Spiritual Perspective. Spiritually, you see that though your personal sense of order is OK, sometimes a "Higher Order" must supercede it.

Transiting Moon Square Uranus

A difficult transit but short term. Your normal sense of originality and freedom - your inventiveness - is not appreciated by others today. This is not because your originality is bad - on the contrary, it is probably very good - but people are not in the mood for it. Try again another time rather than resisting, rebelling or fighting. Family members can consider you too eccentric or rebellious today - but again this comes from mood and is not necessarily so.

The Spiritual Perspective. Be aware whether your originality is coming from a good place. Perhaps it is coming from a desire to shock rather than to be original.

Transiting Moon Square Neptune

A difficult transit but short term. Dreams, intuitions and so-called gut feelings need much verification today. The general mood could distort your reception of spiritual energy. Don't reject your dreams or intuitions, but put them on the shelf for further verification. Not an especially good day for communicating spiritual insights to others (especially women and family members) as they are not in the right mood to receive it. You need to do extra work to get them in the right frame of mind before attempting these things. You will also need to work harder to get into a meditative state. This is not your fault, only that there are more obstructions in the way. Keep trying as this will develop spiritual power.

The Spiritual Perspective. Much of what we say above applies here too.

Transiting Moon Square Pluto

A difficult transit but short term. Libido is not up to its usual standard. Your efforts to transform yourself must be balanced with your family duties and obligations. Family will resent being ignored today. Family members might not be receptive to giving loans. Elimination could be more sluggish or forced today.

The Spiritual Perspective. Spiritually, you are learning that sex drive waxes and wanes in normal ways. This is in the natural order of things and doesn't necessarily indicate that anything is wrong.

Transiting Moon Square Ascendant

A difficult transit but short term. Family members or women in general don't approve of your appearance or personality. The way you like to dress is out of synch with the mood of the day. Perhaps you feel overly controlled by family.

The Spiritual Perspective. A good day, from the spiritual perspective, to transcend the ego-image and realize that you are much more than that. Who you really are can never be diminished.

Transiting Moon Square Midheaven

A difficult transit but short term. There could be temporary - short term - setbacks to career aspirations. The mood of the day is out of synch with your career aspirations. Nothing wrong with your aspirations by the way, there's just some "bad weather" to be overcome. The conflict between family and career is more dramatic today. You will have to give each its due.

The Spiritual Perspective. Spiritually speaking the ups and downs of career should not deter you from your life goals.

Transiting Moon Opposition Moon

This is your personal Full Moon - you have more emotional energy today. Personal desires are either fulfilled or you see good progress towards their fulfillment. The mood of the day is opposite to the way you normally feel about things. But it gives insight into the emotional perspectives of others. If you can bridge these differences - especially with women and family members - there is much power.

The Spiritual Perspective. Since personal psychic energy is enhanced, there is more karma - either positive or negative - to your actions, thoughts and feelings. Thus your choices are more important today.

Transiting Moon Opposition Sun

A difficult transit but short term. The feminine and masculine perspectives are sharply defined and very stark. Neither one nor the other is either right or wrong - they are just operating from two different - diametrically opposed perspectives. In many cases this will lead to gender battles or problems between the parents, or between the men and women in your life. If you are a man you will want to separate yourself from the women in your life and if you are a woman you will want to separate from the men. But if you can bridge the differences, there is great power. This is not an especially good aspect for love or libido. There could be short term tension in the marriage or domestic situation. The natural conflict between family duty and career aspiration is highlighted. In many cases you will have to "do what is right" though you don't feel it and though the sentiment is against you. Family members, women in general, and the overall sentiment of the day might not support your sense of self esteem - shine silently and take a low profile.

The Spiritual Perspective. Spiritually speaking Oppositions are not seen as "stressful" but as "complementaries". The opposite perspective that you are forced to look at, really complements your own - if you can see the unity behind both. The opposite perspectives of the genders is a natural order thing and is useful to us.

Transiting Moon Opposition Mercury

A difficult transit but short term. Not an especially good day for communication - especially with women, family members or the public at large (but other things in the Horoscope could modify this). Your logic and thought process - perhaps your ideas - are opposed by the public sentiment. You feel inhibited in communication. Thought processes could be slower than usual. Though your mind be brilliant and your logic impeccable, it might be better to wait until public sentiment changes before presenting your ideas.

The Spiritual Perspective. Beneath the mood of the moment is a thought, idea or concept. Look to see if there is any validity to it.

Transiting Moon Opposition Venus

A difficult transit but short term. Family members (perhaps family responsibilities) oppose your friends or lover. Family duties vie with your social obligations and you need to balance both. You find it more difficult to express your love sentiments or your artistic inspiration.

The Spiritual Perspective. A good day to practice unconditional love - it will build the spiritual muscles.

Transiting Moon Opposition Mars

A difficult transit but short term. Libido is not up its usual standards. Though you know you should exercise you don't feel like it. Your proposed actions could be out of synch with the public sentiment or with family members. There could be arguments in the home or with family members. Tempers run high..

The Spiritual Perspective. The spiritual message here is that overt action is not always the solution to problems. Sometimes it is sometimes not - inaction could be called for today.

Transiting Moon Opposition Jupiter

A difficult transit but short term. Public sentiment and family members could distort the financial and philosophical judgement. Perhaps there are extra expenses in the home that impact on the bottom line. Your personal philosophy of life and view of the world seem contradicted by the events of the day. Make important financial decisions on another day.

The Spiritual Perspective. Spiritually speaking, there could be a short term "crisis of faith". Rejoice, faith is nothing without tests to it.

Transiting Moon Opposition Saturn

A difficult transit but short term. Allow more time to get to appointments. Delays are common under this transit. Your sense of order and discipline is contradicted by the events of the day and by the public sentiment. Family members could rebel against your authority or attempts at order. A day to develop more patience - a good humored patience.

The Spiritual Perspective. Order, Duty and emotional spontaneity seem diametrically opposed today, but in reality they are not. Duties are best done from a good and joyful mood, and a duty well done does bring emotional satisfaction. There is a need to see the unity in these two apparent opposites.

Transiting Moon Opposition Uranus

A difficult transit but short term. Your sense of freedom and innovation provokes a negative response from the public, women or family members. Your tendency would be to "over rebel" and this could cause even more negative response. Allow people their freedom to disagree with you, but go your own way. Mood changes could be more sudden and pronounced today.

The Spiritual Perspective. Spiritually this is a day to practice tranquillity and peace.

Transiting Moon Opposition Neptune

A difficult transit but short term. Gut feelings seem to contradict intuition and higher guidance. On days like today you can see the difference between a real intuition and a mere "feeling". Intuitive leads seem to push you "against the world" - against the mass sentiment. Or, perhaps they contradict the mass sentiment. Family duties or family members oppose your spiritual urges. The intuition and the dream life need further verification.

The Spiritual Perspective. Meditation and spiritual disciplines could be more difficult today, but important to understand that "spirit" is not angry with you, only that the astrological weather is more turbulent.

Transiting Moon Opposition Pluto

A difficult transit but short term. Libido is not up to its usual standards. You feel coerced or manipulated - and need to be careful not to indulge in similar behavior. Urges to transform are opposed by the mass sentiment, public mood or family members. Try to avoid arguments today as passions can be very intense. If nothing else in the Horoscope denies, this is not an especially good day to take out loans, mortgages or refinancings.

The Spiritual Perspective. Spiritually speaking, this is a day when your efforts of transformation are "tested" by everyday life. Don't despise this testing as it is very valuable - you can see your progress and what more needs to be done.

Transiting Moon Opposition Ascendant

This position either puts the Moon in the 6th or 7th House. If the Moon is opposing the Ascendant from the 6th House health and work concerns obstruct your desires for personal pleasure or self esteem. If the Moon is in the 7th House it shows that social goals take you away from your personal needs. You think of others first (unless this is denied by other transits or aspects in the Horoscope.)

The Spiritual Perspective. Spiritually speaking, your image and appearance are tested by the events of everyday life and this is a good thing. Very often our critics reveal good ideas for improvement (though it might not be pleasant to hear the criticism) - catch the blessing here - it is there.

Transiting Moon Opposition Midheaven

Emotional and family issues - duties and responsibilities - detract from your attention to career.

The Spiritual Perspective. Spiritually speaking, a career is built by both overt actions and inner actions. Dreaming and doing are two ways to further a career. This might be a day for dreaming. Doing can come later. Everyday life events will test the career today, and this is valuable in that you can see how far you've come and what more needs to be done.

Transiting Moon Trine Moon

A happy transit - but short term. You are in a good mood today. Your feelings are in synch with the universe. There is harmony at home and with the family (unless other things in the Horoscope deny). You easily share moods and feelings with others.

The Spiritual Perspective. Spiritually speaking it is good to pay attention to this feeling of emotional harmony - give it as much attention as possible as this will enlarge the feeling. Also it will help you to recall it at other times when things are more difficult.

Transiting Moon Trine Sun

A happy transit - but short term. There is harmony with the opposite sex today. The general mood supports self esteem and your urge to shine. Libido is stronger and in general you have more energy (unless other things in the Horoscope deny). You are more creative and enjoying life more.

The Spiritual Perspective. The main issue is how you will make use of this positive energy.

Transiting Moon Trine Mercury

A happy transit - but short term. A good day (unless other things in the Horoscope deny) for communicating with the public or the masses. Your speech and communication resonates. Your logic is emotionally accepted. Your thoughts and mental processes are appreciated by others - especially women and family members.

The Spiritual Perspective. A word rightly spoken has unimaginable positive results.

Transiting Moon Trine Venus

A happy transit - but short term. This is a transit of "emotional harmony". Love is in the air. Romance can bloom. There is romantic opportunity. You feel more romantic. You express your feelings in a harmonious way. Women play cupid in your life.

The Spiritual Perspective. Enjoy the wonderful love feelings in the air, but also enjoy the times when love gets tested. The harmony and the tests are both working for your good.

Transiting Moon Trine Mars

A happy transit - but short term. Libido is increased. You are in the mood for exercise and sports. Your actions resonate with the general mood and are appreciated. You feel more courageous and decisive. "Gut feeling" actions tend to be successful.

The Spiritual Perspective. You are seeing that Mars is not evil per se, its only a question of getting into right alignment with it.

Transiting Moon Trine Jupiter

A happy transit - but short term. A wonderful financial transit. Luck is on your side. The general mood supports financial goals and your desires for expansion. Your religious beliefs and philosophical attitude strike a chord with the general public. Religious illumination can come from common people and from everyday commonplace events.

The Spiritual Perspective. Much of what we say above applies here as well.

Transiting Moon Trine Saturn

A happy transit - but short term. A good day to bring order and discipline into your home or life. The general mood supports your sense of order and you do things thoroughly and with attention to detail. Management decisions will tend to be good. You are clear headed and stable (unless other transits are denying this.)

The Spiritual Perspective. A day of revelation as you see that Duty and Feelings CAN work well together. You are seeing the true spiritual state of things. Organization and good management need not be onerous if one has the right attitude. Good to remember these feelings when the stressful times come.

Transiting Moon Trine Uranus

A happy transit - but short term. Your originality and inventiveness strikes a chord - resonates - with general public, with women and with family members. Your innovations are appreciated. There is teamwork with family members and in the home.

The Spiritual Perspective. A good day to trust your gut instincts - they lead to creativity and innovation. Changes tend to be happy - if nothing else in the Horoscope denies.

Transiting Moon Trine Neptune

A happy transit - but short term. Intuition is right on target. Trust your feelings today. You will learn why one second of intuition is worth years of hard labor. You are also very inspired and creative. Fine art, poetry, music and mystical type activities allure you - perhaps pursue you. Family members, and the world in general, seem to appreciate your spiritual insights.

The Spiritual Perspective. Much of what we say above applies here too.

Transiting Moon Trine Pluto

A happy transit - but short term. Libido is strong and well received.

Efforts at self transformation receive good support from women and the general public. A good day (unless nothing else in the Horoscope denies) to borrow money, pay down debt or increase your line of credit.

The Spiritual Perspective. The main issue here is how you will use your extra energy. Will it be constructive or profligate?

Transiting Moon Trine Ascendant

Women and the general public appreciate your image and the way you dress. You present a pleasing picture. You are accepted for who you are. Dress intuitively today.

The Spiritual Perspective. Though the body is not you, it is good to treat it well - just as you would treat any animal well.

Transiting Moon Trine Midheaven

The general sentiment favors your career goals and aspirations. Career is boosted by women, the mother or family members.

The Spiritual Perspective. You can more easily fulfill your spiritual mission today. There is help.

Transiting Moon Sextile Moon

A happy, but short term transit. It makes for good moods and emotional stability. You will have opportunities to share feelings with women, family members or the general public. There are opportunities to create domestic and family harmony as well.

The Spiritual Perspective. Nice to remember today's emotional harmony when the difficult times come. There are lessons we learn in harmony and lessons we learn in discord - today is about the former.

Transiting Moon Sextile Sun

A happy, but short term transit. There are opportunities for harmonious interactions with the opposite sex and to create harmony with them. Libido is stronger. Energy levels are higher.

The Spiritual Perspective. The main issue here is how you use your extra energy. Let it be for good and constructive purposes.

Transiting Moon Sextile Mercury

A happy, but short term transit. There is more intellectual clarity. You will have opportunities to communicate to the public, women or family members - and to communicate in a proper way. Your ideas, thought process and logic resonates with the public and the family.

The Spiritual Perspective. There is opportunity today to bring the mind and the feelings into harmony. Working together, they become a powerful force for good.

Transiting Moon Sextile Venus

A happy, but short term transit. Love opportunities happen. You have opportunities to express your feelings of love in a harmonious way. A good day (if nothing else denies) to create some harmony with the family or to entertain from home.

The Spiritual Perspective. There is great beauty in the humdrum, everyday things of life and this is a day where you can become more conscious of it.

Transiting Moon Sextile Mars

A happy, but short term transit. You are in the mood for exercise, sports and physical fitness. Your actions find favor with the public and with the family. Libido is increased. Your courage is admired by others.

The Spiritual Perspective. The main issue here is how you will use the extra energy that you have - will it be constructive or destructive?

Transiting Moon Sextile Jupiter

A happy, but short term transit. Financial confidence is strong. There are good financial opportunities coming. Family and women will support financial goals. There are opportunities for religious, spiritual and philosophical revelation. Your code of ethics finds favor. Educational opportunities come.

The Spiritual Perspective. A good day for prayer, meditation and higher studies. Much more easy to experience the Divine today.

Transiting Moon Sextile Saturn

A happy, but short term transit. You will have opportunities (and the mood) to order the home and take care of those necessary household tasks. Family is co-operative in your efforts to create order. You are a stabilizing force for the volatile emotions of others.

The Spiritual Perspective. You have opportunity to perform duties with good feeling and enthusiasm - to merge the sense of duty with "right feeling". Generally we think of Duty as something onerous and we do them half heartedly - today you can see that moods and emotions need not conflict with your duties.

Transiting Moon Sextile Uranus

A happy, but short term transit. You will have opportunities to express innovation and originality. Your need for freedom wins respect from others. You are in the mood for science, mathematics, astrology and group activities.

The Spiritual Perspective. Gut instincts and feelings can lead to new inventions and new knowledge today.

Transiting Moon Sextile Neptune

A happy, but short term transit. The intuition is good and is well received by others. There are opportunities to communicate spiritual or inspired information to others - in a proper and harmonious way. Others are more receptive to your inspirations than you may think.

The Spiritual Perspective. Much of what we say above applies here too.

Transiting Moon Sextile Pluto

A happy, but short term transit. Libido is stronger. There are opportunities to borrow, raise capital, or gain financial cooperation from family members and women. You will have opportunities to help others transform themselves. Your perception into the deeps of other people's emotions and moods is right on target.

The Spiritual Perspective. The main issue here is how you will use your extra energy - in a constructive or destructive way? Will you earn good karma or negative karma?

Transiting Moon Sextile Ascendant

A happy, but short term transit. You will have opportunities to improve your image and appearance. You are pleased with the way you look and so are others. Women and family members are open to help you find personal fulfillment.

The Spiritual Perspective. You have opportunities to love and appreciate your body today. So often we just take it for granted and perhaps criticize it. Regardless of its condition, it has been your faithful friend and servant and should be acknowledged.

Transiting Moon Sextile Midheaven

A happy, but short term transit. Career opportunities come - either from the family or women. If nothing else denies this is a good career day.

The Spiritual Perspective. Gut instincts can help further the career and more importantly your spiritual mission.

TRANSITS OF MERCURY

In the world view of Astrology, mind and intellect are not the "great enemy" as we hear in certain esoteric teachings. Since every planet, without exception, is the embodiment of a Divine Principle - an aspect of Divinity - mind and intellect too are Divine. But the mind that is not purified - a mind that is full of error - is certainly a problem - will certainly cause distress. But let the mind be purified of error and it is our great friend and ally on the path.

Mercury will bring intellectual clarity, information and ideas to any planet it contacts. Sometimes this comes internally and just as often through speech, a letter, a magazine or book. If the other aspects are good, the information will be good information - useful. If, other factors are denying (a square from Neptune for example) the information can be deceptive and will need verification.

Information makes the world go round. Without good information (we call it intelligence) one cannot fight or win a war, or make a good investment, or even drive to some unknown place. This is Mercury's function. When he is operating properly he brings good information - he is the messenger of the Gods. When he is not operating properly (this can be due to afflictions in the Natal Horoscope or by transits) his information can be faulty, biased or deceitful - he becomes the God of Thieves (one of his titles in the ancient world).

Mercury will also bring a sense of discrimination to any planet that it contacts. There will be a greater discernment in the affairs governed by the planet. The affairs governed by the planet will become more rational and less emotional. For example Jupiter's tendency is to give, give, give indiscriminately. With Mercury in the picture, the native will apply more discrimination in the giving - the giving will be more nuanced - the native might want to know what the largesse will be used for, or perhaps think "I have only X amount to give, and many people or organizations who are in need - let me study the situation and give only to the most needy and the most worthy".

If Mercury contacts the Sun, a creative idea that was vague, now has "words, thought and shape". The concept of the creativity comes. It now has existence on the "mental plane".

Very often people think that it is some "thing" that they need - perhaps a sum of money, a car, a home. But it in many cases what they really need is an "Idea" - and this is Mercury's function.

Intellectual wealth is perhaps the only true wealth. It can never be taken away, for no matter how much you use it, the original is always there. This is what Mercury brings to the table by transit.

Transiting Mercury Conjunction Moon

A happy but short term transit. Ideas come to you in dreams or intuitions. You learn by osmosis. You are in the mood to receive ideas and to learn. You arrive at logical conclusions by intuitive means. Family members are more open to logic and reason - they can be reasoned with. Important family news comes to you. You are more able to verbalize your feelings and emotions. When you speak or write, you feel what you are expressing.

The Spiritual Perspective. Sometimes its not "things" we need, but ideas and spirit is supplying these ideas today.

Transiting Mercury Conjunction Sun

A happy but short term transit. Ideas related to your creativity, children, self esteem or life path come to you - this can come from within or by mail or phone. Intellectuals support career goals and personal self esteem. The logic behind what you want to do comes to you - no longer is it a "blind urge". Creative ideas - and ideas for personal pleasure - also come. Siblings or neighbors come visiting.

The Spiritual Perspective. Sometimes its not "things" that we need - but ideas. And this is the essence of this transit. Spirit brings us good by bringing the "right ideas" at the right time.

Transiting Mercury Conjunction Mercury

A happy but short term transit. You are starting a new mental and intellectual cycle. Very good for beginning a new course of study or to launch a new communication into the world. You are setting new intellectual goals for yourself now. The way you think and reason is in vogue these days - in line with the way the world is reasoning and thinking.

The Spiritual Perspective. The mind/intellect is strengthened today. It has more voltage. Thought is expressed with more clarity, power and conviction. While this is all very positive, the danger here is that you go too far in the direction of "head knowledge" while ignoring heart knowledge. Clear thinking is very important in life and you have this today. But not everything can be solved by "figuring things out".

Transiting Mercury Conjunction Venus

A happy but short term transit. New ideas that further the love life come. If you are a creative person new creative ideas come. You are receiving important information about friends or the lover. You know how to speak and reason in harmonious non-offensive ways. Friends or the beloved will call or write. Good for creative writing. (If the aspects are stressed to this conjunction there will be a tendency to "over-analyze" love - and to relate more from the head than from the heart - this can dampen romance.) Platonic friendships flourish too.

The Spiritual Perspective. Those on the spiritual path will have revelation that the head and heart, logic and love, need not be antagonistic. In fact they are harmonious in essence, but they merely approach things in different ways.

Transiting Mercury Conjunction Mars

A happy but short term transit. You want to be everywhere at once. You cover much ground today. Ideas and information relating to your sex life, exercise regime or athletics interests comes to you. You tend to translate ideas into action very quickly. You act on your ideas.

The Spiritual Perspective. For those on the spiritual path, there is a discernment that mind and body - though different - need not be in conflict. The body acts on what the mind thinks and knows.

Transiting Mercury Conjunction Jupiter

A happy but short term transit. Wealth and financial ideas come. Traders see new techniques in their trading or receive trading ideas. More rationality is applied to the financial life. Wealth should be enhanced today.

The Spiritual Perspective. At certain times the doors of heaven open up and we have opportunity for revelation. This is one of those days. Spirit shows us that wealth is not really "things" but ideas. Wealth emanates from the mind.

Transiting Mercury Conjunction Saturn

A happy but short term transit. Ideas come that help you organize and order your life. New management ideas come - specifically designed for you.

The Spiritual Perspective. Today spirit reveals that the "order", the sequence, in which things are done play a big role in the end result.

Transiting Mercury Conjunction Uranus

A happy but short term transit. Ideas for new inventions or innovations come to you. The logic behind your feedings of rebellion are revealed. Intellectuals in the world support your originality and innovation. There is more communication with friends and with organizations you belong to.

The Spiritual Perspective. The revelation today is that "liberation and freedom" are of the mind. It must begin here. You have the power to liberate others - in their thinking - today.

Transiting Mercury Conjunction Neptune

A happy but short term transit. Spiritual ideas come to you. There is communication with spiritually oriented people - gurus, ministers, psychics, channels etc. The logic behind your intuitive leads is shown to you. A good day for inspired types of writing. Meditation will bring clear spiritual messages and guidance.

The Spiritual Perspective. Illumination will be of the mind today. You will receive it and have the ability to impart it to others.

Transiting Mercury Conjunction Pluto

A happy but short term transit. Ideas relating to sex, transformation and dealing with debt come. Intellectuals support your efforts at personal transformation. Letters regarding debt, refinancing or insurance come.

The Spiritual Perspective. Spiritually, you have the power to transform other people's thoughts and ideas today. Also you attain to a deeper understanding of your personal underworld - almost an "impersonal" understanding - and this is good.

Transiting Mercury Conjunction Ascendant

A happy but short term transit. You will try to look "smart" today, rather than sexy. New ideas regarding the body, personal appearance, diet and sensual pleasures will come. You communicate well.

The Spiritual Perspective. The mental body, though always a factor in the physical appearance, is much more of a factor today. A beautiful mind, beautiful thoughts, will readily and easily create a beautiful body.

Transiting Mercury Conjunction Midheaven

A happy but short term transit. Intellectual interests and communication are a high priority today. You are honored and recognized because of your mind, thought processes or ideas. Career is boosted through teaching, writing, marketing and communication.

The Spiritual Perspective. You have a rational understanding of your career and mission in life - almost an "impersonal, matter of fact" understanding - devoid of emotionalism. Those of you seeking to understand your mission in life, your special purpose will receive important information - probably through the written or spoken word.

Transiting Mercury Square Moon

A difficult but short term transit. You are not in the mood for logic, learning or intellectual activities. Learning is more difficult because of this. You can think, but your emotions don't reflect your logic. Your moodiness could be blocking important information that you need to hear. You hear news that disturbs you emotionally. Family don't respond well to logic - try love and good feeling.

The Spiritual Perspective. The challenge here is to get the astral and mental bodies in synch with each other - this is done by meditation and transcendence.

Transiting Mercury Square Sun

A difficult but short term transit. Your will and your sense of self are being attacked, or downgraded by intellectuals. Arguments are more likely to happen. Your path - that you know is right - seems very illogical. Logic (internal or external) argues against having fun or some creative project. There could be arguments with the children too.

The Spiritual Perspective. The right course today is one where both the mind and the sense of purpose are in harmony. There are activities where this consensus exists. Those are the best activities to follow.

Transiting Mercury Square Mercury

A difficult but short term transit. The way you think and express yourself - your mental and intellectual processes - are out of synch with the logic of the world at this time. There could be many useless arguments. Rather than argue, present your ideas at another time when there is greater receptivity.

The Spiritual Perspective. It can be very useful to confront ideas that are in conflict with your own. This doesn't mean that you have to agree with them, but by seeing the other perspective you can more finely tune your own thinking.

Transiting Mercury Square Venus

A difficult but short term transit. The head and the heart are in conflict. Love pulls you one way, but logic pulls you another. There could be arguments with the beloved today. Difficult to express romantic feelings in an intellectual and impartial way. Intellectuals speak in ways that offend your sense of aesthetics.

The Spiritual Perspective. On a day like this success lies in the ways where the head and the heart are in agreement - look for those ways, they are there.

Transiting Mercury Square Mars

A difficult but short term transit. Intellectual arguments and clashes are likely. Take a few deep breaths and count to ten before answering a provocateur. You can be headstrong and rash. Decisions can be made too impulsively. Thoughts and ideas shouldn't be translated into immediate action - take some time to reflect. Intellectual interests clash with sexual and athletic interests.

The Spiritual Perspective. It is possible to state one's ideas firmly - but there need not be any anger or heat about it.

Transiting Mercury Square Jupiter

A difficult but short term transit. Financial judgement can be awry. Other people's logic (perhaps even your own) might counsel courses of action that are not really in your best financial interest. You are in conflict between the benefits of short term and long term good. The middle way is generally best. Watch the spending today. Financial judgement can be overly optimistic today. Try to avoid religious and philosophical disputes. Logic argues against your religious and ethical beliefs - perhaps there is a crisis of faith.

The Spiritual Perspective. Religious disputes are seldom settled by argument so stop wasting your time. "Not by might, not by power, but by my spirit" do things occur.

Transiting Mercury Square Saturn

A difficult but short term transit. Managerial decisions taken today can draw criticism from your own logical processes or from those of others. To instill order and organization into your life requires you to go against your own logic. Letters or calls you receive conflict with your sense of order. There is a price tag on doing the right and responsible thing.

The Spiritual Perspective. There is a price tag on doing what is right - part of it is that it attracts arguments and disagreements. If doing right were "easy" there would be no merit to it. See the arguments as adding to your good karma.

Transiting Mercury Square Uranus

A difficult but short term transit. Your inventions, innovativeness, originality - your need for freedom - contradicts the logic and ideas of the present time. It can draw much verbal argument and criticism. You are rebellious against the current intellectual climate. Students feel rebellious at what they are learning in school.

The Spiritual Perspective. Criticism of your new invention or new innovation or original idea could have a good purpose behind it - often it leads to improvement of the innovation or idea.

Transiting Mercury Square Neptune

A difficult but short term transit. Intellectuals, the prevailing intel-lectual climate, and even your own logical processes clash with what you are receiving spiritually - with inner revelation, intuition or what a trusted Guru says. There is a crisis of faith. Don't try to force these things through verbal argument. Stay in silence and events will eventually show you the truth. This is the classic confrontation between intuition and logic. A real intuition will always - ultimately - prevail.

The Spiritual Perspective. Today you can see clearly the stark differences between the intuitive and mental planes. The mental plane is temporary, the intuitive is long term.

Transiting Mercury Square Pluto

A difficult but short term transit. Your efforts to transform yourself, to borrow money, increase your credit line draw intellectual fire from others. Your interests in the deeper things of life - death and rebirth, reincarnation, life after death etc. also draw intellectual criticism. Intellectual interests pull you one way, but your deeper interests pull you another. Understand that efforts at self transformation almost require a person to be exposed to criticism. Try to avoid argument - or at least reduce the argument.

The Spiritual Perspective. Personal transformation is rarely a "neat and tidy" business. When you make deep changes to yourself, you are disturbing the status quo in your world, hence the inharmony. But this is only temporary.

Transiting Mercury Square Ascendant

A difficult but short term transit. The way you dress or appear draws verbal criticism from others. You have trouble "looking smart". People underestimate your intelligence - but this is their problem.

The Spiritual Perspective. Sometimes criticism of your appearance can lead to improvements. See if there is any validity to the criticism and take appropriate action.

Transiting Mercury Square Midheaven

A difficult but short term transit. Intellectual interests conflicts with your career aspirations and duties. Your career path or position draws fire from the intellectuals around you.

The Spiritual Perspective. Criticism of your career path, if valid (or even partially valid) can lead to important improvements. This is the spiritual message here.

Transiting Mercury Opposition Moon

A difficult but short term transit. A classic struggle/conflict between logic and feeling. Not a good day for studying, learning or commu-nication - your heart isn't into it. Misinterpretation of what others say is more probable. Perhaps others are saying things that put you in a bad mood. Perhaps your normal ways of feeling come under "logical" or verbal attack. Not so good for communicating with family members either. Logic pulls you in one direction, but your feelings pull you the opposite way.

The Spiritual Perspective. Spiritually, oppositions are seen as complementaries - the natural partners of your position. The head and the feelings seem opposed but underneath they are one - two perspectives on the same thing.

Transiting Mercury Opposition Sun

A difficult but short term transit. When you try to shine or feel self confident you come under attack verbally or through logic. Your feelings of self esteem seem to go against logic (and indeed it was meant to be that way - but now you really feel it.) Urges to fun and creativity pull you one way while intellectual interests pull you in another. Intellectuals are not supporting your life goals or self esteem right now.

The Spiritual Perspective. Real self esteem comes from being able to shine in spite of criticism or intellectual opposition. These attacks can actually enhance your self esteem and life goals when viewed from the correct perspective.

Transiting Mercury Opposition Mercury

A difficult but short term transit. Your normal way of thinking and reasoning is out of synch with the current vogue of thinking and reasoning. Your logic works out one way, while other people's logic leads to opposite conclusions. Now you are learning of the duality of the intellectual process - it all depends on your assumptions. Not an especially good communication day. Phone and mail could be disrupted. Getting around town could be more difficult. Happily this is all short term.

The Spiritual Perspective. It is good to confront different ways of thinking - different ideas - from your own. This doesn't mean that you are wrong, but it can enlarge your perspective.

Transiting Mercury Opposition Venus

A difficult but short term transit. A classic struggle between the head and the heart. Love pulls you in one direction, logic pulls you in the opposite. The best course of action is a position that embraces both these positions. Intellectual interests pull you in one way while romantic and social urges pull you in another. More difficult to express love feelings today. Arguments with the beloved are likely but will be short term.

The Spiritual Perspective. The head and the heart are never really out of synch - they are just two ways of dealing with the same thing. They only seem to be out of harmony.

Transiting Mercury Opposition Mars

A difficult but short term transit. Intellectual interests pull you one way while sexual and athletic interests pull you in another. Your urge to action seems to defy all logic. Your actions could come under verbal attack and criticism by others - especially intellectuals. Hasty actions could be a problem.

The Spiritual Perspective. Spiritually speaking this is a day for uniting two opposite principles - the thinking principle and the acting principle. Thinkers tend to eschew physical action as their forte is thought. Clear thinking requires a stillness of the body. Action people tend to avoid too much thinking as thought would impede their ability to act. Both principles are necessary for successful living. Both are important. Sometimes we need to lean one way and sometimes another. Today is such a day.

Transiting Mercury Opposition Jupiter

A difficult but short term transit. Financial judgement may not be up to par today. Financial moves - even your generosity and good deeds - come under verbal attack. Your religious beliefs could also come under verbal attack and criticism. But if they are real and you are sure of your position, you won't be affected. Avoid religious disputes and hasty financial moves.

The Spiritual Perspective. Spiritually there is a need to integrate and unify the "lower and higher" minds today. The lower mind is concerned with facts, circumstances, conditions - it has a short term, but very necessary, perspective. The Higher Mind is not so much concerned with "facts" as with "principles" and the meaning of these facts. Ideally, they should operate in harmony, but today, one seems to deny the other. But this is only appearance. Look deeper. Perhaps the facts will modify your beliefs. Perhaps your beliefs will give a new meaning to the facts.

Transiting Mercury Opposition Saturn

A difficult but short term transit. Intellectual interests and duties conflict with each other. You know you have to clean your house, but there is an interesting lecture or seminar that you want to attend. You know you have to go to work and pursue your career path, but there's a great book you want to read. Managerial decisions could come under undue verbal attack or criticism - think before acting.

The Spiritual Perspective. This transit shows a need to balance the mental desires (which are valid and true on their own level - just as valid as physical desires) with the realities of life in the now moment. Many will be able to see how the mind can "distract" from important duties, if left on its own. On the other hand, false duties and responsibilities - those that are not truly our own - can impede intellectual development. We need to get into the center here and discern.

Transiting Mercury Opposition Uranus

A difficult but short term transit. Your originality, invention or innovation comes under undue (perhaps harsh) verbal attack or criticism. A good idea to understand the objections so that you can either discard them (if there's nothing to it) or improve your idea (if others have valid points). There could be verbal arguments with friends or in a group you belong to. There are intellectual objections (either internal or from others) to important (and perhaps valid) changes that you need to make.

The Spiritual Perspective. Change rarely comes easily. It disturbs the status quo. Blockages to change can come from many areas - either emotional, physical or mental. Today the impediments come from the mental plane.

Transiting Mercury Opposition Neptune

A difficult but short term transit. A classic confrontation between logic and intuition - logic and higher spiritual perception. If you follow intuition you'll be subject to harsh criticism - but that's only initially. If you're willing to weather this storm intuition (if it is true) will prevail. Not an especially good day to rationalize your inspirations or spiritual ideals. The logical forces in the world seem non-accepting.

The Spiritual Perspective. Since intuition comes from a level way above the thought processes, it is understandable that the mind would consider your intuition as "ridiculous" etc.

Transiting Mercury Opposition Pluto

A difficult but short term transit. Your urges to transform, to delve into the deeper things of life, to deal with debt issues conflicts with your intellectual interests. A sexual escapade is likely to draw fire and criticism from others. Arguments are more likely today. Guard your tongue and don't make matters worse.

The Spiritual Perspective. Transformation rarely comes easily - there are natural obstructions to it. It is more like childbirth than anything else. The discomforts we feel are like labor pains. But today you might feel these discomforts on the mental level.

Transiting Mercury Opposition Ascendant

A difficult but short term transit. Intellectual, health and social interests pull you away from attention to yourself and your personal needs. Self confidence is not as strong as it could be. Perhaps your personal appearance - the way you dress or did your hair - draws fire and criticism from others around you.

The Spiritual Perspective. You will probably have to work harder to "stay in your body" today. You seem "spaced out", distracted. Your mind is elsewhere. Make an effort to practice "mindfulness" today. You might not be giving the body the attention that it needs and deserves (because your mind is focused on "more important" things) and this can draw criticism to you.

Transiting Mercury Opposition Midheaven

A difficult but short term transit. Intellectual interests pull you one way while career duties pull you another. Career aspirations or job performance is likely to be overly criticized - be more careful.

The Spiritual Perspective. The career is not receiving your full mental attention and you are distracted by other things. You will have to make special effort to focus here. The danger here is that you might temporarily forget the reason for your incarnation and this can lead to mistakes.

Transiting Mercury Trine Moon

A happy but short term transit. A good day for learning and communicating. Family members are more able to learn too. You can emotionally empathize with the logic and ideas of others. Intellectuals support your moods and feelings. Moods are likely to be good - unless other things in the chart deny.

The Spiritual Perspective. Though our feelings and logic are often at odds, there is no essential conflict between these two principles. Each is valid in its own sphere. Often the best course of action occurs when the logic and the feeling agree with each other - as you have today.

Transiting Mercury Trine Sun

A happy but short term transit. Your self esteem, creativity and joy of life draws praise from others. New ideas come to you that support your life path, self esteem and creativity. Children have an easier time learning. Speculations are favorable.

The Spiritual Perspective. Our inner Sun shines whether others agree with us or disagree with us. But it is more pleasant (on a psychological level) when others are agree. Today is such a day.

Transiting Mercury Trine Mercury

A happy but short term transit. If nothing else in the Horoscope denies, this is a good communication day. The mind and intellectual powers are strengthened. Learning and teaching go easier. Your thought process and ideas are in synch with the general thought process of the world. You have an ability to reach others on an intellectual level. You also receive information much easier. For students, a good day for study or taking tests.

The Spiritual Perspective. While the intellectual nature is not the ultimate, from a spiritual perspective, its clarity and strength play an important role in our well being. A mind free of error will make sound judgements, and good decisions. It will be a valuable ally in our spiritual quest.

Transiting Mercury Trine Venus

A happy but short term transit. If nothing else denies, this is a good love and romantic day. You receive information or calls or letters that evoke the love force in you (a love letter?). Your intellectual interests support your social and love goals. Singles could find love in the classroom or at a lecture or seminar. You express your love feelings well. Your head and your heart are in synch.

The Spiritual Perspective. The head and the heart are merely two different ways by which we can understand and appreciate the world. Music is a good example of this, but it applies to many other things. Music can be appreciated by the heart and feelings without the mind. The beauty and the rhythm touches us and there is joy. We don't need to understand the technicalities - the joy is in the music itself. But the educated person can also enjoy music from his or her head - he or she sees the chord progressions in the song, the intricate mathematics involved in the music, the style with which the musician expresses these mathematical patterns of beauty. And yes, there is a joy in this. Either way of music appreciation brings a joy. But when we can enjoy the music with BOTH our heads and our hearts, the joy is magnified. This is the kind of a day where you can appreciate the world with both your head and your heart. The mind and heart are not in antagonism, but in unity - each appreciating things in its own way.

Transiting Mercury Trine Mars

A happy but short term transit. Ideas are easily translated into actions today (if nothing else in the Horoscope denies). Your actions are logical and based on good judgement. Reflexes are sharper and you excel at sports or exercise. New and happy ideas come to you that enhance your physical energy, sexuality and courage.

The Spiritual Perspective. This shows a harmony between the mind and the body - the head and the body. There is a well being that comes when these two are in alignment and this is one of those days. Good to remember this feeling for the future as you want to make this "the norm".

Transiting Mercury Trine Jupiter

A happy but short term transit. A good financial day. Wealth ideas or important wealth information come to you. Financial judgement will be sound - if nothing else in the Horoscope denies. Communication activities - sales, marketing, PR etc. - support the bottom line. Higher studies go well. Your ability to communicate religious or philosophical ideas - abstract ideas - is strengthened. Your personal philosophy of life, religious beliefs and view of the world is seen as logical and reasonable by the world.

The Spiritual Perspective. This transit shows that the upper and lower mental bodies are more in synch - if there are no other transits that are denying. This good alignment enhance the judgement and overall mental abilities.

Transiting Mercury Trine Saturn

A happy but short term transit. New ideas or information comes to you that helps you take charge of your life - helps you to set a desired order and organization in your affairs. Managerial decisions are sound and reasonable. Sales, marketing and communication activities support career aspirations. The mind will be stable and deep - a good day to handle accounting chores, or other mental work that requires care and precision.

The Spiritual Perspective. A right and good order is essential to happiness in life, but these things don't just happen - they need thought and consideration. This is a good day to think these things through. The mind "wants" to be helpful in this regard.

Transiting Mercury Trine Uranus

A happy but short term transit. New and inventive ideas come to you. Your inventions, innovations and overall originality draws praise from would-be critics. There is good and happy communication with friends. A good day to study science, technology or astrology. You have excellent judgement about group dynamics today.

The Spiritual Perspective. Originality and insight usually comes in a flash of inspiration, but then comes the hard part - working it out - making it rational. A good day to rationalize - make logical - your innate originality - a good day to explain it to others in a clear way.

Transiting Mercury Trine Neptune

A happy but short term transit. Your intuition, spiritual guidance and spiritual ideals are logical and reasonable. You have good ability to communicate these things to others - you can present them in a logical way. A very good day to study scripture, poetry or other inspired literature - also a good day to teach these things to others. Your head and your intuition are in synch. Logic is intuitive. What is reasonable is also probably what is most spiritual - if nothing else in the Horoscope denies. You receive important spiritual guidance and knowledge today.

The Spiritual Perspective. Spiritually speaking this is a day for revelation. The mind is very much in synch with the spiritual world and spiritual realities. A day for getting "head knowledge" of the spirit, rather than "heart knowledge".

Transiting Mercury Trine Pluto

A happy but short term transit. Your ability to concentrate and focus is greatly enhanced. New ideas and information come to you that help you deal with debt, borrow money, raise outside capital and improve your efforts at self transformation. You will see some of the logic behind the deeper things of life - such as death and rebirth, reincarnation, life after death. Occult type literature is appealing now. Sexuality is enhanced by good communication. Spiritually speaking we can see that passion per se is not evil. So long as it is yoked to the mind and the spirit - to the rational process - passion will provide the fuel to the attainment of goals that have been "reasoned" out beforehand.

Transiting Mercury Trine Ascendant

A happy but short term transit. Your image, the way you dress and package yourself draws praise from others - you get verbal verification. Intellectual interests are pleasurable. New ideas to improve your body, image and sensual pleasure comes today.

The Spiritual Perspective. The body is a living organism with its own innate intelligence. It is possible to communicate with it - and with its various organs - and many a healing system is based on this. This is a good day to practice this as there is good natural communication with the body.

Transiting Mercury Trine Midheaven

A happy but short term transit. Your career aspirations draw praise from others. Intellectual pursuits support your career goals and boost the prestige. The career is furthered through sales, marketing, teaching, writing and PR. New and happy information regarding the career comes to you.

The Spiritual Perspective. Your mission in life, the reason for your incarnation will get clarified and intellectually understood. Sometimes (more often than not) we follow our path without consciously understanding it. It is much more fun when we can understand the why's and wherefore's of our spiritual mission, and this is more likely to happen today. While you may not receive full revelation, you will receive more understanding than previously.

Transiting Mercury Sextile Moon

A happy but short term transit. If nothing else denies, it is good for the overall mood. You will have opportunity to create harmony between the mind and your feelings.

The Spiritual Perspective. As with the Trine, you learn that logic and feeling need not be in conflict and you have opportunities to align these two principles in you.

Transiting Mercury Sextile Sun

A happy but short term transit. Opportunities come to communicate about who you are and what you're all about. Creative ideas come. Self esteem and self confidence is boosted. You can easily communicate with children. Fun loving pursuits will draw praise from others.

The Spiritual Perspective. As with the Trine, you see that head knowledge has its place in both your creative life and career.

Transiting Mercury Sextile Mercury

A happy but short term transit. The mind is strengthened. Communication ability is stronger. Your ideas and logic are in synch with the logic of the world. If nothing else denies, judgement will be sound. Your ideas are accepted by the intelligentsia.

The Spiritual Perspective. As with the trine, the mind/intellect is strengthened today - it has more voltage available to it. If nothing else denies, head knowledge will probably override heart knowledge - and sometimes this is how it should be.

Transiting Mercury Sextile Venus

A happy but short term transit. If nothing else denies, the head and the heart are in synch. There are opportunities for love communication. You express your love feelings logically and rationally. Good communication enhances love. The thought process of the beloved adds to the love.

The Spiritual Perspective. As with the Trine, love and logic are in harmony. There are lessons that we learn from conflict and lessons that we learn from harmony - today is a day for the latter.

Transiting Mercury Sextile Mars

A happy but short term transit. There are opportunities to create better mind-body coordination. Thoughts and ideas are easily translated into actions. You get pointers or receive information that enhances athletic or exercise performance. Libido is enhanced.

The Spiritual Perspective. You have opportunity to bring the mind and the body - the intellect and the physical instincts - into harmony and balance today. This is how they are supposed to work. Each has its role to play. Some people mistake thinking (or talking about something) as if it were "doing". But these are two distinct things that should work in harmony. When its time to act, act and don't think. When its time to think, think and don't act.

Transiting Mercury Sextile Jupiter

A happy but short term transit. Financial and intellectual judgement is good. Opportunities to boost the bottom line or expand your business through sales, marketing, teaching or PR will come. You will also have opportunities to communicate your religious, philosophical beliefs to others. A good day for bible study, the study of scripture and for philosophical discussions.

The Spiritual Perspective. The lower and higher minds - the lower and upper mental bodies - are in synch today. Each has a different role to play in your life, but there is harmony between them.

Transiting Mercury Sextile Saturn

A happy but short term transit. There will be opportunities to learn new ways to order and organize your life. Also to boost your career. Managerial decisions will be sound today. The mind will be deeper and more stable. Things learned today will be learned thoroughly.

The Spiritual Perspective. Spiritually speaking, as with the Trine, there is opportunity to understand the Order of Nature and one's "personal order" better.

Transiting Mercury Sextile Uranus

A happy but short term transit. There will be opportunities to learn more about science, technology and astrology - also to receive new ideas that will enhance your inventions, innovations and overall originality. There will be happy communication with friends. Your judgement on group dynamics is sound.

The Spiritual Perspective. As with the trine, it is a good day to explain your new ideas to others and to otherwise think more about them - make them rational and coherent.

Transiting Mercury Sextile Neptune

A happy but short term transit. There will be opportunities to create harmony between your logic and intuition - between spiritual values and rational values - you will see that there is no real contradiction between these things. A good day to communicate or receive spiritual guidance or inspired types of material. Your ideals will seem logical to others.

The Spiritual Perspective. Spiritually speaking this is a day where your intuition is likely to be verified by others, either through the written or spoken word.

Transiting Mercury Sextile Pluto

A happy but short term transit. The mind will be deep and penetrating today. You will have opportunity to learn more about the deeper things of life - sex, death and rebirth, reincarnation etc. You will also have opportunities to learn more about debt, taxes and insurance issues.

The Spiritual Perspective. On a spiritual level you will learn more about the real meaning of death and transformation - either through the written or spoken word.

Transiting Mercury Sextile Ascendant

A happy but short term transit. There will be opportunities to "look smarter" today - to present an image of intellectuality. Intellectual pursuits are pleasurable and enhance the self esteem and confidence.

The Spiritual Perspective. As with the trine and conjunction, you have a better ability to communicate with your body. Listen to it, it has important messages for you. Also, you can talk to it and it will respond. Remember, the body is an intelligence in its own right.

Transiting Mercury Sextile Midheaven

A happy but short term transit. There will be opportunities to enhance the career through sales, marketing, teaching, communication, PR etc. There will also be opportunities to receive new ideas about how to bolster the career.

The Spiritual Perspective. As with the Trine, this is a day where you are likely to receive more understanding about your career and spiritual mission for this life. This will usually come through the written or spoken word - but it can also come in meditation.

TRANSITS OF VENUS

Venus, the Genius of Love and Beauty, will impart these qualities to any planet that she contacts. Her transits are always considered benefic - that is, pleasant. Her beneficence and largesse are not as large as Jupiter's - the greater benefic of the zodiac - but still they are benefic.

Thus if she contacts Mercury, for example, the speech, the writing, the overall communication will be more beautiful, elegant, and harmonious. Rather than just expressing a thought in a logical or matter of fact way, it will be phrased elegantly, with well formed and proportional sentences, rhythm and cadence. Where normally, the person might express him or self sharply or cuttingly - with Venus around, the speech will be less hurtful, softer.

If she contacts the Moon, the moods and emotions will be expressed more beautifully. There will be more harmony in the home and internal harmony in general.

Venus rules the sweet taste. She rules luxuries and pleasure. So her transits sweeten and bring pleasure - harmony - sensual delight and sensual beauty - to everything she contacts.

Of course the reader needs to understand, that other factors in the Horoscope and in the transits can add or detract from Venus' transit. But all things being equal, this is what she will do.

From the spiritual perspective, the sensual delights that Venus brings are not considered important per se. Spiritually, they are seen as side effects of other things - the normal manifestation of spirit - and not as anything important in their own right. But Venus' power to bring harmony and love to the feeling and earthly nature are very important. When discord abounds, spirit cannot come through. The doors are closed. So Venus' action, opens the doors to the Divine - and thus greater things can come through.

Venus has various levels of expression. On her lower mundane level she gives a desire for luxury, sensual indulgence for its own

sake, a desire for pleasure. Often, she will bring vicious over indulgence.

But on her higher levels of expression she brings an aesthetic
sensibility, a love for harmony, a desire to beautify the world, and of
course love between humans. When humans are in beauty, in love, in
harmony with each other they are close to the Divine. They are lifted
out of themselves into a deeper and better realm.

Transiting Venus Conjunction Moon

A happy but short term transit. .You are in a romantic mood.
Feelings are loving. If nothing else denies, there is harmony in the
home. Marrieds are able to bring romance into the mundane
everyday life - which usually is not romantic. A good day for entertaining from the home or for attending family gatherings. Also good
for decorating the home or buying art objects for the home.

The Spiritual Perspective. The Principle of love and beauty and the
Principle of feeling are in perfect synch. Meditations on love will
tend to go well today, efforts to be more loving will succeed. More
importantly those who are working for a realization of Divine Love,
will tend to attain. Once realization is attained it will be much easier
to hold your state when the aspects are more challenging.

Transiting Venus Conjunction Sun

A happy but short term transit. Romance blooms. There are romantic
opportunities and meetings. Social urges are in synch with your life
work and life goals. Young women come into the life. Your sense of
beauty is increased and artists will be more inspired. If nothing else
denies it is a good financial day as well.

The Spiritual Perspective. Another good day to realize the Love
Divine. Those who have been working on this, will tend to attain
today. It is also a good day to realize the Eternal Beauty of the Divine
- that beauty is its essential nature.

Transiting Venus Conjunction Mercury

A happy but short term transit. Your ideas, communications, and logical process evokes love in others. Others fall in love with your thought process and mind. A very good aspect for creative types of writing. You express yourself in beautiful ways. Today, communication and thought is not just about clarity and truth - but about beauty as well.

The Spiritual Perspective. Spiritually speaking, the Principle of thinking and communication is in synch with the Principle of Beauty. Today you can see why the poet says that "Truth is Beauty and Beauty is Truth". They are the same things realized by different faculties. When we look with the mind, we say it is "truth". When we perceive with the heart we say it is "beautiful". Poetry is truth perceived by the heart. Science is beauty perceived by the Mind.

Transiting Venus Conjunction Venus

A happy but short term transit. You are having your yearly (usually) Venus Return. A new social cycle is beginning. Old goals have probably been met and now is the time to set new ones. Your social and love urges are very much in synch with the current environment. A good romantic day.

The Spiritual Perspective. Spiritually speaking when an old cycle closes, all the goals and lessons of that cycle tend to be attained. So, you are now ready to expand your love life, your social life, your present relationship to a new and hopefully better level. It is a time to renew your present relationship at a higher turn of the spiral. Also because the love force in you is being strengthened today - it has more voltage - you tend to attract more love, by the karmic law.

Transiting Venus Conjunction Mars

A happy but short term transit. Libido roars. Sexual performance is pleasing. (This must be read in the context of a person's age and stage in life - but even older people will have more than their average libido.) Physical movements are graceful as well as powerful. Your courage, aggressiveness and bold actions are appreciated by the opposite sex. A good day to launch a "charm offensive" - or to take more aggressive action in love.

The Spiritual Perspective. Spiritually speaking, the Principle of Love and Beauty is in synch with the body - the Principle of action. It is on days like these that we realize that Spirit loves our bodies and that we can do no less. The body is not something to be despised or abused, but to be loved for what it is - an instrument of something higher.

Transiting Venus Conjunction Jupiter

An unusually happy but short term transit. A lucky day. Good for both love and money. Friends, lovers, the spouse are supporting financial goals. You are living affluently today. Your ethics, religious and philosophical beliefs are expressed beautifully and evoke love in others. Artists are unusually creative.

The Spiritual Perspective. Spiritually speaking what we call "luck" is only the right application of "law". Often people (because of transits such as these) are in a state where it is easier to apply the law, and so "lucky" things happen. With your Higher Mind (Jupiter) inspired by love (Venus) you are more in tune with higher principles and do the right things - you generate good karma for your self.

Transiting Venus Conjunction Saturn

A happy but short term transit. Your sense of order and organization will be expressed beautifully and harmoniously. You exert discipline in a way that is non-offensive and popular. Tough managerial decisions are handled diplomatically. Friends, lovers or the spouse are supporting your need to order and organize your life.

The Spiritual Perspective. In the world, love and order, love and discipline, are seen as antagonistic principles. But this need not be so, as you learn today. They can be complementary. A good order - a good system - a good discipline - is worthy of love. Also, any discipline can be made more pleasurable if we bring love into it.

Transiting Venus Conjunction Uranus

A happy but short term transit. No need to conform or toady up to others to win love. Just be your original and inventive self and love will find you. You are loved precisely because of your originality and so-called eccentricities. Sudden love or romantic opportunity can come. Friends will call. Group activities are enjoyable and can lead to romantic opportunity.

The Spiritual Perspective. Spiritually speaking many original and genius type people fail because they don't appreciate their own gifts. Sometimes they don't realize how awesome they are and that few people have what they have. The so-called "eccentricity" that you might be despising, is actually a great blessing to you. Today is a good day to love and give thanks for your own originality and unique perspective.

Transiting Venus Conjunction Neptune

A happy but short term transit. You love the whole world. You are unusually romantic. You love even though there is no object of love - its as if the object of love is irrelevant - love is good just for its own sake. You will receive inspired ideas in the fine arts. If you are not a practicing artist you will probably be involved in fine art in some way. Your love ideals are very high and what passes for love among mortals seems droll. Your spiritual ideals evoke love in others. Intuition leads to love today.

The Spiritual Perspective. Those who are not on a spiritual path can find their path today. Those already on their path will deepen it.

There is great love for both your path and for the Divine today. The commandment to "love God with all your heart and mind and your neighbor as yourself" is much easier to fulfill today - you have help.

Transiting Venus Conjunction Pluto

A happy but short term transit. Sexuality is happy and evokes love in the partner. In finance you prosper as you prosper others. Ways to prosper others come to you. You make money for the shareholders and inspire their love. Friends, partners, lovers or the spouse help to pay down debt, refinance, or lend you money. Love finds you as you pursue efforts of transformation and the prosperity of others.

The Spiritual Perspective. Pluto rules the "underworld" in ourselves and in others. For the neophyte this is not a "pleasant" or very lovable place - hence it is "hidden" from us. But if we would improve it, we must begin to love it and understand what it is. This love will gradually transform this area. Love doesn't mean that you necessarily approve of it - but you love it anyway. Today is a good day to begin, the cosmos is helping you.

Transiting Venus Conjunction Ascendant

A happy but short term transit. In a woman's chart, there is more glamor and beauty to the appearance. In a man's chart there is involvement with young women. Romance blooms for either sex. New personal items - jewelry, clothing or accessories - come. Personal pleasures - good food, good wine, personal luxuries - call to you. A day when you want to pamper yourself.

The Spiritual Perspective. Spiritually speaking it is very easy to love your body today. No need to force it or make conscious effort - it just sort of happens. Because your love for your body is strong, others too will love it.

Transiting Venus Conjunction Midheaven

A happy transit. For the next 30 days or so career is boosted. There is favor from bosses, elders and those in authority over you. A day to ask for favors from elders, the government and authority figures. Social contacts boost the career. You mingle with people of power and prominence - people above you in status.

The Spiritual Perspective. Spiritually speaking, it is easier to love your career, your life work and your spiritual mission for this life. Many will find their spiritual mission under these kinds of transits - if not today, in the future, under similar transits. The feeling of love will guide you.

Transiting Venus Square Moon

A difficult but short transit. Romantic urges and the daily domestic life are not in synch. There can be domestic inharmony. Difficult to bring romance into the domestic life. Though you might love a person, you can't seem to express those feelings properly - moods interfere. (This is true in reverse too.) Avoid family gatherings or entertaining from home if possible. Family probably doesn't approve of a current love or friendship. The lover is out of synch with your family.

The Spiritual Perspective. Spiritually speaking there is a need to consciously realize love working through all the daily affairs of life - in spite of negative appearances. There is a need to see through the illusion of conflict and to realize that this conflict is actually bringing something superior to pass. For the spiritual person this transit will enlarge the concept of "romance" - the daily affairs of life, the squabbles, the mundane rote tasks are "part and parcel" of real romance and are seen as "very beautiful" by the Higher forces.

Transiting Venus Square Sun

A difficult but short transit. Your ego, self esteem and creativity is not in synch with your social urges or is not appreciated by the lover or partner. Tone things down. There could be some conflicts with children today. Your path of joy conflicts with social urges or with the lover. Your will and your way doesn't find favor with others - friends, lovers, spouse etc.

The Spiritual Perspective. Many people think that their Christ nature (Immortal Ego) will bring them universal approval and love. While this is true spiritually, here on the mortal psychological level, it might well bring the opposite, and this is one of those days. The Solar Nature - the Immortal Ego - the True Self - is cruising to its Destiny with ease, grace and power. From its perspective these attacks are negligible, not an issue, an illusion and delusion. It pursues its path - its orbit - regardless. So the way to deal with this is to adopt the perspective of the Higher Nature. Look at these attacks and problems from its perspective and they will dissolve into harmony.

Transiting Venus Square Mercury

A difficult but short transit. There could be arguments with friends or the lover. Your ideas or thought process is out of synch with the lover's. You could be intellectually correct but find it difficult to express your thought diplomatically or harmoniously. A good day to practice this.

The Spiritual Perspective. Spiritually speaking, the cosmos presents you with a classic conflict between the head and the heart. It will take more spiritual effort on your part to resolve this - for basically it is an illusion. Spiritually speaking the head and the heart are aspects of one, unified being - only they have different perspectives on things. Their goals are basically the same, only they arrive at them in different ways. This is as it should be. The resolution to this conflict can happen in various ways. Perhaps you will have to modify your action - limit action - to areas where the head and the heart DO agree. Perhaps you will have to steer a middle course between both positions. Sometimes, it is better to delay action, until a consensus is reached.

Transiting Venus Square Venus

A difficult but short transit. Your sense of beauty and social grace is not in synch with the general sense of beauty. There could be a short term crisis in a love relationship or friendship. What you consider loving is not considered loving by friends or the lover. If there are no other transits supporting this, the problem will pass quickly.

The Spiritual Perspective. Spiritually speaking, your innate love force is not as strong as usual, thus you don't feel that you receive as much love as you should. You need to make special effort - spiritual effort - to strengthen the love force to overcome this. Meditations on love are good. Sometimes this is resolved by achieving other goals not related to love. For, these problems will resolve very shortly on their own, and you may as well make good use of your time and energy.

Transiting Venus Square Mars

A difficult but short transit. Libido is either overdone or under-done. Sexual expression is not found pleasing by the lover and doesn't evoke feelings of love. Your urges to exercise or athletics conflict with your social urges. Aggressiveness in love or in social matters doesn't find favor. Independent actions are also out of favor - try to consult first.

The Spiritual Perspective. Spiritually speaking, the cosmos presents you with a choice between love and power - kindness and grace, or the use of brute force. There are times in life where we MUST use power. There are times in life where kindness and grace - love - will solve things. Today, you're not sure which is the proper path to follow. Neither position is too palatable. You might have to use some combination of both, or delay actions until you feel clear. From the spiritual perspective these situations are good in that it will lead to greater understanding of these things.

Transiting Venus Square Jupiter

A difficult but short transit. The problem here is too much of a good thing. Perhaps you overspend, or over indulge in the good life. Perhaps you are over-generous with the beloved in a way that you can't really afford. Financial urges conflict with social urges. Your religious or philosophical ideas are not appreciated by the lover, spouse, partner or friends. Perhaps you need to express them more diplomatically. Philosophical differences impede the love life.

The Spiritual Perspective. Spiritually speaking this is a day to strengthen your religious and philosophical beliefs. It is easy to be moral and pursue justice when one is surrounded by praise, not so easy when these actions or beliefs bring condemnation and attack. Yet, if they are true, you must suffer through the attacks. Your spiritual connection will be stronger. Your virtues will also get stronger. You must not allow the natural desire for love to take you down immoral pathways.

Transiting Venus Square Saturn

A difficult but short transit. You need to bring order and organization into your life but when you do, you face conflict or objections from the lover, friends or spouse. If there are diplomatic ways to go about this then take it - if not it might be wise to delay these projects. Managerial decisions - though they are impersonal and even right - seem hurtful to friends the lover or spouse - or the sentiments of the people around you. Doing the right thing is often the most romantic thing as well, but this is hard to see in the short term.

The Spiritual Perspective. Two important Cosmic Principles seem to be in conflict - the loving thing to do seems to conflict with the need for right order - the right thing to do. If you go with either side you will cause problems later on. The middle road is best. Perhaps it is possible to do the right thing, but from a space of love - to soften an unpleasant action. Perhaps, if you meditate, you will see a way to satisfy both sides of yourself. Those on a spiritual path will experience an expansion - a new insight into both "love" and "right order".

Transiting Venus Square Uranus

A difficult but short transit. Your need for freedom impedes the love life or a current relationship. Your lack of commitment is not appreciated. Inventions or innovations are not appreciated by the lover, friend or spouse. Perhaps they see you as compulsively experimental - or innovating in a way that makes matters worse not better.

The Spiritual Perspective. On a spiritual level, the cosmos is giving you opportunity to strengthen your originality and innate uniqueness. Oh, anyone can be original when they are surrounded by love and praise. But the real innovators and inventors are the ones who persist in spite of criticism and attack. In fact, from the spiritual perspective, there is probably some benefit to the criticism. Perhaps, underneath, it reveals a way to improve your product or service. Also, such criticism, if handled properly will strengthen the character. Too often when we launch a new product or invention we do so from a motive of attracting love, adulation, praise or fame. The real motive should be releasing something new and better to help people around you - the human species as a whole. A good day to check your motivations and cleanse them.

Transiting Venus Square Neptune

A difficult but short transit. Intuition and artistic inspiration need more verification today. Idealism can be misplaced or misapplied and can be hurtful to the lover, friends, or spouse. Your spiritual ideals are out of synch with your friendships and love life. It feels to you that loved ones impede your spiritual progress.

The Spiritual Perspective. For the spiritual person today will bring an expansion of the understanding of love and spirituality. The conflicts - the opposition - to your spiritual ideals, is part and parcel of the workings of Spirit. Perhaps your ideals need correction - perhaps they need some fine tuning - perhaps it is strength that is needed. The conflicts will provide all these things if you stay in Higher Consciousness.

Transiting Venus Square Pluto

A difficult but short transit. Your sexual intensity is not appreciated by the lover or spouse. Perhaps you are overly intense. Perhaps jealousy and possessiveness has entered the picture. A love affair or friendship is in danger now. Social contacts are not that helpful in borrowing money or raising outside capital. Try another time. Your efforts to transform yourself could threaten a friendship, marriage or current love affair.

The Spiritual Perspective. Everyone has a "secret underworld" in their consciousness. Its not a pretty sight. Not color co-ordinated or well proportioned. There we find our cultivated tendencies from many, many lifetimes. Perhaps you are glimpsing some of it today, and you feel a sense of revulsion. This sense of revulsion can radiate out and obstruct the love and social life - by the karmic law. But revulsion, though understandable, will not help you in "cleaning these stables" - love and light will help.

Transiting Venus Square Ascendant

A difficult but short transit. The way you dress, color coordinate, accessorize etc. might not find favor with loved ones or friends. Also it might not be appropriate for the current social situation. More difficult to glamorize the image the way you want it. There can be an "out of synch" feeling with the lover, friend or spouse - you want to do one thing and he/she wants to do another. Tone down ego and take a lower profile.

The Spiritual Perspective. Spiritually speaking you might not be loving your body today and it is reflecting out as criticism by others. You can correct this by loving your body "just as it is" - by praising it for all the faithful service it gives you. Of course, you need not go overboard here. Your body is not you - but you can love it the way that you would love a pet horse or cat.

Transiting Venus Square Midheaven

A difficult but short transit. Social urges pull you in ways that interfere with the career aspirations and duties. The lover, partner or spouse is nor supporting current career moves or your attention to career. Bossed and elders are cross about your social urges. Try to give both as much as possible.

The Spiritual Perspective. Our career and mission in life is something that we deeply love. But there are times and situations where we don't love it - the chores, the difficulties, overwhelm us and we lose, temporarily, that feeling of love. This is one of those days. We can compare it to a Mom and her beloved child. She loves the child, but on certain days, when he's particularly naughty, she seems cross with him. These "cross" feelings are superficial, her underlying love is still there. So it is with your career and spiritual mission. You need to keep "soldiering" on. These feelings will pass - and very quickly.

Transiting Venus Opposition Moon

A difficult but short transit. Romance and social urges pull you one way, but family duties and obligations pull you in the opposite way. The lover or friend is out of synch your family and vice versa. More difficult to express feelings of love. Marrieds find it more difficult to bring romance into the everyday life. Re-schedule family gatherings or entertainments from home.

The Spiritual Perspective. Both Venus and the Moon represent our "feeling nature". Venus represents our higher feelings - our feelings of love, beauty and harmony - while the Moon represents our "normal feelings", our daily moods and emotional instincts. So it is harder to attain to the "feeling of love" today. The passions, the moods, the instinctive nature are not in sync with the love feelings being broadcast by the cosmos. The spiritual person WILL be able to feel love, but through more meditative effort. And this is what is called for. Probably memories of the past are being triggered that block love feelings. Perhaps there are painful memories, not yet resolved, of past loves that ended badly. These need to be looked at today.

Transiting Venus Opposition Sun

A difficult but short transit. Romantic difficulties. You are out of synch with the lover, partner or spouse. Feelings of self esteem and self confidence are not appreciated by friends, the lover or spouse. Creativity and joy pull you one way while romantic urges pull in another. If you can bridge these differences (not easy) romance can bloom.

The Spiritual Perspective. The masculine and feminine principles seem out of synch today. Though in truth they are always in union and harmony, they do have different perspectives on things. These different perspectives are "natural order" - correct. Today you are seeing the different perspectives very clearly, and this is good. If you accept both perspectives as true, you will be led to higher spiritual ground where both these perspectives are integrated into a unified whole. Now, one perspective is the right path, now the other.

Transiting Venus Opposition Mercury

A difficult but short transit. Intellectual interests - the life of the mind

- pull you in one way while love and social interests pull you in another. You want to attend class, but the lover wants to go to a party. There could be verbal arguments with friends or the beloved today - be careful. The mind and the heart are not in synch. Logic pulls you in one direction, but love pulls you in another. The logical way might not be the most loving way.

The Spiritual Perspective. A classic conflict between the head and the heart is happening - a conflict between logic and love - head knowledge and heart knowledge. In some cases, either the head (the logic) needs purification, or the heart. The conflicts are coming from "impurities" in either - sometimes both. Cleanse the impurities through spiritual methods and harmony will soon be restored - in spirit there is no conflict between the mind and the heart. Both are merely different ways of arriving at a certain goal. Each has its place and each works in harmony with the other.

Transiting Venus Opposition Venus

A difficult but short transit. The way you show love is not in vogue at the moment. Friends and lovers are not appreciative. They think you should show it in other ways. Your personal aesthetic sense is also not in fashion today. Your taste comes under question.

The Spiritual Perspective. Because Venus is now in her "full Moon" phase of your personal cycle, many love goals have been achieved. And it is this very achievement that seems to weaken your personal love force. Its as if you ask, "Is that all there is?" Sometimes (not always) the worst thing that can happen to a person is to get what he or she asks for. But this too leads to good. By going through the experience you gain wisdom and perspective. Your love nature gets expanded. Right now, what was once a "seed of love" has blossomed into a full blown tree. You can see it clearly. It is manifest. You can see the good points and the bad points. And because of this, you can make corrections and adjustments for the future.

Transiting Venus Opposition Mars

A difficult but short transit. Not conducive for love or sexuality. There can be passionate conflicts with the beloved. Athletic interests conflict with social urges. The need for adventure and independence hinders the love life and a current relationship. Independent action - unilateral action (and you may be forced to do this) is seen as unloving or inconsiderate. The love life is tempestuous. Too much aggressiveness in love is not advisable.

The Spiritual Perspective. Spiritually speaking this is a day where more work needs to be done to harmonize the male and female principles within you. It is right and proper that each has a different perspective - an opposite perspective - from the other. This is what makes creation possible. Neither is right nor wrong - but sometimes one way is right and sometimes another. Also remember, from the astrological perspective, that opposites are the natural marriage and love partners. Also this is a day where you have to confront the difficult decision of whether to use force and power in a given situation or to use grace, kindness and love. In life, sometimes force and power is necessary, and this might be one of those times. But first try kindness.

Transiting Venus Opposition Jupiter

A difficult but short transit. Love and financial urges pull you in opposite directions. Difficult to fulfill financial obligations and please the beloved (or friends) at the same time.

The Spiritual Perspective. Spiritually speaking, your religious and philosophical beliefs conflict with love and it is difficult position to be in. Don't let the need to be popular force you into unethical behavior. On the other hand, love might reveal flaws in your religious, philosophical beliefs and you will have opportunity to amend them. Your belief system (if it is correct and congruent to reality) is a very wonderful thing. But these are merely "guides" on the path of life. There is a need to be able to apply them in specific situations - and in situations of conflict, which you have today. So long as you are true to them in principle, you will apply them correctly in the specific situation.

Transiting Venus Opposition Saturn

A difficult but short transit. Love and social urges pull you one way while Duty pulls you in another. Your need to assert order, organization and discipline could make you unpopular. Today you learn that the right thing is not always the popular thing. Love urges and career responsibilities also conflict. Strive for the middle way.

The Spiritual Perspective. Love and Duty seem like antagonistic principles, but really (when seen correctly) they are not. They are complements. Duty - doing the right thing by your loved ones and yourself - is often the highest form of love. When you love, you will do your duty. This is a day when you need to understand these things more clearly and the cosmos, in its infinite mercy, has given you a real life "drama" in which to learn.

Transiting Venus Opposition Uranus

A difficult but short transit. Your need for freedom and unconventional beliefs can shake up the love life or friendships. You can be overly rebellious with friends or the beloved. Today you learn that originality doesn't always bring popularity - in fact it can bring the reverse.

The Spiritual Perspective. Real originality and innovation stems from love. The soul desires to make like easier for others and thus creates new innovations, inventions, technologies and reforms. But in the short term, these things can bring storm and criticism from others and this is one of those days. Today is a day where you will have to work hard to love your originality and uniqueness - to appreciate these things in yourself, because the world doesn't seem to appreciate it. Also, love (through criticism and perhaps even attack) might guide you to making improvements in your reforms, inventions and innovations. Underneath the unpleasantness is a great treasure.

Transiting Venus Opposition Neptune

A difficult but short transit. Intuition needs verification. Love pulls you one way while your spiritual urges, ideals and inner guidance pulls you in another. Your idealism is not especially popular and you will see that there is a steep price tag to any spiritual ideal. But if the price wasn't high, would it be worth it?

The Spiritual Perspective. Neptune rules the love divine - the impersonal love of spirit that loves everything and everybody "equally". Venus rules "personal love", human love. This is the love that loves "X" ardently, but doesn't love "Y". So the Cosmos presents you with a conflict between these two principles. Impersonal love sometimes can hurt the personal love life. The lover feels " Oh he/she loves me, but he/she also loves the squirrels, the trees, the ocean and all those other people as well....I'm nothing special in his/her eyes". So these issues need clarification. Can someone who loves "impersonally" be involved in a normal human relationship? If I love with the love divine, will I lose my whole romantic life? Ultimately even the personal love life needs to be surrendered to spirit and this is one of those days. The truth is, since we are multi-dimensional beings, we can love with the love divine and still have "romantic" feelings for special people. Both can happen at the same time. But this is a day for getting spiritual revelation on this subject, and this comes through "surrender".

Transiting Venus Opposition Pluto

A difficult but short transit. Passions run high in love. There could be a crisis in a current love relationship. There is a need to avoid jealousy and possessiveness. Sexual intensity doesn't evoke love today. Try a softer approach. Urges to transform yourself are not popular with friends, the lover or spouse. Perhaps they are seen as overly selfish and self indulgent.

The Spiritual Perspective. Personal transformation is one of the important works of those on the spiritual path. We are meant to become "more than man" - to become immortals with immortal bodies. This is a long and slow process and doesn't happen overnight. This transformation process will face many challenges - and today is one of them. As a person changes, relationships will inevitably change. Crisis in relationship is normal. Good relationships will adjust to the change and survive the crisis. But flawed ones won't. You need to continue to love others, but keep on with your transformation process.

Transiting Venus Opposition Ascendant

This aspect usually occurs with Venus in either the 6th or 7th House. With Venus in the 6th House, health and work take you away from needs for sensual pleasure. You may have to forgo that fatty meal or rich desert today. The demands of the work place could also be more intense. With Venus in the 7th you need to think more of others than of yourself. The way you look or dress might not be popular with friends or the beloved.

The Spiritual Perspective. It is harder to love your body today as you are more focused on others. This reduction in love has karmic consequences as others (like a mirror) seem disapproving of your body or image. And then a vicious cycle can begin, the more they disapprove, the more you disapprove of yourself, and on and on and on. You need to make special effort - meditatively - to love and appreciate your body today.

Transiting Venus Opposition Midheaven

A difficult but short transit. Love and family concerns pull you one way while career duties pull you in another, you are caught in the middle. You will have to work hard - be ingenious - to satisfy the family, the lover or the boss.

The Spiritual Perspective. Spiritually speaking, Oppositions always reveal "unity". The opposing forces are really two sides of a coin and complement each other. Life is an "alternation" between opposites. This alternation between love, family and career is, in reality, a healthy thing. It might not be "comfortable" on a psychological level, but it is healthy.

Transiting Venus Trine Moon

A happy but short term transit. There is emotional and domestic harmony today (unless other things in the Horoscope deny). You are in the mood for love. Love feelings are expressed harmoniously. You feel loving. A good day for entertaining from home or for family gatherings. Your aesthetic sense in home decor is very strong and it is good for buying objects of beauty for the home or to otherwise beautify it. Marrieds can easily make the domestic life more romantic. Singles find that their lover or friends are in synch with the family. A good day to bring a lover to meet the family. Family supports romantic urges and perhaps plays cupid. You show love by giving emotional support and like to receive it in return.

The Spiritual Perspective. You can see that love can make the most mundane - even dreary - events "romantic" and beautiful. Nothing is romantic or beautiful in or of itself, only love makes it so.

Transiting Venus Trine Sun

A happy but short term transit. Love blooms. There are romantic meetings and opportunities. You are loved for who you are - for you sense of self esteem and self worth - for your creativity - for just being you. Love elevates self esteem. Creativity is excellent today. Career is boosted by young women and social contacts. The beloved supports career aspirations. You get along better with children.

The Spiritual Perspective. The union and harmony of the masculine and feminine always produces "creation" of some kind. These creations can happen on many levels - ideas, feelings or physical things. So this is a creative kind of day.

Transiting Venus Trine Mercury

A happy but short term transit. You not only express yourself clearly but also elegantly and beautifully. Your logic true but also diplomatic and friends or the beloved fall in love with your thought process as much as with you. There is love talk today - or communication from the beloved or friends. A wonderful aspect for teachers or creative type writers.

The Spiritual Perspective. The head and the heart are in "synch" today. Thus actions and decisions are more likely to be correct and powerful (of course, other things in the chart should also be taken into account, but of itself this transit is a positive.) Some spiritual teachings teach that the "mind is the enemy", but today you see otherwise. The mind, when purified, is your friend and ally. Today is good day to love your mind (your intellect) and appreciate it for what it is.

Transiting Venus Trine Venus

A happy but short term transit. Your aesthetic sense is in vogue today. The way you show love evokes loving responses from others. The social life blooms.

The Spiritual Perspective. Your love force is strengthened today. It has more voltage. Since more love comes out of you, you receive more, by the karmic law.

Transiting Venus Trine Mars

A happy but short term transit. There is sexual harmony today. Sexual expression is pleasing to the partner and evokes love. The lover, friends or partner supports unilateral or independent action. Your approach to love is just right - neither too aggressive nor too passive. You can be forward when you need to be and passive when that is called for. Your movements are more graceful and fluid. Love opportunities can happen at the gym or as you play sports.

The Spiritual Perspective. Spiritually speaking, today is a day for seeing what sexual and gender harmony should be like. We need to be able to see the ideal before we can make any proper goals. The student of painting needs to see works of the masters so that he or she can see the potential of his or her own gift. Likewise, the student of life, needs to see what the ideal is, though it often doesn't last, in order to see his or her own potential in this area of life.

Transiting Venus Trine Jupiter

A happy but short term transit. A lucky day. There is both love and money in your life. Friends, the lover or partner are supporting financial goals and perhaps bringing financial opportunity. You are wealthy both materially and in friendships. Speculations would be favorable - if nothing else in the Horoscope denies. Your religious beliefs, philosophy of life, code of ethics evoke love in others. Today is a day for love and affluence - for leading the good life.

The Spiritual Perspective. Spiritually speaking you are lifted up into a more rarified level - a level where love and affluence are the norm and there is no lack of either. Though this feeling might not last, remember it and savor it, so that you can return in the future. Eventually, you want this to be your normal state. Though we must always consider other things, this is the kind of transit we would want if we were planning a wedding, social gathering, or spiritual rite that involved either Venus or Jupiter.

Transiting Venus Trine Saturn

A happy but short term transit. The right thing is also the popular thing today. Your need to order, organize and manage your life - to take charge of it - evokes love in others. Managerial decisions are well received. Love and Duty go hand in hand. Your sense of responsibility is appreciated. Career is boosted by the lover, spouse and social contacts. Young women are helping the career.

The Spiritual Perspective. The Principles of Love and Duty are in harmony today (if there is no denial from other transits) and so you can see deeper vistas of both. The more you love the more you want to do your duty. The more dutiful you are the more love that comes to you. Right Order is something holy and good and should be loved. This is a day where love for elders and authority figures is naturally stronger. You appreciate them for who and what they are - they have a place in the scheme of things. This extra love brings their favor to you by the karmic law. You find that they love you more.

Transiting Venus Trine Uranus

A happy but short term transit. Your originality, inventiveness and eccentricities evoke love in others. Inventions are popular with the spouse, friends, and lover. Friendships are more romantic than usual. Romantic opportunities happening with friends or in organizations you belong to. Your need for freedom and "no commitment" is not a deterrence to love.

The Spiritual Perspective. It is easier for you to love your originality, uniqueness and innovativeness today. You have a natural appreciation for it, and you see it reflected (by the karmic law) in others. Truly, your uniqueness is a great blessing and treasure. Though you are one with all that is, made of the same essence and substance, yet you are special and unique. There is noone quite like you.

Transiting Venus Trine Neptune

A happy but short term transit. You are very inspired, intuitive and altruistic today. Love is your religion. Feelings of love lift you to the spiritual heights and bring artistic inspiration, intuition and spiritual knowledge. Your spiritual ideals evoke love in others. Love opportunities come from your intuition or at spiritual type gatherings.

The Spiritual Perspective. Personal love and Divine Love are in synch today. You have a natural love for spiritual things and for your own spirituality. Your love for the Divine is intense and this will probably bring spiritual types of experience - God experiences. When we love the Divine with ALL our heart and mind, it will certainly come into us. In Truth, the love for the Divine is the greatest romance we can have.

Transiting Venus Trine Pluto

A happy but short term transit. Your intense sexuality is warmly received and evokes love in the partner or lover. The passions of love are high and positive (unless other things in the Horoscope deny.) Friends and social contacts help you pay down debt. You are good at prospering others today. Your efforts at self transformation evoke love and appreciation.

The Spiritual Perspective. As we have mentioned, the process of transformation is a messy business and can bring all kinds of challenges. But the end result of transformation, is very much like child birth - a new creation happens and it is beautiful. Regardless of where you are in the transformation process, today is a day where you can "see through the mess" to the end result. (Some of you will actually see the end result today.) Also you have more power and inclination to love the "underworld" in yourself and this aids the transformation process - it actually changes the underworld into something finer and better.

Transiting Venus Trine Ascendant

A happy but short term transit. You look good. You have a special sense of style today. Perhaps new clothing or accessories come to you. There are good relations with young women. Your physical appearance draws praise. A good day to go to the hairdresser or otherwise beautify the body.

The Spiritual Perspective. On a spiritual level, this is a day where you can love your body. (Probably you will quite naturally.) While your body is not you - you are much more than that - still it is your faithful servant and friend - isn't it worthy of love? A good day to praise and give thanks to it - to praise all the organs and systems one by one. The body will respond beautifully.

Transiting Venus Trine Midheaven

A happy but short term transit. The love and social life supports the career. There is harmonious interaction between the two spheres. Love opportunities can come as you pursue career goals and career goals can be furthered as you pursue social goals. Young women are boosting the career.

The Spiritual Perspective. This is a time where you can easily fulfil the dictum of "let each man love his destiny". Truly when the Destiny is seen for what it is - stripped of human, social opinion and judgement - it is a beautiful thing, worthy of love and devotion. Love your career today, love your bosses. Love your mission for this life. Realize that you have been blessed and honored by it.

Transiting Venus Sextile Moon

A happy but short term transit. The mood is good (if nothing else in the Horoscope denies). There will be romantic opportunities near home or through the introduction of family members. There will be opportunities to bring romance and beauty into the every day life. Everyday life CAN be romantic if we have the right attitude towards it.

The Spiritual Perspective. Spiritually speaking there is an opportunity today to heal old emotional wounds and grievances - will you take it? It is up to you. If you don't take this opportunity, many more will come, so there's no rush - but why prolong suffering?

Transiting Venus Sextile Sun

A happy but short term transit. Love opportunities come. Opportunities to harmonize with the opposite sex and to express creativity happen. Your creative expression evokes love in others. No matter who you are, what you look like, you are someone worth while and are worthy of love. You are loved because of the Highest that dwells in you.

The Spiritual Perspective. Spiritually speaking you have an opportunity to see the beauty of your own higher being as it is. You can see it in yourself and in others.

Transiting Venus Sextile Mercury

A happy but short term transit. The mind and intellect is strengthened. You will have opportunities to express yourself creatively and diplomatically. There is communication with friends and the beloved. Love opportunities come as you pursue intellectual interests. You are loved for your mind as well as your body.

The Spiritual Perspective. Spiritually speaking this is a day where there is opportunity to realize the essential harmony between logic and love, the mind and the heart. Both come from the same place when they are pure. Logic is love expressed by the mind. Love, is logic expressed through the heart. This realization (today brings opportunity for this) will keep you steady during times when the head and the heart seem to conflict. (It is really the impurities that are conflicting and not the essence.)

Transiting Venus Sextile Venus

A happy but short term transit. A good love day. Your feelings of love are reciprocated. Love opportunities are coming and you can handle them. Love opportunities come at the usual places - parties, gatherings, weddings etc.

The Spiritual Perspective. Spiritually speaking, because the love force in you is being strengthened today you are more able to radiate love. As a karmic consequence - very natural - you attract more love.

Transiting Venus Sextile Mars

A happy but short term transit. Sexual activity is well received by the lover or partner and evokes love in them. Erotic opportunities come. Love opportunities come at the gym or as you pursue your athletic goals. Bold, independent action evokes love. You can be more forward and direct in love today.

The Spiritual Perspective. You have opportunity to harmonize the masculine and feminine principles within you and thus, the outer world, will reflect this harmony back to you - usually in the form of happy social or sexual experiences. Also you find it easier to discern when kindness or firmness is needed in a given situation.

Transiting Venus Sextile Jupiter

A happy but short term transit. A wonderful transit both for love and money. Overall happiness increases. You find love as you pursue financial or educational goals. You find earning opportunity as you pursue social goals. Speculations will tend to be favorable - but other factors in the chart can modify this - definitely follow intuition with this. Your religious and philosophical beliefs evoke love in others. Philosophical discussions are good foreplay in love.

The Spiritual Perspective. Spiritually speaking real love should happen on all levels. It is not just physical and emotional. We must love (appreciate) a person's higher mind - their philosophy and religious beliefs as well. This is a good day to expand your love to the mental (upper mental) levels. If you can't love another's Higher Mind, than love your own.

Transiting Venus Sextile Saturn

A happy but short term transit. You have the ability (and opportunity) to bring order and organization into your life in a tactful and diplomatic way. Tough managerial decisions can bring love and appreciation rather than condemnation today. Social urges and contacts boost the career.

The Spiritual Perspective. Spiritually speaking this is a day where you can take time to appreciate the order that you have created in your life. Oh, it might not be perfect and sure it can use improvement. But first you need to appreciate the good points here. This will naturally lead to improvement. Also good to appreciate the elders and authority figures in your life. You need not white wash their imperfections, but certainly they have some good points.

Transiting Venus Sextile Uranus

A happy but short term transit. A good day for friendships and group activities. Group activities can lead to romantic opportunity. Your independence and freedom is appreciated by others. Inventions and innovations evoke love in others. You are loved precisely because of your uniqueness and offbeat ways.

The Spiritual Perspective. Spiritually speaking this is a day where you can appreciate and love your own genius and originality - the uniqueness that you are. There is no one in the world quite like you - in fact no one in history is quite like you. Your so called eccentricities are really blessings and part of your uniqueness. When you love this aspect of your self, your originality will be more accepted by the world.

Transiting Venus Sextile Neptune

A happy but short term transit. Idealism is very strong. Artistic inspiration is inspired. Intuition and psychism is strengthened. Your spiritual ideals evoke love and admiration in others. A good day for meditation and creative type activities. You will have opportunities to see inspired artistic productions.

The Spiritual Perspective. In order to succeed spiritually a person must LOVE their path - whatever it is. Finding your path is very much like falling in love. This a good day to remember the love you feel for your path - also for the Will of the Divine.

Transiting Venus Sextile Pluto

A happy but short term transit. Sexual intensity evokes love. Sexual activity will tend to be happy. Love passions are high. Friends, lovers, or the spouse are helpful with debt issues. Efforts at self transformation evoke loving responses. You have greater ability to prosper others today.

The Spiritual Perspective. The cosmos will give you opportunity to love the "underworld" in yourself today and this will help to change this nature into something more positive. It will speed up the transformation process. The underworld in us came about from lack of love in the first place, so love will help to change it. Many spiritual people have negative attitudes about sex and today is day where these can be corrected.

Transiting Venus Sextile Ascendant

A happy but short term transit. A good love aspect. You look good - others admire your appearance. Your body, image and overall demeanor evokes love. Opportunities come to beautify the image. A good day for the hairdresser.

The Spiritual Perspective. Spiritually speaking you have an opportunity to love your body - to appreciate it for all the self less service it renders to you. In many ways it is your best friend. If you love your body, others will also love it.

Transiting Venus Sextile Midheaven

A happy but short term transit. Friends, lovers or the spouse support career goals and aspiration. Love opportunities come as you pursue your career goals.

The Spiritual Perspective. Spiritually speaking this is an opportunity to love your career and your mission in life. Whether you are in a career that you love or not, this is a good time to love it. Even the worst of careers has some good points and this is a good time to remember them. And your love and appreciation will certainly lighten even the worst of careers. Those of you who are consciously doing your Divine Mission can also take time out for some appreciation. Often we just "soldier on" doing what needs to be done regardless of how we feel. But injecting good feeling here will be a help.

TRANSITS OF MARS

Both the Sun and Mars will add energy and dynamism to any planet that they contact. But the energy of the Sun is a more harmonious type of energy. It is like sunshine on a plant. It gives overall life and energy. Mars on the other hand gives the energy of passion, of action. It is solar force concentrated in a certain way - in a certain direction. The Sun will give warmth to any planet it contacts, but Mars will give heat. The Sun will give light and illumination, but Mars will give passion. The Sun wants everybody to be happy and entertained, but Mars wants everybody in activity - doing - achieving - either purposes of construction or destruction. The Sun is the King on his throne who commands the armies under him. But Mars is the actual army - the generals and the fighting men. They will do the actual fighting. A planet exposed to the Sun is taking a sunbath on a sunny summer day. For the most part it is pleasant and warming - though over exposure can be dangerous (then the Sun starts to partake of Martian energy). A planet exposed to Mars is like a mustard plaster applied to a sore back. Yes it is good for the organ, but it is hot, biting and not very pleasant. The Sun is the energy of sunshine. Mars is the energy of fire. Sunshine tends to be benefic. Fire must be handled just so. Handled properly fire is benefic. Misused it can burn and do damage.

So any planet that Mars contacts will be "heated up" - very hot. It will be energized and active. Physical actions - direct, independent actions - will start to happen in the affairs governed by the planet. If not handled properly, these actions can lead to pointless conflict, violence or accidents. If handled properly there will be great (and quick) achievement. Mars will add courage to the affairs governed by the planet it contacts. And, if abused, it can tend to undue haste, rashness and errors based on this. Impatience, conflict and violence are the main dangers with a Mars transit.

There are times in life where brute force is necessary. There are times when the logic of Mercury and the social grace and skills of Venus are of no avail. Only Mars - brute force - correctly used - in a surgical way - will solve the problem. When a dangerous virus enters the body, the white blood cells, the agents of the immune system, will not negotiate, reason or "have a cup of tea" with this dangerous intruder. They just kill it. The body has a wisdom that we can all learn from. To have a "mistaken" compassion for this virus, would be a lack of compassion for the rest of the body.

Without this ability to maintain its integrity, no body can survive in this earthly realm. By definition, life means, the ability to defend itself - to be self sustained. And this self defense mechanism is the Mars force in the human body, in society and in the cosmos.

A transit of Mars will often force a decision to use brute force - either physical, emotional, legal or mental. Only the native can discern if this is necessary. And, the native will be held accountable for any misuses or abuses of this power.

Transiting Mars Conjunction Moon

A Neutral transit. Much depends on how you handle the energy. The moods and emotions are hot and excitable. You are in the mood for action - for doing things - for sports and adventure. You are in a risk taking mood. There is more energy to get things done today. But temper is the main danger. Watch your tone with children and family members - they might think you're angry and not understand that you're only in a certain mood. A great period (a few days before and after) for getting things done around the house - for renovations, furniture moving, and repairs.

The Spiritual Perspective. As we mentioned above, heated emotions - anger - is the main spiritual danger. Events are likely to bring up old "anger memories" from the past and these should be looked at. Are you responding from the present situation or from accumulated memories of the past? Even very spiritual people can have "anger flare ups", but the spiritual person never "lives in that". He or she gets out of it as quickly as possible. Don't blame yourself for your anger flare up - accept it and observe it. But get out of it quickly through meditation and prayer.

Transiting Mars Conjunction Sun

A Neutral transit. This brings both more energy and more sexuality. You are bold, brave, looking for adventure. You excel in sports or exercise regimes. You are speculative and risk taking. And while you have more energy to achieve things - you do the work of ten people and in half the time - you do not suffer fools gladly - and will let them know how you feel. Slights to your ego can provoke violent responses. The light that you are is not just a passive thing - it brings power and the ability to achieve. The main danger today is rash or impulsive action - actions that you will regret later on when things calm down.

The Spiritual Perspective. Spirit is many things, and power is one of its attributes. Though it is not politically correct to say this, dominion is an attribute of our being. This attribute is strongly emphasized now and the issue is how you will use it. Misuse of power always brings negative karmic consequences. Not using power when you should, will also bring negative consequences. This transit is a lesson in the right use of power - neither avoidance nor abuse.

Transiting Mars Conjunction Mercury

A difficult transit. The mind is overheated and excited. There is a tendency to snap judgements and impulsive decisions. There could be difficulty in understanding another's mental position. There is a strong tendency to arguments - many of them needless, if you had taken the time to really understand what was being said. On the positive side, you learn quickly and are not afraid to make a decision. You are a formidable debater.

The Spiritual Perspective. This transit is about intellectual power and the right use of it. The pen (and the word) is mightier than the sword. Right use of these powers will bring good and blessing to yourself and others. Abuse will bring negative karmic consequences. You need to be razor sharp in your discernment, voice tones and body language. You need to use just the amount of power to do the job - no more and no less. To use less power means that the job doesn't get done. Too much power will create gratuitous hurt. Neither is good.

Transiting Mars Conjunction Venus

A Neutral transit. Much depends on how the energy is used. Love passions are high today. There is love excitement. There is a tendency to "love at first sight" and to leap into relationships blindly and impulsively. You are definitely aggressive in love matters now - not someone who is waiting around for the phone to ring. If you like someone you will let them know. You are an adventurer in love and adventure means risk. Sexual expression will sizzle. The passions of love need to be kept positive or this could lead to conflicts with the beloved.

The Spiritual Perspective. The feminine, love principle, in you is being super activated by the male principle. This always leads to creation of some sort. Sometimes the love agenda needs bold actions in order to go forward. Women are more in touch with their male side today and men are more in touch with their feminine side - but always keep in mind, being "in touch" doesn't mean that you become the opposite gender.

Transiting Mars Conjunction Mars

A happy transit. You are having a Mars return now. An old physical and sexual cycle is ending and a new one is beginning. (The exact nature of the cycle will also depend on what House Mars rules in your Horoscope.) You might change your exercise regime. You might change your athletic interests or sexual interests. Old building projects are completed and you are ready to begin something new. In general physical and sexual energy is enhanced now. You are more independent, thrill seeking, and bold. You are more action oriented.

The Spiritual Perspective. The Mars Principle in you - the physical side of you - is receiving a lot more voltage today. The challenge is to use this properly and in a balanced way. Abuse of this power can lead to violence, accident or pain caused by rashness and impatience.

Transiting Mars Conjunction Jupiter

A Neutral transit. On the one hand you can attain wealth suddenly. You are taking action on your financial plans and projects. You make quick financial decisions. You are financially fearless. You achieve financial goals quickly. But the danger here is rash and unduly risk taking financial decisions. Your generosity will be impulsive and perhaps ill considered. Spending likewise. If intuition is with you your snap decisions will work out. You tend to "plunge" into investments, purchases and wealth schemes in a big way. You are on a financial adventure and the risk is part of the excitement.

The Spiritual Perspective. The Higher Mind is receiving a lot more voltage today. It is hyperactive. Try to avoid religious or philosophical conflicts this period. This is the aspect of the "holy warrior" - the "jihadist". Remember, that the real "holy war" is within and not without. In order to succeed in the religious and spiritual life one needs zeal and ardor. And this you have in abundance today. This zeal enables you to overcome many of the formidable spiritual obstructions that we encounter on the path. But this zeal, when abused, can lead to horrible pathologies - inquisitions, holy wars, intolerance and hatred of other faiths and belief systems. Yes, have zeal for your own path - but be tolerant of others too.

Transiting Mars Conjunction Saturn

A Neutral transit. You have the energy and the drive to bring order and organization into your life. The bringing of legitimate order will go smoothly, but if the order is illegitimate you will bring conflicts upon yourself. This is a good period for executing career plans - taking the physical steps necessary to make them happen. Take a deep breath before making important management decisions or career changes - you might be too impulsive and draw fire on yourself.

The Spiritual Perspective. This transit is another lesson in the right use of power. Order is a spiritual principle - it is Heaven's First Law. We all come here to create order out of chaos. Hopefully our personal order will be in harmony with "Heaven's Order" and not some personal thing that we try to impose on the world. Order sometimes needs to be imposed with power, with firmness and sometimes brute force. This could be one of those times. Spirit presents you with a challenge. Either you impose righteous order and discipline now, or you create problems for yourself (and those under your dominion) later on. If you don't discipline that child or employee now when you should, you will be held karmically responsible for the problems that happen later on - for your action now could have prevented these problems. Did you neglect discipline because of fear? Social ostracism? Misguided kindness? Bad judgement? You will reap the consequences. On the other hand, if you over discipline or use too much force, you will also have negative karmic consequences. This is not a time for "cruelty" but for measured use of force - enough to get the job done and no more.

Transiting Mars Conjunction Uranus

A dangerous and volatile transit that needs to be handled "just so". There will be desires for sexual experimentation - and these need to be kept constructive and not destructive. There is a tendency to test the limits of the physical body too. These things are good, but need to be done mindfully. You can be overly rebellious and this can draw violent responses on you. You might rush into a new invention or innovation without due consideration of consequences. There could be conflict with friends or in a group you belong to. But the good part is that you have the courage of your convictions. You are ready to take action on your original ideas, inventions or innovations. You make new friends suddenly.

The Spiritual Perspective. "There is a time for everything under heaven." A time for war and a time for peace. A time to obey authority and a time to rebel. A time to cooperate with a group and a time to strike out on your own. You are likely to be in a time for the latter. Again this transit is a lesson in the correct use of power. If you are rebelling against unjust authority, do not use more force than necessary. Examine your motives. Examine your procedure. Are you being more violent than you need to be? Are you being cruel? Are you being selfish and provocative? Are you rebelling just for the sake of rebelling? Are there ways to attain the same result with less pain and rebellion? If so, you must try those ways first. Are you in the right here? Is there something to the position of the authority figure? Understand all the angles and ramifications of the situation and use the correct amount of force - neither too much nor too little. Always remember that the Divine loves the person, group or people you are rebelling against and will not suffer injustice on your part.

Transiting Mars Conjunction Neptune

A Neutral transit. Spiritual ideals, altruistic feelings, are now put into action. This will be the test of them. Action - living these things in the world - will teach you the viability of these ideals. A very good period for Hatha Yoga, Eurythmy, Sufi dancing or dancing in general. Through graceful actions one reaches the divine. If your ideals are deluded, this transit will reveal it to you.

The Spiritual Perspective. Much of what we said above applies here too. This transit brings great spiritual ardor and zeal - a necessary ingredient for successful spiritual practice. If there have been obstructions in your meditation or prayer life, this is a time for "breaking through" - you have more force available to you. You have a "passion for the Divine" these days and this passion must be channeled properly - aimed towards the Divine. Abuse of this energy can lead to holy wars, intolerance and spiritual warfare. It can undermine and distract you from your spiritual goal.

Transiting Mars Conjunction Pluto

A powerful and dangerous transit that needs to be handled "just so". Libido is magnified a thousand fold. Your focus and overall intensity is also magnified. You can achieve great things athletically, financially and in your efforts at transformation. Efforts at transformation will require physical actions. Temper is the main danger here. Also fanaticism. This is not a diplomatic, nicey nice, energy. You want what you want when you want it. You feel like you want to eliminate all opposition to your plans and projects. You will brook no dissent. If you're not careful this can lead to violence. But the correct use of the energy is within - to eliminate flawed character traits, thought or emotional patterns - that block your ongoing. A wonderful period for detox, exorcism, depth psychology.

The Spiritual Perspective. Much of what we say above applies here as well. Your lusts, both spiritual and carnal, are greatly intensified. If this energy is directed towards the Divine you will make incredible spiritual break-throughs in prayer and meditation. No obstruction can withstand your zeal and one pointedness. If the energy is directed towards less noble purposes it can lead to pain, suffering and destructive behavior. This transit is about the correct use and direction of power.

Transiting Mars Conjunction Ascendant

A Neutral transit. You are more active and athletic today. You are in the mood for adventure. You dress in a more masculine athletic way. You have more energy and thus can achieve more. Personal magnetism is strong. You are assertive and will pursue sensual pleasure ardently. There is a tendency to a "me first" attitude.

The Spiritual Perspective. The mortal, carnal nature will be much stronger than usual. The desires and appetites of the flesh can over power good spiritual judgement if you're not careful. It is more difficult to assert the dominion of the spirit over the body today - it will take more effort. Spiritually, you can experience a "War of Armageddon" - a titanic battle between your God Nature and your Animal Nature (the Beast). On the other hand, if the desires of the flesh are non-destructive and not out of alignment with your spiritual principles, you can indulge them today.

Transiting Mars Conjunction Midheaven

A Neutral transit. You are very active careerwise. The workplace is hectic. There is much competition for your place and position and you are defending your turf - and perhaps looking to capture another's. Career is like a military campaign. You are bold and aggressive. If other transits support - your boldness will win the day.

The Spiritual Perspective. You have a new reverence and respect for the male genius - the military genius - athletes and activists. Perhaps (as many beginners on the path do) you disrespected them in the past - considered them unspiritual or superfluous. But this is changing now. Perhaps this new insight will come from having more dealings with these kinds of people in your career or in regards to your spiritual mission. The reality will often differ from your "idea" of these people. Pacifism, though a noble virtue, will not always lead you to the heights. When war is necessary you need to be ready. Spiritual warriors don't make war the way ordinary people do - they use the weapons of light. It is a whole different way of making war, but it is nonetheless war.

Transiting Mars Square Moon

A difficult transit. There are family conflicts. You will have to work hard to keep the temper down - both in yourself and in relations with family members. The tempers of family members are also high. You are in a combative mood. Temper flares in spite of yourself. Emotions are "trigger happy". A good day for meditation to keep things calm. Stay above the fray.

The Spiritual Perspective. Much of what we said above applies here. Anger, temper and conflict are the main dangers. Old pain and anger memories from the past are getting re-stimulated now. In most cases, the anger is not coming from the present situation, but from an accumulation of many situations. The good news is that these things are now "conscious" and you can cleanse and transform them through prayer and meditation. The main spiritual lesson of this transit is that one can take forceful and bold actions without temper or psychological violence. When one uses power from an emotional state - and not from a conscious state - there is always "imbalance" and negative karma created. For, there is a tendency to go overboard.

Transiting Mars Square Sun

A difficult transit. There can be conflicts with men. Ego and self esteem issues can trigger heated responses. Rash and impulsive actions should be avoided. You have more energy but you are also more rash. Speculations are ill advised. Libido can be over expressed. Try to slow down today (it won't be easy).

The Spiritual Perspective. The star that you are, the solar being of you, is always shining regardless of circumstances and conditions. This is its nature. Conflicts do not dim its light or diminish its self esteem. Sometimes conflict can have a useful spiritual purpose - it can reveal how powerful the solar being in you really is. It is good to learn how to handle people or situations that attack you for being "who you are". It is not pleasant to be sure, but when handled properly, there is much spiritual gold.

Transiting Mars Square Mercury

A difficult transit. There will be tendencies to arguments and verbal abuse. The mind is over heated and combative. You (or others around you) are more interested in asserting intellectual power than at arriving at truth - the true purpose of the intellect. Avoid hasty decisions or snap judgements. Over-stimulation of the mind can lead to insomnia or other nervous problems. It will take hard work to soften your tone when you speak.

The Spiritual Perspective. Much of what we said above applies here. The mind and body, the intellect and the passions are not in synch today. It is like a house divided against itself. Bringing harmony here will require spiritual effort - more prayer and meditation - more light and understanding. There is a larger harmony of which this temporary disharmony is part.

Transiting Mars Square Venus

A difficult transit. Not especially good for love nowadays (but other things in the Horoscope can modify this.) There are conflicts with friends, the lover or spouse. Your love feelings can attract anger and attack. Your aesthetic taste draws fire. Reschedule parties for another day.

The Spiritual Perspective. The Principle of Love and Beauty is not in synch with the physical body and with the Principal of action. The masculine and the feminine in you tends to be out balance - actually in conflict. This tends, by the karmic law, to reflect as outer conflicts. It will take more prayer and meditation - more spiritual effort on your part - to harmonize things. Sometimes these conflicts are permitted by the Higher Power in order to "clear the air" and to reveal imperfections so that you can correct them.

Transiting Mars Square Mars

A difficult transit. Your independence and actions are not in synch with the actions of the environment. Overall energy is not up to par. Libido is not up to par and can be over or under expressed. There can be conflicts with men. Aggressiveness evokes aggressive responses in others. Actions evoke counter actions. Slow down this period.

The Spiritual Perspective. When energy is not up to par, we either over compensate or under compensate, and thus right physical expression - right actions - are more difficult to express. There is a greater need to "stay in the body" - to stay "mindful" and alert today. How do you feel when you try that exercise or yoga posture that you always do so effortlessly? Yes, always it is effortless, but today is different. Do you feel pain? Resistance? Don't force. Perhaps the pain is just a message to stop or slow it down. Another important lesson today is that action and force are not always the way to the goal - sometimes yes, sometimes no. Sometimes, non-action, will take you there. This might be one of those days.

Transiting Mars Square Jupiter

A difficult transit. Avoid rash or impulsive financial actions. The desire for a "quick buck" is dangerous now. There are strong tendencies to philosophical and religious arguments. Avoid religious fanaticism or the feeling of the "holy warrior". Truth is truth and will eventually assert itself. Athletic interests conflict with financial and educational interests.

The Spiritual Perspective. As with the opposition and conjunction, this transit brings great religious zeal and ardor. This is basically a good thing - a necessary ingredient for spiritual success - but can be abused under this kind of transit. It is right to love your own path -

and even to love it above any other. But make sure that this love doesn't cause you to have contempt for other paths - or to attack them. There is likely to be religious and philosophical revelation today which you want to put into practice immediately. While it is always good to practice our faith, it might be wise to let the revelation or insight "digest more" before leaping into action.

Transiting Mars Square Saturn

A difficult transit. Your efforts to impose order, organization and discipline can evoke anger and antagonistic actions from others. Managerial decisions come under fire. You are fending off competition at work or in the career. Avoid over reactions. Career aspirations conflict with your athletic interests.

The Spiritual Perspective. We are here to create order out of chaos. But noone said that it would be easy. A good order will survive most attacks on it, and this is a period where your personal order - the way you arrange your life - gets "road tested" by the cosmos. Like a car being road tested, it gets unusually "rough handling" to see how well the "order and system" performs. Don't take things too personally today.

Transiting Mars Square Uranus

A difficult transit. There are conflicts with friends or in a group you belong to. Inventions and innovations are seen as threatening and come under fire. Your rebelliousness and freedom loving urges are seen as provocative and draw fire. Friendships are tested. Athletic interests conflict with social interests. Be more mindful and alert today. Avoid risk taking where possible.

The Spiritual Perspective. While it is good to be original and unique, this originality is not going to be "universally loved" or accepted. The price for individuality is often high - as you learn in periods like this (this transit is in effect for about a week). But the gift of being original is worth any price and you should pay it gladly. Also the cosmos is "road testing" your new inventions, innovations, or ideas. It gives them some rough handling, not as punishment, but to reveal how well these things perform under pressure. The stress will reveal any flaws in these things so that you can make the proper corrections.

Transiting Mars Square Neptune

A difficult transit. Your intuition, inspiration and spiritual idealism is seen as threatening and likely to draw fire and anger from others. There is more difficulty in translating your ideals into actions. Intuition needs verification.

The Spiritual Perspective. As a person follows his or her spiritual path, there are many adventures. At times we are led into "green pastures" and the "land flowing with milk and honey". But at times we are led into desert spaces hounded by armed and angry Egyptians or Philistines (this is meant as allegory). Still we must continue and rely on the Divine Guidance. The Divine will supply the solution for the attackers. Also, it good that your intuition be road tested as it is this period. It must become a reliable instrument - a reliable faculty - always operating even in the most difficult circumstances - and this reliability factor is attained through this kind of "road testing".

Transiting Mars Square Pluto

A difficult transit. Libido is either over or under expressed. Efforts at self transformation draw anger from others. You will have to work harder to stay calm and cool. Surgeries should be avoided now - unless they are emergencies. Avoid risky activities where possible. Re-schedule them for another time.

The Spiritual Perspective. The process of transformation - of giving birth to your own ideal of self - is not an easy process. Often, as you make important changes, it will draw attack from others (and these others are really reflectors of your own inner attitudes), and this is one of these periods. This is a time to learn spiritual courage and to persist regardless of the attacks and criticism.

Transiting Mars Square Ascendant

A difficult transit. Your overall demeanor can draw anger from others. Your ego and self esteem come under attack. Slow down today. Avoid rash actions. Take a lower profile.

The Spiritual Perspective. Physical energy is not up to par this period and so the sense mechanisms, physical judgement, physical faculties are operating with less power - this can lead to mishaps if you're not careful. Just as a computer or any other electrical instrument will malfunction when there is a voltage drop (or too much voltage) so too will the physical instrument. Do what needs to be done today, but take a more reduced schedule. Avoid risk taking activities if possible.

Transiting Mars Square Midheaven

A difficult transit. You are working very hard. The demands of the career tax your physical strength. You are fending off competitors to your place and position. Your status is under attack.

The Spiritual Perspective. If you are doing your spiritual mission - in your right place and position in life - no one can take it or threaten it. Yes, you might face resistance or attacks, but you can never lose your rightful place. Understanding this will help you be more philosophical this period. Let the dogs bark at the moon, the moon is not touched and continues in her orbit.

Transiting Mars Opposition Moon

A difficult transit. There is emotional tension now. Relations with the family could be much better. Tempers flare at home. Your sentiments and moods draw anger from others. Your urges to independence and adventure (and to athletics) pull you one way while family duties and obligations pull you in another. Your tendency is to choose one over the other and thus cause problems in one or the other area of life. The best way - though it will be difficult - is to give both urges some expression. You are not in the mood for sex and this can cause some problems at home.

The Spiritual Perspective. The Principle of Feeling and the Principle of Action are not in synch today. You're not in the mood to do what you need to do - and you can't seem to do what you feel like doing. This can produce some frustration and anger. Also old memories of the past are getting re-stimulated and this is a good day to look at these and cleanse them. Underneath the anger is some pain - look at it - and heal it. There are many, many ways to do this - prayerfully and meditatively.

Transiting Mars Opposition Sun

A difficult transit. Libido is either over or under expressed. There can be conflicts with men. Not a period to try to break athletic records. There can ego conflicts. Take a low profile. Avoid undue risk taking - financially or otherwise.

The Spiritual Perspective. As with the square, the true being that you are - the Divine Immortal - seems to face hostility and attack merely by being who it is. But the Sun doesn't change its orbit merely because some humans are kicking up a fuss. Neither does the Solar Being in you change its Destiny. There is nothing higher in life than being "truly yourself" - but there is also nothing harder to achieve than that. If it were easy, where would the achievement be?

Transiting Mars Opposition Mercury

A difficult transit. Thought and action conflict with each other. A great idea might not be workable. Watch your tone when you speak as it can be taken as provocative and draw anger and aggressive responses. Athletic interests pull you one way and intellectual interests pull you another. See if you can combine both in some way. The need for adventure and action pulls you one way while your logic pulls you in another. There is a middle way if you search for it. Intellectual arguments are more likely today.

The Spiritual Perspective. The Principle of Thinking and the Principle of Action are not in synch today and it will take more spiritual effort on your part to bring them into harmony. Thus the logical thing seems "impractical" or undoable, while the "doable" seems illogical. The coordination of the mind and body is not up to its usual standards. When you should be "doing" you might find yourself thinking and when you should be thinking you might be "doing". The practice of Mindfulness will be a big help. Also, knowing that these principles are ALWAYS in harmony on the spiritual level will be a big help. You are experiencing "appearances" and not reality. The apparent discord is masking a deeper harmony.

Transiting Mars Opposition Venus

A difficult transit. There can be disputes with the lover, spouse or friends. Romantic urges pull you one way and sexual urges pull in another. Romance and sex are seen as two separate things - when in fact they are not - but this is the situation you are confronted with. The person you are sexually attracted to - you don't love. The person you love is not sexually attractive. There is conflict between the sexes these days. The male and the female perspectives seem irreconcilable.

The Spiritual Perspective. As with Square, the masculine and the feminine principles "appear" to be out of synch and this will manifest as romantic or social problems or disputes. At times like this - and it is difficult - we must remember the spiritual truth here

- that these principles are always in harmony on the spiritual level. If you are experiencing discord, bring your mind to the spiritual truth and watch it dissolve. On a deeper level, the cosmos wants greater discernment from you. Sometimes the way to gain ends is through the "feminine way" - through grace and charm - and sometimes it is the "masculine way" - through direct action and brute force. Neither way is inherently better than the other, but sometimes one way is better and sometimes another. We need to be able to do both. Today you might need to exercise a little bit of "both" ways - depending on the situation. Will being kind really help the situation? Perhaps "tough love" is called for.

Transiting Mars Opposition Mars

A difficult transit. Libido and overall energy are not up to their usual standards. Your sense of action and adventure is not in synch with the current climate of action and adventure. Personal aggressiveness evokes a corresponding aggressiveness in others. There are conflicts with men and between men.

The Spiritual Perspective. Your physical and sexual energies (depending on your stage in life) are at maximum now. Perhaps you are overdoing things and this is drawing fire from others. Sometimes we don't realize our own strength and something that seems innocuous to us, can be devastating to another. These karmic kickbacks have the effect of seeming to "weaken" us, even though we are essentially strong. We waste precious energy fending off the reactions of others. Our apparent weakness is coming from strength.

Transiting Mars Opposition Jupiter

A difficult transit. Your religious, philosophical and financial goals seem unworkable - cannot be translated into actions. Wait a while until this aspect passes (in a few days to a week) before acting on these things. Religious and philosophical conflicts are more likely now. Beware of attempts to try to convert the world - or to convert people by force. Fanaticism is a problem. Not a good period for speculation or important financial decisions. Your financial goals pull you one way while your need for action and adventure pull you in the opposite way. Your religious beliefs and financial plans get tested now.

The Spiritual Perspective. As with the square, religious zeal - so necessary for spiritual success - can be misplaced or abused. This zeal - a powerful force - the cause of all religious success AND the pathologies of religion - needs to be handled with the utmost delicacy. And this is a period where the Cosmos puts you to the test. Your religious, philosophical path is very much like a marriage. A person can love his or her own spouse without despising all others.

Transiting Mars Opposition Saturn

A difficult transit. This transit is like trying to drive forward while your emergency brake is on. Slow going. Your desire for fast paced action and progress conflicts with your need for order, organization, stability and security. Managerial decisions can draw anger. There is opposition to your control over life. Your career position or social status comes under fire. You need to work harder to achieve career goals.

The Spiritual Perspective. As with the square, the cosmos is testing your ability to create order - and your present order. Its as if they are getting "road tested" - given some rough treatment - so that whatever flaws there are will be revealed. Then you can make the necessary corrections. Being an "ordering force" in your environment is a Divine Quality, it was never meant to be always "easy". It is both an art and science, and if we overdo or under do we will know it during these kinds of periods.

Transiting Mars Opposition Uranus

A difficult transit. Your need to be original, free, unfettered draws fire from the environment. Perhaps you are too provocative - or too rebellious in the expression of these things. Originality and freedom has a price tag - which you are learning about these days. It is not a free ride. There are consequences. There could be conflicts with friends or with an organization or group you belong to. Perhaps even within the group - though you might not be involved. Inventions and innovations are being tested this period too. They can sound fine in theory but not be workable in action. Rejoice in these testings as you have opportunity to correct the flaws. Avoid risk taking this period. Avoid stressful activities especially if they are elective. Of course, what you need to do should be done.

The Spiritual Perspective. Much of what we say above applies here.

Transiting Mars Opposition Neptune

A difficult transit. Your spiritual ideals and intuitive guidance draw fire from others. Following the spirit is one of the great privileges of life - but there is a price tag attached, which you are seeing this period. Intuition needs verification. Don't be in a rush to come to conclusions about intuitive guidance, dreams or prophecies. Try to stay in the body this period - especially when exercising or driving. Avoid dreaminess in everyday life. You can let yourself go when you're at home in your chair meditating - but in the world, stay in the body.

The Spiritual Perspective. Much of what we say above applies here too. Those who meditate will have their abilities tested as it will be much harder to focus with all the storm going on - but even the attempt will build strength.

Transiting Mars Opposition Pluto

A difficult transit. Your efforts at self improvement and self transformation meet with anger and hostility from others. They are more difficult to put into action this period. Libido is either overdone or under-done. Passions and tempers are higher these days. Avoid undue risk taking - especially with other people's money. Avoid rash borrowings. Your urge to eliminate the undesirable in your life can be overdone and could meet with stiff resistance. Avoid tense or potentially violent situations and people. Avoid risky activities, such as surgery - especially if you have free choice in the matter. (In some cases the surgery is not a free choice, then you must do it.)

The Spiritual Perspective. Much of what we say above applies here too. Spirit is using opposition from others to help the transformation process - it will speed up the expurgation of "underworld" forces - for they are being re-stimulated and brought to the surface. Though this isn't pleasant, it is good - in the same way that an enema or colonic is good. Effete physical and psychological material needs to come out.

Transiting Mars Opposition Ascendant

A difficult transit. There could be power struggles in a love relationship. Self esteem and self confidence comes under attack. Take a lower profile. Avoid risky activities especially if they are elective.

The Spiritual Perspective. Physical energy is probably not up to par and so more rest and relaxation is called for. Not a day for trying to break athletic records (unless you have help from other transits). Sometimes "doing nothing" achieves more than "overt action" - this could be one of those days.

Transiting Mars Opposition Midheaven

A difficult transit. Your status or position comes under fire. Competitors vie for your place or position. You must fend them off. Athletic interests, the need for adventure and sex pull you away from career aspiration and duties.

The Spiritual Perspective. This is more of a day for building the foundations of career - or more precisely, for removing inner impediments to the career and life work - than for overt career action. Unless these inner impediments - psychological impediments - are removed, your actions will be futile.

Transiting Mars Trine Moon

A happy transit. You are in the mood for independence and constructive action. You are in the mood for exercise, athletics and sex. A wonderful period to renovate or repair the home - to do heavy work in the home or to have it done. Work will be done properly. You can assert yourself without being angry or overbearing. Moods are optimistic. There is harmony with men, if nothing else in the Horoscope denies.

The Spiritual Perspective. The Principle of Action and the Principle of Feeling are always in harmony on the spiritual level, and this is a period where you can see how this manifests. Its as if you are given a glimpse of a heavenly state of affairs in this department this period. This is how things actually are, even during the stressful periods - only in the stressful periods the harmony is more "disguised". On its level the Sun is always shining, but on cloudy days here on earth, we don't see it.

Transiting Mars Trine Sun

A happy transit. Libido is stronger than usual and is expressed harmoniously. You excel in sports, athletics and exercise regimes. Energy levels are higher. You are independent and fearless. No situation can daunt you. You are active. Action seems the solution to most problems. If nothing else denies, this is a wonderful period to launch new projects into the world.

The Spiritual Perspective. Your Solar Self - your true self - executes its plans and processes with greater ease today. What others call bold and courageous actions are merely "normal" operations of this being. The Mars forces of the world - the police, the military, builders, athletes and the like are cooperating with your plans and purposes.

Transiting Mars Trine Mercury

A happy transit. This brings intellectual power and strength. Learning is quick and easy. Decisions are made quickly and they are good. You express yourself forcefully but not in an overbearing way. You get your point across. You are a formidable debater. Your ideas are easily put into practice. Reflexes are sharp and quick. The mind is quick. You have power to sway the masses - you can light a fire under others.

The Spiritual Perspective. Much of what we say above is applicable here. The Principle of Thought and the Principle of Action are always in harmony, but this period you can realize it easier.

Transiting Mars Trine Venus

A happy transit. If nothing else denies, this is a transit of romance and especially of sexual fulfillment. You are more forward and aggressive in love matters today. You go after what you want. You are not about to wait around for the phone to ring. You make romance happen. There is happy social activity. Romantic risk taking pays off.

The Spiritual Perspective. The male and female principles are in harmony in you and this reflects out as happy love and social experiences. The extent of the romantic and social harmony depends on well you have handled the "difficult" times. If you handled them well, the present rapture will be greater than normal.

Transiting Mars Trine Mars

A happy transit. Physical energy and libido are enhanced. You are more adventurous, bold and independent. You excel at sports and exercise. You are action oriented and get things done quickly.

The Spiritual Perspective. You have more physical energy available to you and the only issue is how you will use it - will it be constructive or destructive? Used to good effect or merely wasted in prodigality? Its something like having money in the bank that you can use any way you like. The money can be invested for a greater return or squandered on silly things. Those on the spiritual path will use the energy wisely.

Transiting Mars Trine Jupiter

A happy transit. If nothing else denies, you make bold financial moves that work out. You are more active in the pursuit of financial goals - also more risk taking. This is a period for constructive actions on the financial front. You are a defender of the faith today and you do so effectively. Constructive actions expand your Horizons.

The Spiritual Perspective. Your Higher Mind - the Upper Mental Body - is greatly strengthened today. What we call "good fortune" comes from this realm. Your ability to see the principle behind things brings good fortune - and right quickly at that.

Transiting Mars Trine Saturn

A happy transit. There is much power behind your efforts to assert order, organization and discipline in your life. You have the firepower to take charge of your life. Management decisions are made quickly. Career success comes through taking constructive and bold actions. You thrive on competition this period.

The Spiritual Perspective. You are an ordering force in your environment in full possession of your powers. You are backed up by mighty spiritual forces.

Transiting Mars Trine Uranus

A happy transit. Your originality, inventions and innovations are backed up by men and have much fervent support. Constructive actions taken now will boost these areas. If you feel hemmed in, stuck in a rut etc, this is the period to break out. Group activities are action oriented. You are more aggressive in the pursuit of friends.

The Spiritual Perspective. The Cosmos gives you a glimpse of what happens when the Principle of Originality is in harmony with the Principle of action. You need not "struggle", "rebel" or kick up a fuss to be original and innovative. It just happens easily and effortlessly. (Keep in mind that other transits could contradict this, and create some disturbance - but if nothing else denies, these activities will be effortless and easy.)

Transiting Mars Trine Neptune

A happy transit. Spiritual ideals, intuitive guidance, artistic inspiration are easily put into practice this period. Constructive action will further all these areas. It is a time for acting on your ideals.

The Spiritual Perspective. The Cosmos gives you a glimpse of the wonderful things that can happen when intuition is in synch with the Principle of Action. Ten years - even 20 years of hard labor - can be done in a trice. This is how things will be all the time as you advance on your spiritual path.

Transiting Mars Trine Pluto

A happy transit. There is great power and force behind your libido and efforts at self transformation. You can attain almost any goal now. A wonderful period to eliminate the unnecessary from your life - whether it be character traits, weight, possessions, or effete material in the body. A powerful period for exorcism and detox programs. Meditators will make spiritual breakthroughs now.

The Spiritual Perspective. Much of what we said above applies here too.

Transiting Mars Trine Ascendant

A happy transit. Physical energy is increased. You are more forceful in the pursuit of personal pleasure, fulfillment and sensual delights. There is more personal magnetism and more attraction to the opposite sex. You assert yourself without being over bearing or arrogant. Athletic type accessories suit you now. Red allures you.

The Spiritual Perspective. With more energy available to you the challenge is to use it wisely and constructively. Think of it like money in the bank - you can invest it or squander it.

Transiting Mars Trine Midheaven

A happy transit. Career is furthered through constructive and bold actions. Men are supporting career goals. The police or military are kind to you - if nothing else denies.

The Spiritual Perspective. If you are clear on your spiritual mission this is the time to act - action will bring understanding eventually. If you are not clear, act on your highest understanding of your mission - this will lead to more understanding later on.

Transiting Mars Sextile Moon

A happy transit. Through exercise and physical activity you will be able to change your moods from negative to positive - also to change the family and domestic situation. Positive actions - bold and coura-geous actions - will improve the current mood or domestic situation. Sexual opportunities will come.

The Spiritual Perspective. You have the opportunity to harmonize your feelings and your actions - actions done with "right feeling" will be more powerful. Feelings that can be acted on are likewise more powerful today.

Transiting Mars Sextile Sun

A happy transit. Physical actions - including exercise or sports - will improve self esteem, enhance creativity and improve relations with children. Libido and overall energy is stronger. Self confidence is stronger. Constructive and bold actions will also boost the career and your life goals. The light that you are wants to express itself through action this period.

The Spiritual Perspective. As with the Trine, this transit affords opportunity to act powerfully in line with your life's spiritual mission - the agenda of your Immortal Self is easily accomplished. (If nothing else denies.)

Transiting Mars Sextile Mercury

A happy transit. The mind is stronger. Decisions are made quickly. Learning is faster. Communication is assertive but not overbearing. You will have opportunities to translate your ideas into actions. If you feel mentally sluggish, try exercising or vigorous physical activity for a while - mental acumen will be enhanced.

The Spiritual Perspective. As with the Trine, increased mental ability should be used constructively.

Transiting Mars Sextile Venus

A happy transit. There are happy sexual opportunities today. There are opportunities for harmonious interaction with the opposite sex. If you are in the love doldrums take positive actions to improve things - this is not a time for passivity.

The Spiritual Perspective. If you take the opportunity to harmonize the male and female principles in your consciousness, this will reflect in happy outer social experiences. Because the transit is easy you will more easily accomplish this.

Transiting Mars Sextile Mars

A happy transit. Both libido and overall physical energy are enhanced. You will have opportunities for bold and constructive action this period. You will have opportunities to express your physical energy - either athletically or through building or exercise. Physical activity will enhance and not detract from your energy. A good day for body building.

The Spiritual Perspective. As with the Trine, the challenge today is to use your extra physical energy in positive and constructive ways - in the service of your Higher Nature. Let it be used to bring good rather than difficult karma on you.

Transiting Mars Sextile Jupiter

A happy transit. You will have opportunities to take positive and bold actions towards your financial goals. Wealth is increased through positive and bold actions. This is a day where you make your luck. You will also have opportunities to act on your religious and philosophical beliefs. Faith without works is dead.

The Spiritual Perspective. As with the trine, your religious and philosophical nature - your upper mental body - is greatly energized. Your religious zeal is capable of bringing great spiritual and prayer break- throughs this period.

Transiting Mars Sextile Saturn

A happy transit. You will have opportunities to take positive career actions this period. Career is furthered through bold and independent actions. It is time to take the initiative and act quickly. Positive and bold actions will also help you assert order, organization and discipline into your life.

The Spiritual Perspective. As you strive to create order in your life and affairs - a very cosmic and spiritual thing - you find help available, whether it be physical or moral.

Transiting Mars Sextile Uranus

A happy transit. You will have opportunities to take positive and bold actions that promote your freedom and originality. You will also have opportunities to implement new inventions and innovations. Be proactive with friends this period.

The Spiritual Perspective. As with the trine, the cosmos gives you a glimpse of what things can be like when you are true to yourself - to your own originality and uniqueness. Help will come from surprising sources.

Transiting Mars Sextile Neptune

A happy transit. You will have opportunities to act powerfully on your spiritual ideals, intuitive guidance and creative inspiration. Meditators will have spiritual breakthroughs this period as there is more energy behind their efforts. You will have opportunities to eliminate spiritual, psychological or mental obstructions.

The Spiritual Perspective. Much of what we said above applies here too.

Transiting Mars Sextile Pluto

A happy transit. Libido is enhanced. The ability to focus likewise. You will have opportunities to eliminate that which is no longer necessary in your life - whether it be effete material in the body, character traits, bad habits or addictions. This is the period to "make clear the pathways of the Lord". Your power is enhanced and most likely will be channeled in a positive way.

The Spiritual Perspective. As with the trine, this is about the right use of power. Rightly used power will bring you every good thing and create good karma for you. Abused, it will be a boomerang.

Transiting Mars Sextile Ascendant

A happy transit. You will have more opportunities to express yourself physically. Exercise regimes and sports are more likely. You will dress more athletically.

The Spiritual Perspective. As with the Trine, the challenge is to use your extra physical energy in constructive ways - in ways that benefit yourself and others.

Transiting Mars Sextile Midheaven

A happy transit. You will have opportunities to take constructive and bold actions to further your career and ambitions. Positive actions boost the career. Men are supportive careerwise.

The Spiritual Perspective. Action on your spiritual mission and career will lead to understanding. Sometimes we need to "just do" before we can understand. Understanding is a later stage in the process.

TRANSITS OF JUPITER

Jupiter, the great guru, of the zodiac is going to expand, enlarge, exalt and make great any planet that is contacts. It is the great benefic of the zodiac. Its contacts are always pleasant and good. On a mundane level, he is like a cosmic Santa Claus, who just gives, gives and gives. This is his nature. Jupiter is not concerned about a person's worthiness or unworthiness for a thing or condition. As far as he is concerned everyone, every child of God, is worthy of all good. He will give it.

On a mundane level, we read this as "good fortune". He is the bringer of good fortune, the so-called lucky breaks, the lotto or lottery winnings, the big, larger than life gift, the fortunate social connection. In mundane terms, he brings a sense of overall happiness and success. There will be a feeling of optimism and confidence connected with all the affairs governed by the planet that he contacts.

But in truth, a Jupiter transit is much more than these things. All these happy mundane events that occur are merely side effects of something much deeper going on. For on a spiritual level, the Jupiterien Rays are bringing revelation into a given area of life (into the affairs of the planet that he contacts). Its as if the planet is now sitting at the feet of a great and wise Guru - someone who under-stands the Law behind a thing - and "receiving the law" - the secret, invisible Principle that brings success and expansion. If a person is on a spiritual path and conscious, he or she will gain a conscious understanding of the Principle behind the affairs of a certain area of life. When this principle is understood, good fortune can be consciously brought to bear at any time. Jupiter will bring a permanent good fortune - something that can never be lost. Grasping the law behind a thing - whether it is in finance, or in a profession or art - is always more joyful than the actual sum of money, or work of art, or promotion that one receives. Those things are temporary. The Law behind it is eternal.

If the person is not on a spiritual path, not conscious, Jupiter will still be acting, but he or she will be unaware of what is really going on. I have found, that in these cases, the person starts behaving - in an unconscious way - in ways that will bring success or prosperity. The person will start becoming more generous, or more jovial and optimistic - which attitudes tend to attract success. But this kind of behavior is more of the nature of being "under the influence of a drug", and when the drug wears off - Jupiter moves away from his contact - the person is right back where he or she was before. A little richer, with more things, perhaps in a higher station in life, but inwardly the same.

Even Jupiter's stressful transits bring good - this is how benefic he is. But the problems usually come from excess - too much of a good thing can be just as stressful as too little.

Transiting Jupiter Conjunction Moon

A happy transit - generally long term. Blessed and Fortunate. In many cases it brings the fortunate purchase or sale of a home or money from real estate. The family prospers and will tend to be generous with you. You are generous with the family. Often it shows the enlargement of the home or the family circle - through births or marriage. There is good emotional and financial support from the family. Often this shows a happy move (if nothing else in the Horoscope denies). Moods are very optimistic these days and it is this very optimism which brings about good fortune where otherwise there wouldn't be any. Religious and philosophical illumination comes to family members - and to you through dreams.

The Spiritual Perspective. This is an aspect of "realization". Many of us understand spiritual truths and principles in an intellectual and abstract way - but these understandings are superficial and non-functional. It is only when these truths are realized in the "feeling nature" - the Moon nature - that they become real and functional in our lives - we begin to live these truths - act on them. This naturally brings good fortune, which is just a synonym for "lawful spiritual behavior". It is no accident that Jupiter - the planet of religion and philosophy - is exalted in the sign of Cancer, ruled by the Moon. Abstract religion, though better than nothing, can never be as powerful as "realized" religion.

Transiting Jupiter Conjunction Sun

A very happy transit. You are enlarging the borders of your tent. Your overall consciousness and sense of self is very much expanded. Self esteem and self confidence are strong. Lady luck is with you in speculations. Financial windfalls - major ones - or financial opportunities come. There is greater recognition and appreciation for who you are and your abilities. Though you have always been a star, now your light shines even brighter. There will be more travel and more of the good life. Creativity is very much enhanced. There is happiness from children.

The Spiritual Perspective. Much of what we said above applies here. You achieve more, gain more, because you are becoming more. Your sense of self is enlarged. Old limits fall by the wayside and new vistas open up to you. This enlargement of the Self (the self can never be larger or smaller than it is - but your awareness is enlarged) generally brings happiness and joy.

Transiting Jupiter Conjunction Mercury

A very happy transit. The mind is expanded. The horizons of the intellect widen. The ability to communicate and to teach is expanded. Financial opportunity will come from your communication abilities. Wealth ideas come to you. You have a greater grasp of religious and philosophical truths and this translates into more mental ability. Many people buy new cars or computers or communication equipment under this transit. However, the tendency of the mind now will be to enlarge and exaggerate and this could create unrealistic decisions.

The Spiritual Perspective. Here we have a situation where the Upper and Lower Mental bodies are "merged" - hard to tell one from the other. When we throw a coal into the fire, the coal very soon loses its identity and we can hardly see it. So, the lower mental is swallowed up in grand ideas - spiritual ideas - lofty truths and is enamored of these things. Its natural tendency will be to express them rationally through the written or spoken word. It has a grander eloquence as well.

Transiting Jupiter Conjunction Venus

A very happy transit. One of the happiest transits a person can have. The love nature is expanded. Great love is coming into the life - a significant relationship. The social circle expands in a happy way. You are socially in demand. Objects of art or beauty are coming. This is also a wonderful financial transit, bringing "easy and happy" money - perhaps through wealthy friends or through social contacts. A transit of social and financial rapture.

The Spiritual Perspective. The happy events that happen on the physical plane are just the natural consequence of an expanded and enlarged "ability to love". Since our capacity to love is enlarged, love (and all the things that love brings) easily comes to us by the karmic law.

Transiting Jupiter Conjunction Mars

A very happy transit. Libido is increased and is expressed happily. Athletes break records these days. Physical energy and stamina is increased. Bold, courageous and independent actions bring good luck. You have the ability to "make luck" happen. New - and probably high end - sports and exercise equipment comes to you.

The Spiritual Perspective. Note the difference in perspective that a high energy level brings. You feel you can do anything. Impossibilities become possibilities. Projects that you "ruled out" in the past, now seem eminently workable. Its not so much that new ideas are revealed to you - probably you've always had them, but pushed them away as "impractical and undoable" - now they become doable. Spirit is revealing the role that energy plays in your life and why it is important to maintain high levels - not to go "prodigal" and fritter it away.

Transiting Jupiter Conjunction Jupiter

A very happy transit - especially if this is to your Natal Chart. This is your Jupiter Return - a once in 11-12 year occurrence. (If this is in the Solar Return chart, it is not a major aspect as it will only reinforce the original tendencies of that chart.) You are closing out an old financial cycle and beginning a new one. Usually goals of the old cycle are now manifest so that you can set goals for the next cycle. Financial desires are achieved now. This also represents the close and beginning of a religious, metaphysical cycle. You have absorbed the lessons of the previous cycle and are ready to begin anew on a higher level. Many people will change pastors, churches, or gurus these days.

The Spiritual Perspective. Much of what we said above is applicable here. When a cycle ends, the desires of that cycle tend to manifest. So this is a period of great achievement. A good wealth and educational period. Now you must set new and higher goals - on the next rung of the spiral - for the coming new cycle.

Transiting Jupiter Conjunction Saturn

A happy transit. Your ability to manage, organize and set order in your life is greatly enlarged. You are seeing that wealth is often produced by "cutting back" or right management of resources as it is by mere earnings. Career is reaching new highs now. Often there is a promotion at work or in your social status. Often there are new career offers that come. If you have been prudent and doing the right things all along, this Jupiter transit will reward you with more wealth, recognition and honor.

The Spiritual Perspective. The cosmos is now rewarding you for past (and perhaps unsung) achievement, discipline and hard work. While you were doing these things, you thought you were unnoticed and unappreciated. But on the inner level your efforts were investments earning interest. Now you will collect on them. You see that no genuine effort at self improvement is ever wasted.

Transiting Jupiter Conjunction Uranus

A very happy transit. There is more freedom in your life now - happy freedom. Wealth - big wealth - can come suddenly and unexpectedly. You can go from rags to riches in a trice these days. Wealth can come to you in the form of new inventions or original innovations. Big ticket, technological gadgets or equipment come to you. New and significant friends are coming into the picture. New and wealth producing knowledge is coming.

The Spiritual Perspective. The word "original" means thinking from the "origin" of things. This is the source of all real creativity, invention and progress. Ultimately all scientific discoveries come from the "origin" in ourselves. The "Sky Father" (Uranus) within. A person who "truly consults his own powers" says Emerson "is incapable of copying anyone". He or she is "hopelessly unique". So now that this part of the nature is being energized and expanded it is not a surprise that we mentioned above, tends to happen. This is a natural - karmic - consequence. It is under transits such as this that those on spiritual path can realize that "man does not live by bread alone, but by every word that proceedeth from the Father". It is not "things" that we need - but this "living word" - this awareness and insight.

Transiting Jupiter Conjunction Neptune

A very happy transit. A very spiritual transit. Spiritual illumination is coming. Inner powers are expanded. Prophetic abilities are vastly increased. The spiritual life, meditation practices, the spiritual ideals bring great happiness and fulfillment. Wealth ideas come. Intuition brings wealth. Artistic creations bring wealth. There will be travel by sea. The grace of the Divine is all around - a tangible, palpable presence.

The Spiritual Perspective. Much of what we said above applies here too. What you are experiencing is the natural consequence of the expanding of your spiritual nature and understanding. You are more easily able to discern the "Will of the Divine" and to trust and know that this Will is GOOD. You are not afraid to surrender to it and thus many wonderful blessings on many levels flow through.

Transiting Jupiter Conjunction Pluto

A very happy transit. The libido is vastly increased. Debts are easily paid or easily made. You can attract outside investors to your ideas or projects. You see value in dead or distressed things that bring profit to you. You see how to profit from turnaround situations. You can go from rags to riches now. This is a transit of big success - mass success. There is much help available in your efforts at self transformation. Powers of concentration are greatly increased and thus you are able to attain almost any desire.

The Spiritual Perspective. Some of these underworld forces in yourself that you have been heretofore despising and rejecting are now shown to be great blessings when used properly. The light of revelation and spiritual understanding shines on them. These "dead and disgusting" things are really gold deeply disguised and you can have as much of this gold as you like. Your personal process of transformation - of giving birth to your own ideal self - is greatly accelerated now - and this too can bring large and sudden success.

Transiting Jupiter Conjunction Ascendant

A very happy transit. You are living the good life. You are eating in fine restaurants and the best of foods and wines. You are traveling and otherwise enjoying life. Self esteem and self confidence is good. You are jovial and optimistic. Sensual fantasies are fulfilled. Big ticket personal accessories come to you - clothing or jewelry. You are dressing for success - donning the image of wealth. Financial windfalls come. The only problem here is excess - too much of the good life will show up on your waistline. Keeping the weight down is a problem. People often move under this transit. And, often, they enlarge their personal quarters - their office or the room where they spend most of their time in. Women of appropriate age tend to more fertile than usual. This is one of the signatures for pregnancy.

The Spiritual Perspective. Under this kind of transit we learn the love that spirit has for our bodies. It lavishes them with every good thing, with almost no limitation. "The Temple of God is with Man". It is up to us to exercise some restraint and judgement and not overdo things. Too much of the good life will leave us with a price tag later on - and this is not spirit's fault.

Transiting Jupiter Conjunction Midheaven

A very happy transit. There is career success, honor and recognition. Career Horizons are expanded. The rich, the powerful, the high and the mighty are granting their favor and boosting career goals. Often this brings a raise or promotion at work. Politicians with this transit will often gain elective office. There is a favorable outcome in dealings with the government or with people of high status. Overall status is increased.

The Spiritual Perspective. Those on a spiritual path will receive revelation about their spiritual mission for this incarnation. Not only does this transit bring revelation but also the wherewithal to follow this path. Also, because of this revelation such a person's spiritual standing - his or her position in the Hierarchy of Beings - will be elevated. Its as if one gets an "inner promotion".

Transiting Jupiter Square Moon

A difficult and long term transit. Moods can be wildly or unreasonably optimistic and this can set you up for a crash later on down the road. Family duties and obligations can conflict with financial goals and needs. There could be a tendency to overspend on the family or the home - in a way that is disproportionate and which you will rue later on. Undue moodiness - either too high or too low - affect the financial judgement. Avoid important financial decisions until you feel calm and at peace.

The Spiritual Perspective. The principle of feeling and your religious ideas "appear" out of synch this period. You find it more difficult to realize spiritual truths. Or, the feelings distort them in negative ways. The danger here is that you can reverse things. The (everyday)feelings should take their cue from religious and philosophical truth, but here you might try to project your feelings onto your theology. My feelings are right, theology is wrong. "Thy will not my will be done" is a wonderful prayer this period. It will straighten out many things.

Transiting Jupiter Square Sun

A difficult and long term transit. The problem here is too much of a good thing. Self esteem and self confidence is a wonderful thing - but you might overdo it now. Ego drives could force you into expenditures that are ill considered. You will be tempted to make the "grand gesture" - i.e. buy drinks for everyone in the restaurant or fly all your friends to Acapulco for the weekend - take a deep breath before you plunge. Speculations can be ill considered as well. You will be tempted to spend more that you can really afford - or exaggerate your self importance unrealistically.

The Spiritual Perspective. The mortal can only handle so much spiritual power at any one time. Only so much spiritual good. Only so much knowledge and revelation. For the mortal is limited. And sometimes, as during this period, so much good is pouring out on you - that it can unbalance you. The lesson here is that even good things need more moderation. We should only ask spirit for what we are able to handle.

Transiting Jupiter Square Mercury

A difficult transit. It leads to excessive speech and excessive thinking. Ideas can be unrealistically big. There will be a tendency to exaggerate the good to a point where judgement is affected. It will be hard work reining the mind in.

The Spiritual Perspective. The Principle of Expansion appears to be out of synch with the Thinking Principle. Thus the enlargement of thought can be overdone or disproportionate. Or it can be experienced as a "forced expansion" of the mind, when the mind is not ready for it. Ideas are like food - and some ideas, though perhaps wonderful and good, are not digestible by the mind at certain times. It will take more spiritual effort to bring these principles into harmony. Breathing exercises will help control over active thinking. "Be Still and Know that I am God" is wonderful meditation now. Be still.

Transiting Jupiter Square Venus

A difficult transit. The problem here is too much of a good thing; too much partying, too much of the good life, over eating, too much sexual or sensual indulgence and the like. There will be a tendency to try to buy love and to overspend on romance or friends. Social urges - the need to be popular and loved - can conflict with your financial interests. Perhaps you party so much that you neglect your financial needs and urges.

The Spiritual Perspective. Much of what we said above applies here too. Balance and right proportion is the key to happiness - too much of anything is not good. Neither is too little. If you overdo the good life now, its OK, but there will be a price to pay later on.

Transiting Jupiter Square Mars

A difficult transit. Be careful not to bite off more than you can chew on the physical level. If you normally run 5 miles a day, now you will want to run 10. If you can normally lift 50 pounds, now you will want to lift 100. There is a tendency to be too optimistic about what you can do and achieve - unrealistically so. Athletic interests conflict with your financial interests. Religious or philosophical arguments can erupt now.

The Spiritual Perspective. A good day to practice mindfulness in the physical body. Slow everything down. Focus on every action. Watch how your body feels. You'll get more done and will less chance of mishap.

Transiting Jupiter Square Jupiter

A difficult transit. Over-confidence is the main danger here. You tend to exaggerate your wealth and your prospects and to spend accordingly. Generosity is wonderful but you can be overly so now. Your concepts of wealth are out of synch with the general concepts of wealth at the moment. You are a contrarian. Your philosophical and religious beliefs are also out of synch with the style of the period - religious arguments are likely. It will be hard to avoid over-spending or over-expanding.

The Spiritual Perspective. The upper mental body, your Higher Mind, is being expanded in a perhaps unbalanced way. This could easily lead to the excesses mentioned above if you're not careful. Keep both feet on the ground during this period. Make financial moves that are in your comfort zone.

Transiting Jupiter Square Saturn

A difficult and long term transit. This is a classic conflict between the need to consolidate and the need to expand; the need to see the "worst case scenario" and to plan a way out and irrational exuberance. Your need for status and prestige could conflict with financial goals. You may have take a long term decision that has negative financial implications in the short term. Your need to expand must not exceed your capacity and abilities - and herein lies the dilemma.

The Spiritual Perspective. There is a spiritual need to understand these two principles - expansion and contraction - as complements and not as opponents. Life is an alternation between the two. We breathe in - expand - and then we breathe out - contract. One leads to the other. The better our contraction, the better will be the resultant expansion. The greater the expansion, the greater the contraction. Expand, expand, expand is not good - and not natural. But neither is contract, contract, contract. In meditation you will feel the rhythm to these things. Don't worry about temporarily "pulling in your horns" as this will lead to expansion later.

Transiting Jupiter Square Uranus

A difficult transit. Your need to be a free spirit, foot loose and fancy free conflicts with your financial interest or with the financial interests of others. Freedom urges and rebellious tendencies are greatly exaggerated. You are probably overdoing it. Inventions and innovations might not be financially workable these days. Your scientific mind conflicts with your religious beliefs and you can feel rebellious about it.

The Spiritual Perspective. It is essentially a wonderful thing that your innate originality and innovativeness is getting expanded. But perhaps this expansion is happening in an erratic or unbalanced way. There could be the spiritual equivalent of "power spikes" and then abrupt "power lows" in this aspect of your mind. Thus the tendency will be to either over do "originality" - become rebellious, and then to "under do" it. You will need to do more spiritual work to "keep the expansion smooth and steady" - to smooth out the power spikes. This can be a wonderful transit if you do the spiritual work. You can invent many wonderful things.

Transiting Jupiter Square Neptune

A difficult transit. The spirituality and idealism are greatly exaggerated today. Perhaps you misapply these things or apply them in wrong contexts. If the house is burning, you don't have time to pray for a dream, you must take concrete and common sense action. Your spiritual ideals conflict with your financial needs - or they seem to - you are in a moral dilemma. Mystical and dream experiences - or perhaps spiritual teachings - seem to conflict with the teachings of your religion. It is hard work to reconcile the two - though both are dear to you. You could have water problems in your home, office or neighborhood.

The Spiritual Perspective. Spirit is revealing to you this period, the nature of spiritual pathologies - what happens when the spiritual nature is abused or misunderstood by the human, or when one is insufficiently instructed in the ways of spirit. An emotional urge is confused with real intuition. A negative rapport gets confused with real intuition. A spiritual message or dream - correct on its own level - gets distorted by the mortal, unpurified consciousness. Spiritual vision gets abused by thought and political manipulators who try to use it for their own nefarious ends. The laws of the different dimensions get confused. It is under aspects like these that we hear of the stories like "God told me to kill all my five children, or to shoot up my office." But the true spiritual disciple will gain benefits from all this. By seeing the pathology he or she will know how to avoid these things. An absolute inner integrity and a passion for truth will steer you through. Also it is important to remember that just because there are spiritual pathologies out there, it doesn't negate the essential validity of spirit or its phenomena.

Transiting Jupiter Square Pluto

A difficult and longer term transit. Sexuality can be exaggerated and overdone. The need to eliminate the unnecessary from your life likewise. It could be you want to rush the natural processes of elimination and transformation and this will create snafues. You want big success yesterday. Passion and intensity is overdone and can kick back on you. Religious fanaticism is a problem.

The Spiritual Perspective. This transit is a lesson in the correct use of power. The Principle of Expansion seems (in appearance) to be in conflict with the Principle of Transformation. Thus you might over do your efforts of personal transformation and cause even more problems. Death and death issues can be misunderstood or your attitude be unrealistic. You have unusual intensity in everything you do, but the danger is in misdirection. Use of power must be strictly measured - like a surgeon.

Transiting Jupiter Square Ascendant

A difficult transit. Definitely the problem here is of excess. There could be weight problems and over indulgence in sensual pleasure. Perhaps you overspend on yourself, or overly inflate your own self importance. Perhaps you flaunt your wealth or charm in a tasteless flamboyant way. Your attempts at joviality are seen as arrogant.

The Spiritual Perspective. You understand that spirit loves your body and wants the very best for it. But perhaps you make too much of your body - you see it as you - or overweight its importance in your life. The body should be loved, but its role needs to be kept in perspective.

Transiting Jupiter Square Midheaven

A difficult and relatively long term transit. Financial interests pull you away from career goals and aspirations. Your desire for status conflicts with your desire for wealth. The financial powers in your world are not supportive of career goals. Religious and philosophical beliefs also conflict with your next career steps. The need is to steer a middle course.

The Spiritual Perspective. A passion for truth and for the Divine Plan in your life will steer you through this difficult transit. You are receiving new understanding about your mission in life and the reason for your incarnation, but perhaps you are overly inflating it - becoming arrogant about it - instead of accepting the truth with humility. (It is very easy to become arrogant when we get a glimpse - even the merest glimpse - of what the Divine has in store for us.) Perhaps you are trying to implement things too quickly instead of taking a step by step evolutionary approach to it - and this will create difficulties too. There are other scenarios too. Revelation of your true calling could seem to conflict with the religious teachings you were born into. But if you hold this in meditation you will see that there is no "real" conflict.

Transiting Jupiter Opposition Moon

A difficult transit. Financial urges and needs pull you in one direction while family duties, and moods pull you in the opposite. Moods and family concerns pull you one way while your religious and philosophical beliefs pull you to the opposite. The tendency is to choose one over the other and when that happens you go overboard in one direction. If you choose your religious beliefs, path of conscience or financial obligations you can be extremist there - alienating family members. If you go with your mood and family duties you are likely to be over moody, over nurturing, over protective - and perhaps ungenerous. There is a need for balance. There are many wealth opportunities out there but you don't seem in the mood for therm - or you feel that these things will violate your sense of emotional harmony. You find it difficult to apply your religious and philosophical beliefs in every day life - especially in the domestic sphere.

The Spiritual Perspective. The Higher Mind - the Philosophical Mind - seems out of synch with the emotional nature. You find it difficult to "feel" what you believe in - oh you have not lost your belief system, but its hard to integrate it into daily life and hard to feel it. The events of daily life seem to deny your religious beliefs. Many meditators, those experienced on the spiritual path, will feel as if "the presence has departed from them" - of course this is not true, but the Presence is more difficult to feel. In such cases we must transcend our feelings and rely on faith and knowledge.

Transiting Jupiter Opposition Sun

A difficult transit. Financial urges pull you one way while your will and ego pull you in another. There are many financial opportunities out there but you feel they are either beneath you or too above you. Perhaps you lack the confidence to pursue them. Religious and philosophical beliefs may require you to transcend your ego and sense of self importance - and while this might be necessary it isn't comfortable or easy. Your urges for fun and creativity are thwarted by financial duties or by religious or philosophical proscriptions.

The Spiritual Perspective. The Immortal that you really are must follow a path that seems to contradict your own personal religious beliefs - and perhaps the religious beliefs of those in your environment. But this is only a "seeming" and not a reality. The Immortal which is always "One with the Father" is the source of all religious beliefs - it is the ultimate authority. You must follow that and eventually you will see that there is no contradiction, but a deepening of your faith. Time will show that the actions of this Immortal actually vindicate the spirit and intent of your religious and philosophical beliefs. The belief system tends to be "static" while the actions of the Immortal are living and dynamic - and so it is inevitable at times that it will contradict (or seem to contradict) the belief system. A true story. A boy in a religious family, rebels against the family religion. His Immortal calls him to be an Artist, which they take a dim view of. This is God's will for him. In order for him to follow God's Will, he needed (paradoxically) to break with the family religion (which espouses obedience to God's will). These are the kinds of situations you may be confronting. In the end, if you are truly following God's Will, all of this will get harmonized. But in the meantime it can be unpleasant.

Transiting Jupiter Opposition Mercury

A difficult transit. Your sense of the short term good or short term trend conflicts with your sense of the long term good. There is a need to look both and steer a middle course. Facts seem to conflict with spiritual principles. Intellectual interests pull you in one way while financial interests pull you in the opposite direction. The money people and the teachers in your world are not especially receptive to your ideas, communication or thought process. Thinking can be unrealistic on a financial level now. Trades are not fortunate (though other things in the Horoscope can deny this.) The mentality is not at full strength.

The Spiritual Perspective. Two aspects of the mind - the Higher (Jupiter) and the Lower (Mercury) seem out of harmony. The short term perspective, the short term trend, seems to deny the long term view or long term plan that you have. Facts conflict with spiritual faith - a pretty common occurrence. But the reason for it is simple - the facts need to be seen in context. The future will show that these facts actually confirm your spiritual principles and beliefs once you put them in right perspective. Under these kinds of transits the faith will get widened, while our understanding of the every day facts of life will also clarify. Crisis is generally the doorway to deeper truth.

Transiting Jupiter Opposition Venus

A difficult transit. This transit shows a classic conflict between love and money. Your financial best interests pull you in one way but the lover, friends, or social urges - the need to be popular and loved - pull you in the opposite way. Both are important to your well being. You will have to balance yourself between the two urges. The lover might accuse you of being ungenerous. The money people in your life might accuse of being too weak and frivolous. Love pulls you in one direction, but religious and philosophical beliefs pull you in another. You are in a love or social situation that goes against some of your deepest metaphysical beliefs. Lessons are going to arise from this.

The Spiritual Perspective. Love and Wisdom never oppose each other in reality. But from the limited, perspective of the mortal psychological nature, this can often happen. These kinds of transits are tests of faith. There is a need for the mortal to put things in perspective. Yes, we are to love others. Yes, our loved ones are precious. But we must love our spiritual path and the Divine more than personal loves. We must put the Divine (and the way to it) first in our lives. When this happens, relations with loved ones will straighten out one way or another. In fact, we will be more able to love these people in a better way and healthier way.

Transiting Jupiter Opposition Mars

A difficult transit. Your independent or unilateral actions are out of synch with your financial interests and with the money people in your life. Difficult to act on wealth ideas now. Athletic and sexual interests interfere with financial duties and the acquisition of wealth. Also difficult to act on your philosophical or religious beliefs.

The Spiritual Perspective. Often under these kinds of transits people say, "I'm so busy, I've got so much to do, I don't have time to pray or meditate". While this can feel very real on the objective level, it is delusion. True action proceeds after a state of prayer and meditation. First comes spiritual and mental clarity, then comes action. When prayer is true and done properly, actions flow effort-lessly. In fact, spiritually, prayer is considered action in itself.

Transiting Jupiter Opposition Jupiter

A difficult transit. Your normal and personal wealth attitudes are out of synch with the wealth concepts of the world and with the money people in your life. Your wealth attitudes are just not in style right now - but that doesn't mean that they're bad or wrong. The same is true with your religious and philosophical beliefs - they are out of synch with prevailing opinion. Your ideas of expansion are radically different for the way the money people want to expand. Oftentimes the prevailing style has something good to teach us - if so, learn it and incorporate it.

The Spiritual Perspective. The reason you feel that your personal religion is out of synch with what's happening in your environment and life is that it has now matured and is in full power. It is very different from what it was 5 years ago. The infant and the adult have different perspectives on things. Likewise the "adult higher mind" is seeing things very differently from the "baby" of five to six years ago. Because Jupiter is now in its "Full Moon" stage in your life, you are seeing the consequences (good and bad) of what you fervently believed 5 to 6 years ago. Very soon, you will be able to make adjust-ments to it.

Transiting Jupiter Opposition Saturn

A difficult transit. Your sense of order and discipline - your personal sense of security - might not be in your best financial interest - or might not find favor with the money people in your world. You have to examine whether your sense of security is based on blind fear or just innate stodginess or whether it is something real. Your need to bring order to your world is out of synch with the prevailing religious or philosophical beliefs in the world. You feel a need to consolidate and pull back but the forces in the world are pushing for expansion. Pessimistic and optimistic impulses are both strong in you and you're not sure which side is right. Spiritually, this conflict is leading you to a position that transcends either optimism or pessimism but which embraces both.

The Spiritual Perspective. As with the square, there is a spiritual need to understand these two principles - expansion and contraction - as complements and not as opponents. Life is an alternation between the two. We breathe in - expand - and then we breathe out - contract. One leads to the other. The better our contraction, the better will be the resultant expansion. The greater the expansion, the greater the contraction. Expand, expand, expand is not good - and not natural. But neither is contract, contract, contract. In meditation you will feel the rhythm to these things. Don't worry about temporarily "pulling in your horns" as this will lead to expansion later.

Transiting Jupiter Opposition Uranus

A difficult transit. Your urges to personal freedom, to innovation and originality are not in your best financial interests - or perhaps are opposed by the money people in your life. Perhaps these urges also draw strong moral or religious condemnation. There is a need for you to take the middle road, but its not so easy to bridge these differences and to please everybody. There would be a tendency for you to be either overly rebellious or to let bottom line considerations squelch your freedom and originality. There would be a tendency to break with religious or philosophical teachings this period - perhaps in an unbalanced way. There could be conflicts with the clergy or within your church, synagogue or mosque. On a philosophical level, you are caught between the contradictions of modern science and the teachings of your religion. It might help to know that in reality there is no contradiction - only a need for deeper understanding. Know that the contradiction is the actual doorway to deeper knowledge. Social urges might also conflict with your financial or religious urges.

The Spiritual Perspective. Much of what we say above is valid here too. While it is good sometimes to rebel against false teachings - best to make sure that they are really false or that you have understood them. Often people are rebelling against "chimeras" or caricatures of a teaching. They misunderstand the teaching and then rebel against their own misunderstanding. A vain enterprise. Almost all religious teaching is couched in allegory and symbolism. On the surface they are generally filled with contradictions and paradoxes. It is easy to misunderstand the true intent. Often, there is a personality clash with a teacher or mentor type. And, the student confuses the Mentor with the teaching itself. So first make an effort to understand the teaching, then review and discern whether rebellion is called for - and if so, how to do it in a proper way. Uranus is our urge to freedom. Religion is about setting limits so that greater freedom is possible. One "dams up" the vast powers of the mind, in order to generate a different kind of power. But sometimes the urge to freedom in us (Uranus) doesn't see the greater freedom, but chafes at the limits. This is a time to gain clarity here.

Transiting Jupiter Opposition Neptune

A difficult transit. You are in an extremely religious and idealistic period now. The higher things of life - religion, spirituality, mysticism, the search for God - are paramount. In many cases this transit highlights the contradiction between traditional religious teachings and actual mystical experience. Your personal spiritual ideals and intuitive guidance seems to conflict with traditional religion. But the contradictions that you feel are only in your lower mind - if you view these things from a higher place in yourself you will see that there is no contradiction - both mystical experience and traditional religious teachings are valid in their sphere - and actually support and complement each other. On a more mundane level, your spiritual ideals seem to go against your financial interest or are opposed by the money people in your life. You learn that there is price tag - perhaps a high one - attached to your idealism. This period will reveal whether your ideals are important enough for you to pay the price. Intuitive guidance can also seem to go against your financial interest - but know that this is a short term phenomena. Intuition is seeing the big picture and into many years in the future.

The Spiritual Perspective. Much of what is said above applies here too.

Transiting Jupiter Opposition Pluto

A difficult transit. This is classic conflict between the sexual urges and one's moral and religious background. Sexual urges pull you towards a path that is opposite to your personal philosophy or religion - or that is opposite to the religious and moral teachings prevailing at the moment. This tension might lead you to violently break with or try to destroy these teachings. Sexual urges can also conflict with your best financial interests or perhaps come under attack by the money people in your life - or by those involved in your financial life. Your urges to transform yourself might also conflict with religious teachings or with your best financial interest. Often this transit brings a new personal philosophy of life or new world view. The inadequacies of the old philosophy or world view are clearly seen and you change them. In many cases this transit shows a conflict between one's own financial interest and the financial interest of the spouse, partner or shareholders. There is a need to take both sides into account - but it seems difficult to please everyone. Borrowing money or paying down debt could be more difficult than usual. Often this aspect brings a financial crisis as hidden flaws in your plans, strategies or thinking are clearly revealed. You will emerge from this period with a much deeper understanding of finance, sex and religion.

The Spiritual Perspective. Much of what we say above applies here too.

Transiting Jupiter Opposition Ascendant

This is actually a happy transit - especially on the social level. New and important friends are coming into the picture. Perhaps a significant other is entering or has recently entered your life. Your social life is expanding and so you need to put other people's interests ahead of your own. Issues of personal fulfilment, getting one's way, being independent take a back seat to the social life.

The Spiritual Perspective. Sometimes it is good to take attention away from our selves, personal desires, personal goals, and direct it towards the welfare of others. It gives more perspective in life - a more balanced attitude. Of course we shouldn't neglect ourselves (one of the dangers here) but we should think of others too. This is one of those transits where good comes through others and by the good graces of others. As we shift attention to others, they will naturally respond to our needs.

Transiting Jupiter Opposition Midheaven

Though this is considered a difficult transit, there are many wonderful things going on. Career is less important these days and less interesting. You are in a period of inner psychological growth - and later on down the road it will lead to career expansion. Many people move under this transit and the move is usually happy. Many people expand their present residence of buy additional homes. Family life is more rewarding. The family circle expands through births or marriage.

The Spiritual Perspective. There are times to act overtly on one's mission in life and there are times when we need to prepare the "inner ground" for it. This is a time for the latter.

Transiting Jupiter Trine Moon

A happy transit. Moods are optimistic. Relations with the family are happy. There is good family support - both financial and emotional. You in turn are supportive to family members. Usually there is the fortunate purchase or sale of a home, or an expansion of the existing home. The family circle expands either through birth or marriage. You meet new people who are "like family" to you. There is good fortune in real estate. Family connections or family businesses bring wealth.

The Spiritual Perspective. As with the conjunction this is a transit of spiritual realization. Your faith can now become "functional" and a living force in your life. Abstract principles and beliefs have little power if they are not realized - if you don't "feel them". Intellectual knowledge might make you popular (or unpopular as the case may be) on the cocktail party circuit, but otherwise will have little value in your life. But with realization comes power and ability. And this is what is happening for you now. The fact that you can feel your faith, feel the truth of the Higher Law and Teachings, naturally brings happy events into your life.

Transiting Jupiter Trine Sun

A happy transit. You are prospering and lucky. The breaks are falling your way. You shine. You are appreciated and perhaps honored for who you are and what you've done. Self esteem and self confidence is strong. New career opportunities come. You travel more. Happy educational opportunities also come. Speculations are more favorable now - though other things in the Horoscope can deny this. Always follow intuition in these matters. Both men and women are more fertile under this transit. Personal creativity is very strong. There is more fun in the life these days.

The Spiritual Perspective. The Immortal I Am of you - the True Self - and its powers and privileges, seems very much expanded now. Of course, on its level, the I Am never changes - but your perception of it is enlarged. You ARE more, thus you can do more, earn more, know more and have more. I Am is the source of all good in life - the source and the way to it.

Transiting Jupiter Trine Mercury

A happy transit. This transit is especially good for writers, communicators, traders, advertisers and PR people. They have a banner period. The mind and communication powers are enhanced. Your ideas and thought processes are well received by the money people in your life or by those who influence public opinion. Writers are more likely to sell their wares and get published. For those who have books already written, this is a wonderful period to release it into the world or to submit it to a publisher. Students will have good success in school and perhaps earn honors - but other things in the Horoscope can deny this. There is good confidence in the mental abilities now and you are less prone to doubt or second guess your judgement. Many people receive new and high end cars, computers or communication equipment under this transit. Under this transit you will learn that wealth of ideas is also wealth - and translates into what we call material wealth.

The Spiritual Perspective. Because your intellectual horizons are enlarged now, you have access to new and better kinds of ideas. Your mind becomes an instrument of affluence and of enlightenment. Mind is not your enemy but your ally and friend once it is enlarged - can see things from a wider perspective (a more impersonal perspective). The enlargement of the mind itself is a great purifying force for it. Much mental error comes from a perspective of "limitation" - a narrow point of view. Just enlarge the view and errors are naturally cleansed and removed.

Transiting Jupiter Trine Venus

A happy transit. One of the happiest - overall - that a person can have. Enjoy. The social life sparkles and the people you meet are significant and on a higher level. They are cultured, refined, educated and rich. And, even if they are not actually rich, they live as if they were. Often this transit brings marriage or a significant relationship. There are many parties and much going out. You are mixing with high glamor people. Money comes easily - perhaps through social contacts or through marriage. Love opportunities come as you pursue your financial goals - and there is wonderful synchronicity between the social and financial life. One helps the other. Artists will be more successful with their art now. They will sell more and receive recognition. Your social graces and aesthetic sense is very much expanded and is in synch with the money people or religious people in your life. Love is your religion these days - and we could all have worse ones.

The Spiritual Perspective. As with the conjunction (but perhaps not as powerful) the love nature gets vastly expanded. You love more and with greater intensity. The horizons - the limits - of your love nature are transcended. You can love things and people - and situations - that you couldn't love before. You can see beauty where you couldn't see it before. So, naturally, by the karmic law, happy love and social experiences are going to manifest. As above so below. As within, so without.

Transiting Jupiter Trine Mars

A happy transit - especially for athletes and military people. There is great confidence in the physical abilities now. You have more energy, stamina, and self confidence. And all of this leads to increased athletic skills and performance. Libido is roaring. Independent and bold actions lead to success. This is the time to push forward towards your goals - both personal and financial. The path of adventure also leads to riches and other desires of the heart.

The Spiritual Perspective. The enlargement of your physical capacities comes from the mind. The body itself is an infinite thing. We have not yet plumbed all of its possibilities and talents. The body is hemmed in by the limitation of the mind. Thus when the Higher Mind steps into the picture, our concepts of previous limitations just fall away.

Transiting Jupiter Trine Jupiter

A happy transit. Your natural religious and philosophical beliefs are very much in synch with - and supported by - the religious and philosophical beliefs prevalent in the world - especially in your world. Your wealth attitudes are in synch with the money people in your world. You are in a period of abundance and expansion - of optimism and joviality. Happy travel and educational opportunities come. Enjoy.

The Spiritual Perspective. As with the conjunction and to a lesser extent the Sextile, the Higher Mind in you, the "Kingly" mind, the Upper Mental regions of your nature, is much stronger, has more voltage and is thus playing a bigger role in your affairs these days. Thus all that we have mentioned above tends to happen naturally by the karmic law.

Transiting Jupiter Trine Saturn

A happy transit. The career is boosted and expanded. Probably there are raises and promotions at work. You are not afraid to take on extra responsibility and this contributes to your success. Your ability to impose order, discipline and organization in your life is well received and supported by the money people in your world. You will expand your career or business but it will be in a controlled and manageable way. Prudence and practicality is not necessarily a barrier to wealth and in fact can enhance wealth. Your management skills are very marketable right now.

The Spiritual Perspective. Without a proper "order" in life, happiness is impossible. Even so-called anarchists, who seem to deny all order, have to obey this law. What they deny, is the current order in the world, and they would like to impose their own notion of order rather than the prevailing one. Order is the underpinning of all creation and manifestation. Without order, beauty is impossible as well. So, now you are getting a deeper understanding of "order" and are more able to apply it in your life. There are other interesting spiritual things happening as well. You are seeing that "Order" - Limits - can lead to expansion in other ways. One can "limit" the undesirable and expand the desirable. The businessman can limit expenses, losses, and waste and thus create "expansion" through this kind of limitation. The meditator can limit his or her focus on "evil" and expand the focus on "good" and this will also produce greater happiness and expansion. Limitation is a wonderful thing when used properly and with understanding.

Transiting Jupiter Trine Uranus

A happy transit. Your urges for freedom also lead to enhanced wealth. Your new inventions, innovations and originality is well received by both the money powers in your world and by the religious powers. Inventions are very marketable now. You enjoy the best of both worlds - freedom and prosperity. This freedom that you enjoy now is a happy freedom and not the inharmonious freedom that comes through strife and rebellion. New and innovative ideas are coming to you. New big ticket high tech items are coming. New and powerful friends are coming.

The Spiritual Perspective. There is a season unto all things. There is a time to create order and there is a time to destroy an old, outworn, inadequate order and create something new. If this is your situation, you are easily able to do this and have much spiritual help now. Of course, you can never destroy the "Principle of Order" (Saturn) itself, but you can destroy old manifestations of Saturn and then create something new. Of course, spiritually speaking, you will have to be mindful of how you go about destroying an old order. Rather than attack it, you are better off taking you attention from it and building your new order. Your ability to be original and innovative, to see the new trends that are coming into the world, is greatly enlarged and thus more active in your life. Thus all the things we mention above tend to happen. Both astrologers and lay people will have an enlarged understanding of astrology this period. Beginners often have their charts done under this kind of transit. Or they get introduced to astrology in some way - through a book or a friend.

Transiting Jupiter Trine Neptune

A happy transit. A very spiritual period in your life right now. Your spiritual awareness is growing and expanding. Your intuition leads you effortlessly to wealth and all good. New spiritual gifts - psychic ability, healing, the ability to interpret scripture and sacred writing, inspired ideas - are coming to you. Meditation and spiritual practice is not only happy but is probably the most practical thing you can be doing. Your mystical experiences and dream life is well received by the religious and/or academic community and reveals the reasoning behind religious teachings. People often take cruises or buy boats under this transit. You travel more - either in your mind or physically. You access higher planes of consciousness. The higher things of life are paramount now.

The Spiritual Perspective. Much of what we say above applies here. This transit is enlarging your spiritual nature and thus it takes a more active and dominant role in your mind and affairs. All the things that we mention above are merely natural consequences of this. The closer we get to the Divine, the more the Divine reaches out to us and influences our affairs. The supernatural world, the invisible world, is more real to you than so-called reality itself.

Transiting Jupiter Trine Pluto

A happy transit. Many astrologers consider this to be an aspect of "large success" - but large success is a relative thing. The success that comes now will be large according to your personal lights. Libido is roaring (stronger than whatever your norm is), sexual activity is happy and increased. Access to outside capital is increased. Most people will have increases in their lines of credit. Debts are easily paid and easily made. You are prospering the partner, spouse or shareholders and they in turn are prospering you. Your insight into things brings fortune. Efforts at self transformation are happy and successful.

The Spiritual Perspective. The underworld in yourself - the part of you that his normally hidden in you. The parts of you that perhaps you deny or keep under wraps, is a source of much power. Jupiter's action brings illumination and understanding to it, and we are more able to access, these basically impersonal forces, in harmonious ways. The world of spies and undercover agents (for example)seems to us to be a terrible world. For the most part we don't pay much attention to this. It seems all about killing, deceit and duplicity. Yet it is an aspect of our consciousness. There are positive forces in this underworld who use their cunning and assassination skills on our behalf - to protect and defend us. These positive forces are now being strengthened. This transit will also bring much psychological and spiritual growth. Our negative view of our personal underworld is a result of judging from our limited mortal consciousness. But it is a much different perspective when we look at with "Jupiter's" eyes.

Transiting Jupiter Trine Ascendant

A happy transit. It brings the good life on a personal level. Sensual pleasures, good food, good wine, and a jet set type of life. Self confidence and self esteem are strong. You have faith in your personal image and appearance. You dress for success - expensively. Big ticket personal items - clothing, jewelry or accessories are coming to you.

The Spiritual Perspective. In some spiritual circles it is fashionable to hate the body and the carnal nature. It is seen as evil. But this period you learn that spirit loves the body and has no interest in depriving or abusing it. Rather the reverse is so. The danger under these transits is thinking that the body is you and that the happiness of the body is your happiness. The body, which is of the animal kingdom, should be treated well - just as you would a pet horse or dog. It has desires that are natural to it and these should be fulfilled - which spirit is doing now. But like the animal kingdom, it is not in charge of things. Its mission is to carry out policy that comes from spirit, the Higher Nature - not to set policy. This is a subtle distinction. Also, it is good at times to taste all the pleasures of the sensual world and to understand them. Only after you have tasted of all the pleasures of this world can you truly appreciate the pleasures of the spirit, which far, far surpass them. One needs to reach a point in development where one asks "is that all there is?" Then greater spiritual development can happen.

Transiting Jupiter Trine Midheaven

A happy transit. Career is expanding. Career Horizons are expanding. There could be raises or promotions at work. There is more honor and recognition. Social status is also elevated. New and happy career opportunities come. Job changes are happy and for the better. You are enjoying your career. Bosses, elders and authority figures are granting their favor.

The Spiritual Perspective. Those not on a spiritual path will merely experience "career success". But those on the spiritual path will experience that and much more. They will receive revelation into their mission for this incarnation - their true life work - the work they were born to do. There is nothing higher in life than doing that. Also they will find that they have the wherewithal to do this mission. Under these kinds of transits we get a glimpse that "spirit is calling us to greatness" - but can the mortal accept such a grand destiny? Many will have to arrive in stages, and by degrees. Those already doing their mission will make good progress here.

Transiting Jupiter Sextile Moon

A happy transit. Moods are jovial and optimistic. Opportunities will come in real estate, to buy or sell a home, or to move to larger quarters. There are opportunities to create harmony with family members and to improved the domestic situation.

The Spiritual Perspective. As with the trine and the conjunction the Principle of Truth is in harmony with the Principle of Feeling - you have opportunity to create this harmony. Thus it is much easier to realize, on a gut, feeling level, the good that you believe in. Manifestation is more likely. Its as if the feeling nature, the moods, are freed of the shackles of error and are lifted up. This mere "lifting" - this elevation of vibration (the true meaning of the "ascension of the feminine") brings many happy events to pass.

Transiting Jupiter Sextile Sun

A happy transit. There will be happy career and travel opportunities this period. Personal creativity has a market and prospers. Self esteem and self confidence is good. Lady luck is with you but you must be alert to her now. You prosper in honorable ways.

The Spiritual Perspective. There is opportunity to enlarge the sense of self - the understanding of the powers, privileges and prerogatives of the True Self. And because you become more, you start to have more and do more. With this expansion also comes great happiness and joy.

Transiting Jupiter Sextile Mercury

A happy transit. The mind and communication abilities are strengthened. There are opportunities to market your intellectual wares - ideas, writings, books etc. There are teaching and lecturing opportunities coming. Opportunities will come to strengthen your intellectual capacity - these can be educational opportunities or gadgets that help you write or communicate better.

The Spiritual Perspective. As with the Trine, there is opportunity to expand the mind and the intellectual horizons. The mind, the Thinking Principle, is both strengthened and enlarged. The mere enlargement of the mental vistas reveals new and happy opportunities. The person sitting in one room only sees the possibilities of that room. But let him walk outside and he will see myriads of other possibilities. In the vernacular, it is easier to "think outside the box" under this transit.

Transiting Jupiter Sextile Venus

A happy transit. Happy social and romantic opportunities are coming. Perhaps even a marriage opportunity. You are in a loving mood and your love is reciprocated. Opportunities for the good life are also coming.

The Spiritual Perspective. There is opportunity (and encouragement) to enlarge the love and aesthetic nature. This enlargement almost automatically produces social and love opportunity. It was always there only you didn't see it or understand it. Because your love vistas are expanded there are naturally more happy love experiences or opportunities that happen. This is merely the karmic law at work.

Transiting Jupiter Sextile Mars

A happy transit. Overall physical energy and libido are strengthened. You will have opportunities to profit from athletic abilities and/or interests. You will have opportunities to take the bold and courageous actions needed to bring wealth to you.

The Spiritual Perspective. There is opportunity under this transit to enlarge the physical capabilities - the previous limits that you thought you were under are lifted - and so the body, almost naturally, has greater capacity. Its as if you removed some "short circuit" from the body - removed some erroneous idea that held it back.

Transiting Jupiter Sextile Jupiter

A happy and relatively longer term transit. This is a period of optimism and prosperity. Fortunate financial and educational opportunities are coming. There are opportunities to obtain religious or philosophical illumination. There are opportunities to expand your horizons.

The Spiritual Perspective. Your Higher Mind, the upper mental body, has more energy and force under this transit - more voltage. Thus its impact on your affairs is stronger. You will tend to be more moral, more generous, charitable and optimistic these days - to take on more of the natural qualities of this mind.

Transiting Jupiter Sextile Saturn

A happy and relatively long term transit. Managerial abilities are strengthened. There are wonderful career opportunities happening now.. You have opportunity to create more financial security (long term) for yourself. IRA's, 401K's and other retirement savings grow this period.

The Spiritual Perspective. You have the opportunity to see the harmony between the Principle of Expansion and Contraction. You can easily see that "contraction", "limitation" has some very good points - one can set "limits" on "evil" or what is undesirable, and expand and magnify that which is desirable. This understanding, naturally and effortlessly, brings happy experiences to pass.

Transiting Jupiter Sextile Uranus

A happy transit. You will have opportunities to prosper from your new inventions, innovativeness and original ideas. Breaking out of traditional thinking can be profitable. There are also opportunities to meet new friends.

The Spiritual Perspective. As with the trine, your uniqueness and originality as a being is enlarged. The spiritual challenge here is how you will use this - will it be positive and constructive, or merely rebellion for the sake of rebellion? Since this is a harmonious aspect, chances are that you will use it positively.

Transiting Jupiter Sextile Neptune

A happy transit. A spiritual transit. There will be opportunities to market or profit from your inspired ideas, spiritual ideals and intuitive guidance. There will also be opportunities to enhance the Spiritual life and abilities. This is a period of spiritual growth.

The Spiritual Perspective. Much of what we say above applies here as well. Your spiritual nature, your perception of the Divine Will, your spiritual faculties are enlarged and expanded. Thus, the above happens, naturally and effortlessly, by the karmic law. Prayer and meditation will go much easier and have greater impact - and, as the scripture says, if we but "touch the hem of the garment" we are healed.

Transiting Jupiter Sextile Pluto

A happy transit. Libido is enhanced and there is more sexual opportunity. There will be opportunities for large success - to borrow money or pay down debt - to access outside capital - to prosper others. Educational opportunities will come that will assist efforts at self transformation.

The Spiritual Perspective. All the Pluto forces in the nature - the sexuality, the ability to transform, the ability to penetrate beneath the surface of things, are enlarged and strengthened. So with more of this power available the issue is how you will use it. If directed towards higher things, this is a time for spiritual and psychological breakthroughs. The ability to focus and concentrate is much stronger. The "personal underworld" is more easily seen and thus easier to deal with and transform. Spiritually speaking this is wonderful period for "alchemy" - turning negatives into positives.

Transiting Jupiter Sextile Ascendant

A happy transit. There will be opportunities to enhance the image and to lead the good life. In all probability there will be travel and wealth opportunities too.

The Spiritual Perspective. This is a period where you see that spirit loves the body and cares for it. Spirit is not interested in "depriving the body" of any needful thing - just the reverse is so. And this period you will see how spirit lavishes its love on the body. The only issue is that we are not the body, but much more than that. While it is necessary to love the body, we must not love it as ourselves, but more as a dearly beloved pet, who serves us well.

Transiting Jupiter Sextile Midheaven

A happy transit. This transit brings happy career opportunities or opportunities for raises, promotions and honors. There are opportunities to enlist the favor of those above you in status - bosses, elders and authority figures.

The Spiritual Perspective. This is a fortunate period for learning more about your true spiritual mission and calling - the reason for your incarnation. Your true duty to life. Egoic issues tend to block us from this perception, but today you have opportunity to expand beyond the ego and see more clearly. What the Divine has in store for you is greater than anything you can presently imagine - and happier too.

TRANSITS OF SATURN

With Saturn, perhaps more than with the other planets, we need to see two dimensions of it. One, the mundane, psychological perspective, the second, the deeper spiritual perspective.

On the mundane level, Saturn brings a feeling of limits, inhibition and restriction to any planet that it contacts. There is a need to "pull in our horns", to consolidate rather than expand, in any area that Saturn impacts. On a psychological level, it generally feels unpleasant. No one likes to spend less, or deny oneself material things. No one likes restrictions on speech or energy. (Even though, ultimately, these things might be very good for the person.) When it contacts the love nature, there is a feeling (often unconscious) of coldness and separation from others. On a mundane level, Saturn tends to build the character. One can only progress in the affairs ruled by the planet it contacts through real, earned effort - through taking on burdens and responsibilities that we would rather not take on - though it is right that we do take them on.

The affairs of the planet that Saturn contacts tend to be done from a sense of duty, rather than from any feeling of love or enthusiasm - though rightly understood - duty is a high form of love.

If a person has been irresponsible in a given area of life - has been in violation of spiritual or cosmic law - Saturn is the great rectifier - the Lord of Karma - who is going to adjust things - and it can be very unpleasant in those cases.

If a person has been responsible in a given area of life, then a Saturn transit will rarely be traumatic. It will be difficult, one has to earn everything - but Saturn will bring great rewards. Where Jupiter tends to give indiscriminately, Saturn gives only to the worthy. So a person who has worked hard, followed the rules of finance, been upright and honest in his dealings, will actually prosper under a Saturn transit to his financial planet. Saturn will reward his or her past effort. So, Saturn rewards the worthy and punishes the unworthy. He executes the karma, good or bad.

A person who has followed the rules, worked hard, will often reach career pinnacles under a Saturn transit (George W. Bush was re-elected as President, under a stressful Saturn transit.)

From a spiritual perspective, Saturn has two main functions. One, he is going to bring "right order" - the true cosmic order - to any planet that he contacts. Right order is a great blessing. It will always prosper the thing which is put "into order". But the process of bringing right order, is usually not pleasant. Things that have been "out of order" - in disrepair - in our lives are getting put back into order. The machine, or area of life, will have to be taken apart, rewired, parts replaced, and perhaps even be used in a different way. If the body was being misused - a common occurrence - a Saturn transit over the Ascendant or Ruler of the Horoscope - will show where the abuses have taken place and enforce a correction of them. If the person cooperates - usually by undertaking a stern and disciplined regime - the body will be put back into right order and the person will learn the "right use" of this wonderful instrument for the future. And so it is with every affair of life that Saturn is involved in.

Saturn second function - and this is the hardest for people to understand - is his role as the "tester". Sometimes a person has worked hard, followed the rules, done everything right, and still Saturn seems to bring him or her a "rough time". But this rough time is not coming from "karma" or past errors, but rather the universes' desire that the person be made "stronger" - "toughened" in a given area of life. It is much like the way a new car, or design, gets road tested by the manufacturer. The car will be tested under harsh conditions - conditions that most drivers will never face - in order to see how it performs. Does it fail under stress? If so, where? Does it hold up? Great, we can go into production. Likewise with us. Can we stay calm and balanced in a financial crisis? Do we still do the right things? Great, the cosmos will give us bigger financial responsibilities to handle - we will have more money to handle. Did we crack under the stress? Well, we might have to go back to the drawing board and improve our design.

Many people have very high goals and aspirations in life. Nothing wrong with this. But in order to attain these things - to handle them properly - they need the musculature and proper nerve responses. A puny, 90 pound weakling might want to compete in the Olympics, but until he or she develops the muscles and co-ordination, it will only remain a dream. It won't actualize in a proper way.

Many people think they are in love - that their love is real and forever. This is common when people are in the first flushes of romance. It is as if they are on "narcotics". But until their relationship has weathered a Saturn transit, they will never really know whether the love is real or enduring. We only know these things when the tough times come - when the challenges arise. These are the proving grounds. This is Saturn's function.

Transiting Saturn Conjunction Moon

Both a difficult and long term transit. Keep in mind that difficult doesn't necessarily mean bad - the long term result of this transit will be good - its just difficult to handle. For the past year and probably for the year ahead (If this is to the Natal) you had a need to manage and restructure your emotional life, family situation and domestic situations. Not all feelings or moods can or should be expressed. This need to control the emotions could have led to repression and even depression. The tendency to depression is the most dangerous thing now. Moods are pessimistic - perhaps unduly so. The native feels his or her age. The native broods about old age. Positive direction of the moods and feelings are called for but not repression. Often this transit brings disappointments with the family or with those who are like family to the native. The native will feel "cramped" in the home but might not be able to do anything about it - the best solution is to make better use of the space available. Often there is separation from family members. The native may be called upon to take on family burdens and responsibilities - the burdens and responsibilities of duty. They are unpleasant but must be borne. If they are handled properly this leads to emotional growth and to eventual family harmony. Generally this transit is more difficult for women than for men.

The Spiritual Perspective. Much of what we say above applies here. Those on the spiritual path can minimize much of the discomfort here by realizing that the planetary powers are NEVER punitive - only educational. You are not being punished. You are not being singled out. Basically, there is a need to bring "order" to the emotional life and nature - also to the family situation - both are related to each other. There is a need to set limits in the home and with family members. There is a need to control and direct the moods and the emotional responses - especially the negative non-constructive things. Your job now is to learn how this is done in a correct way - not by repression, but by direction. Then, the job is to apply this knowledge to your situation. One can feel anger, sadness, grief, or any other emotion without necessarily expressing it, or dumping it on other people. This only creates negative karma on yourself and worsens the situation. One can fully experience these things in a meditative state and just observe them - and this observation will often dispel them and transform them. There are many other ways to do it. But basically you are in for a period of "emotional house cleaning". Often this bringing of "order" to the emotional life will manifest as some event. A family burden or responsibility is placed on you that cannot be avoided. A sick or ailing family member is put in your care. A child is adopted. Some family member comes to stay with you. There are many other scenarios as well. Extra burdens tend to depress people. But spiritually this need not be so - spirit is training you. Pick up the burden and handle it - as you do so, you will grow in unbelievable ways. This is what we call "a character building" transit.

Transiting Saturn Conjunction Sun

Both a difficult and long term transit. More difficult for men than for women. Self esteem and self confidence are not up to par. Your self esteem is undergoing a reality check. If it is unreasonably high - if there is pomposity or arrogance attached to it - this will now be leveled. You will learn exactly where you are in the scheme of things. The good news is that if you've been undervaluing yourself, your self esteem will be raised. This is a time to take a low profile and avoid power struggles. This is a period (probably for the past year and well into the next year) where you need to work harder and smarter. You become aware of your physical limits and you must focus on the things that really matter. This is a time to progress by real and earned effort and not through chicanery, political connections or demagoguery. Hyping yourself will not work now - success comes through hard work and through your actual abilities and contributions. Often one is under a very demanding boss. Or, one is forced by conditions to work as if there were a demanding and exacting taskmaster over him. This is a time when you feel your age. Even young people will be thinking of old age now and planning accordingly. It is a serious and sober period. You've got to hunker down and accept responsibility. Duty comes before pleasure. But the good news is that this transit gives a long term perspective and if one cooperates with it there is enduring success. One will emerge from this stronger, more organized and more realistic about life and the self. Healthwise more attention needs to be given to the heart.

The Spiritual Perspective. Spirit presents you with another of its many paradoxes. Sometimes, in order to shine the way spirit intends us to shine, we need to take a low profile, become humble, take on onerous duties and responsibilities. The Prince might be sent out to the garden to do some "manual work". The Queen might be assigned "kitchen duty". The literary genius will be subjected to critical editors and readers, who might nit pick on the little things. In order to shine, we need proper training. Even the most talented person needs to train his or her talent, and this is done in "rote" and often boring ways. Repeat, repeat, repeat. This will go on until your Solar Being, the I Am of you, can express itself through a trained instrument - an instrument that can do justice to its genius. Often - another paradox - the main blockage to shining is our own self esteem and pride. Our mortal pride is an obstacle to the real light that we are. And, so Saturn, is going to tame the mortal pride - put it in perspective - so that the real spirit can shine.

Transiting Saturn Conjunction Mercury

Both a difficult and long term transit. (If this is in the Solar Return it is only in effect this year.) But the end result should be very good. There is a need to limit the speech. If you talk without knowing what you're talking about you can expect negative responses. This a period for the deeper study of things. Writing and communication needs to be more precise. You need to dot the "i's" and cross the "t's". Some people experience car and computer problems with this transit. Often there are problems with the mail or shipping companies. Important communications can be delayed. But less talk has many positive side benefits. You learn the reason why "silence is golden". Much of the speech around you (and that you have been indulging in) is frivolous and counter productive. Silence is indeed the better alternative. This is a good period though for making long range plans - long range financial or educational plans. The mind has a long term outlook these days.

The Spiritual Perspective. Much of what we said above applies here too. There is a season to all things under heaven. Now is the time to bring order and system to your mind, your thought process and the ideas that you hold. Though, initially, this can be unpleasant - the mind, when untrained, can be a most unruly creature - the end result will be good. The bronco will buck for a while - resist - run and jump and do all kinds of antics to throw off the rider - but eventually it will calm down and become "tamed" to do useful work. Also, order in the mind, will reduce mental error - the main pathology of the mind and the source of much suffering in the world. The seer knows that most people are not suffering from "physical or material ailments" per se - but from mental error. Thus your ability to reduce this, is going to reduce the suffering in your life. But it's a wild ride for a while.

Transiting Saturn Conjunction Venus

Both a difficult and long term transit (in effect for a year to two years). If this is in the Solar Return it is only in effect this year. Not a very good transit for love and social activities. A current love or marriage is going to be tested. There are difficulties in expressing the love force and others can consider you cold, aloof and forbidding - even though you may not realize it. You will have to work harder - make special efforts - to be warm, friendly and loving. The social circle is now being weeded out. Disappointments with friends or lovers will cause you to narrow your social life down to those who are really your friends. This is a period where you will learn that it is better to have fewer but good friends, than hordes of lukewarm ones. Your urge now is for long term relationships - relationships that will endure the test of time. Not a good period to plan a marriage or schedule a wedding. However, the period is good for business partnerships.

The Spiritual Perspective. Seen from the mundane perspective this transit is unpleasant to be sure. But from the spiritual perspective, wonderful things are happening. Much needed order and realism is being brought to bear on your love nature, love life, and social life. Love, romantic notions, friendships are getting a dose of "reality therapy". Love, which many consider to be a "passion" thing, will be brought to a newer and deeper level. Passionate love rarely lasts over the long haul. One must have a more realistic basis for long term relationships - something that outlasts the passions or emotions. By the time this transit is over you will be more able to enter into long term relationships. There is also another important dimension here. Our love relationships are "Destiny" things. Foreordained. And, often, especially under such a transit, seemingly happy love relationships, which are not part of the Destiny, will dissolve. No one is to blame. Neither party is a bad person. The path is being prepared for the predestined one.

Transiting Saturn Conjunction Mars

Both a difficult and long term transit. If this is in the Solar Return it is only in effect this year. You feel the limits of your physical energy. You are forced to scale back your athletic or exercise regimes to a more realistic level. Libido is not as strong as usual - and sexual excess will get toned down this period. There is nothing wrong with you per se - just a need to scale back on over indulgence. In many cases people will take on a disciplined exercise regime under this transit - but it will be realistic. Independent actions need more planning and thought. You are more risk averse these days - and the lure of adventure is not that compelling. Healthwise give more attention to the sexual organs and the head.

The Spiritual Perspective. There is nothing like cosmic limitation to cause us to become more efficient and resourceful - and ultimately healthier. When it comes to sex and the use of our physical energies many of us have become "prodigal". We have squandered the abundant life force given us in "riotous" living - which can take many forms. This is a time where we pay the price for it, but also make the necessary corrections. Sex, ego and physical activity are not "evil things" - but they need to be put into perspective. When they take up too much a part of our lives they vampirize energy needed for other important things. This is a time where order and right proportion are applied to these urges and energies.

Transiting Saturn Conjunction Jupiter

Both a difficult and long term transit. If this is in the Solar Return it is only in effect this year. But if handled properly will lead to great wealth and success later on down the road. You need to pull in your horns on a financial level. You need to consolidate rather than expand. You need to weed out waste and inessentials in your business and finances. You need to make better use of existing resources rather than blindly try to expand earnings. There is prosperity in cutting back. Bigger is not necessarily better - nor is it necessarily more profitable. There is a need to take a long term view of finances. You are undergoing a financial reality check. Sometimes these lessons are learned through "financial crisis". But there's light at the end of the tunnel - though tough choices have to be made. There is also a reality check going on in your religious and philo-sophical belief system - a good thing too. Probably you have been believing things that aren't really true or perhaps are only partially true - this is a time to re- structure this area of your life and mind.

The Spiritual Perspective. Much of what we say above applies here too. The Principle of expansion (Jupiter) and the Principle of Contraction, Consolidation, Limits (Saturn) appear to be in conflict. The truth is, there is no such conflict as these two principles are always in harmony. But spirit is using these appearances to clarify these issues in your mind. What better way to learn than by "laboratory experience". The main lesson here is not to be attached to either position. Someone on the spiritual path should be equally comfortable expanding, or contracting; equally at ease in the "high life" or the "simple life". He or she does either according to the Higher Destiny and the Divine Timing. Since there is no attachment to either position, it is much easier to flow with the need of a given situation.

Transiting Saturn Conjunction Saturn

Both a difficult and long term transit. If this is in your Solar Return, you can disregard this as this transit is only amplifying your sense of order and discipline. But if this transit is to your Natal Chart - it is very important. It means that you are undergoing your "Saturn Return" - a once in 28-30 year occurrence. This is a most important period in your life right now. You are closing out an old cycle and beginning a new one. In a few years you will be in radically different conditions and circumstances than you are in now. And this would be normal. These "Saturn Returns" bring moves, and career changes. Often they bring crisis as you need to make long term and very important decisions. The decisions you make now will determine your life for the next 30 years or so. The "Saturn Return" occurs when you are 28-30 - this is, astrologically speaking, the transition from adolescence to true adulthood. The 2nd return occurs at age 58-60. Many people are planning their retirement. Many are embarking on careers - especially now that the children are grown up or on their own. Almost always there is a move - often out of state or even out of the country. Whether this is your 1st, 2nd or 3rd return - you need to think about the next 30 years and make "practical" decisions based on this planning. Often this "Saturn Return" period is a reality check - ideas and plans that you have that are unrealistic are revealed for what they are. It is a time for dealing with reality as you find it and as it is revealed to you.

The Spiritual Perspective. What we say above applies here as well. Basically spirit is creating a "new order" in your life. Making the transition from the old order to the new is sometimes unpleasant, but the end result is good.

Transiting Saturn Conjunction Uranus

Both a difficult and long term transit. Your urges to freedom and your innovations are undergoing a reality check. Are they valid? Are they reasonable? Are they practical? You may feel very unfree according to your old notions of freedom, but if you look deeper, you'll find that this unfreedom has opened up other types of freedom. You are forced to deal with authority and perhaps feel uneasy about it. Traditional ways of doing things and traditional beliefs need to be dealt with. Blind rebellion won't work. You need to understand why the tradition or custom arose in the 1st place and then see where you can create freedom within that context. Inventions and innovations need to be practical and workable. They will be severely tested. Friendships will get tested as well. Many ideas and inventions sound wonderful on paper - but never work in practice and this is a time where you will learn this.

The Spiritual Perspective. Much of what we say above applies here. This transit is about integrating two opposite and very powerful urges - the Principle of Order/Limits and the Principle of Freedom/Originality. The object is eventual mastery of both - knowing when to apply what. Knowing not to apply one without regard for the other. Eventually a harmonious balance will ensue.

Transiting Saturn Conjunction Neptune

Both a difficult and long term transit. Your spiritual ideals, dreams, and creative inspirations must be made practical and useable. Ideals that sound wonderful when you are in a Himalayan cave or outside the mainstream of life, might not be so wonderful if they were applied to practical life. The timeless must be synchronized with time. The nebulous must have a body and a form. Very creative and spiritual people - who are usually considered impractical and dreamers - will have to learn more practicality this period.

The Spiritual Perspective. Much of what we say above applies here as well. It is the nature of Spirit to manifest and take form - and Saturn is part of that process. The timeless (Neptune) manifests here on earth in "time", as a process and not all at once. In Spirit everything is NOW, but in the manifestation process, things happen in "time" - in an order - in a sequence - as an evolution. On a psychological level, it can seem difficult to make this adjustment and this is why the transit is considered difficult. These are not really "antagonistic principles" from the spiritual perspective - but partners in the manifestation process. Its as if the "spiritual ideal" get's adjusted to the needs of the earth plane.

Transiting Saturn Conjunction Pluto

Both a difficult and long term transit. The limits of libido will be felt. Sexual activity will be toned down. Quality sex is preferable to quantity. If you've been irresponsible with debt - you can face a financial crisis now. It is much harder to borrow money, attract investors or access outside capital. Your efforts at self transformation encounter much resistance - either from the forces of tradition without or from hardened patterns within. Your interest in the occult or the deeper things of life require a disciplined, long term approach. Dilettantism won't get you very far these days. There can be prolonged power struggles with the system, authority figures or elders under this transit - sometimes these are justified. But only you can discern whether it is or is not.

The Spiritual Perspective. Much of what we say above applies here as well. Divine Order is being brought to bear in your "personal underworld" - into your sex life, your uses of libido, into your efforts of personal transformation and world transformation. This is the time where you learn what is workable and not workable in the world - this is where theory gets modified by practical life experience. While there are many aspects of our personal underworld that might need liberation and expression - there are many other aspects that should NOT be given expression - they need to be understood and managed - and sometimes controlled. They need a strict discipline.

Transiting Saturn Conjunction Ascendant

Both a difficult and long term transit. If this is to the Solar Return it is only valid this year. You seem distant, aloof and separate from others. You feel your age - or perhaps look older than your age. You are thinking of the long term and old age. You dress more conservatively and don't want to stand out. You take a lower profile with your image. On the positive side, you will be more fussy about diet and personal hygiene. Weight loss and detox programs are both more interesting and powerful. You are more inclined to take on a disciplined health regime.

The Spiritual Perspective. Divine Order is being brought to bear on your body, image and personal appearance. This Order is very necessary if your body is going to be good instrument that it needs to be so that you can fulfill your destiny. This is also true of your self concept and ego. Nothing wrong with any of these things - and spirit is not punishing you - but putting things in right perspective and right order. If you have food or substance addictions - if you overeat or under eat - this is the time to get these things under control.

Transiting Saturn Conjunction Midheaven

Both a difficult and long term transit. If this is to the Solar Return it is only valid for the current year. But ultimately it brings good. Career advancement happens only through hard work, real achievement and real merit. Eschew hype, fluff and imagery in the career - only reality - doing the right thing - taking on more responsibility - will advance you now. Strive for excellence. Take a long term perspective. This is not a time for "quickie" success. Rejoice when you make career progress even though the ultimate goal seems very far away. It is the steady and persistent progress that matters now. Bosses, elders, authority figures are likely to be more demanding these days - so be sure your actions are flawless. Many will get promoted under this transit - those who have payed their dues in the past. But this promotion brings more work and more responsibility - this is not a free ride.

The Spiritual Perspective. Much of what we say above applies here. Basically Divine Order - the right and correct order - is being brought to bear on your career and life work. This is most necessary if you are going to fulfil it in a proper way. The way that this order is imposed can vary. If a person has been out of order for a long time, the imposition of "right order" can be shocking and traumatic. But if a person already has the right attitude, this transit is not difficult, but will actually assist in attaining career goals.

Transiting Saturn Square Moon

A difficult and long term transit. If this is to the Solar Return it is only valid for the current year. The cosmos is forcing you now to bring order, stability, and discipline to the emotional life, the old subconscious patterns and habits, the home and to the domestic situation. This is not easy work, but disappointments with family members or feelings of depression force you deal with these things. Often it forces painful choices between sentiment/family loyalty and the career aspirations and what is "the right thing" to do. There is a feeling of being cramped in the home but moving is difficult. Onerous family burdens or duties are placed on you. The only way out is handling them and doing what is right. There is a need to re-organize the home but it involves much displacement of family members or displacements of a comfortable pattern. These reorganizations don't happen easily. It is a time for facing the truth about your feelings and moods and then correcting them. It is time to see the difference between sentiment and real justice and fair play.

The Spiritual Perspective. Much of what we say above applies here. A right and realistic order - a Cosmic Order - needs to be applied to the astral body, the home, family relations, the personal past and the whole emotional nature. This is a big job and we often don't undertake such unpleasantness unless we get a "wake up call" - usually in the form of emotional pain or discomfort. Order needn't happen through unpleasantness for those on the spiritual path - but often it takes these kinds of goads to get us moving. The cosmos is now supplying the goad. In the end, when you, succeed in bringing this order to bear, it will be a great blessing to you, your family and everyone you contact. An out of control emotional nature is merely " a broadcaster of inharmony and dissonance" into the emotional environment. Since these emanations are "forces" there is karma attached to them. Every negative force (it need not be physical) will have a karmic consequence. Thus straightening this area out is going to improve your future karma.

Transiting Saturn Square Sun

A difficult and long term transit. If this is to the Solar Return it is only valid for the current year. Overall energy is not up to its usual standards. Overall health - especially the heart - needs to be watched. The cosmos places resistance to your will and objectives so that you can develop strength and power and correct some of your flaws. Your ego is subjected to a reality check. Oh, anyone can have their nose up in the air, feel grandiose, a master of the universe, when everything is going well and there is much support available. But when times get tough we learn who we really are. This is a time for taking a low profile (and often this isn't pleasant) and doing one's duty - doing what is right because it is right. There will be little ego gratification these days. This is a serious period. One comes up against the limits of one's will and power - a good thing too. Then one learns to work within those limits. This is a time for gradual and evolutionary success. One cannot rely on luck or too much help from others - one earns whatever one has. One succeeds by sheer excellence and merit these days. This is what is called "a character building transit".

The Spiritual Perspective. Much of the above applies here too. The powers of the Divine Immortal get tested this period. From the perspective of your True Self, resistance is seen as a good thing. For when the True Self overcomes it is a lasting success. Even one's enemies (the resistors and adversaries) bow to the victorious one. " He or she made it in spite of all we could do." The difficult self esteem will be transformed to much greater self esteem in the end. Here the Immortal is dealing with the resistance from the past, from "traditional forces", the Pharisees in the Temple, the current order in the world. In the end the spiritual person will see that they are not really enemies, but have their role to play in his or her life and in the world. He or she will be freed of any "unpleasantness" from them - but it will take time. Under this transit one feels that he is performing the "labors of Hercules" - impossible tasks - but not really impossible.

Transiting Saturn Square Mercury

A difficult and long term transit. If this is to the Solar Return it is only valid for the current year. Your ideas, thought processes and writings are getting a reality check - are they true? Partially true? Mostly True? Mostly untrue? You will learn about these things now. Though this can be intellectually painful it is good medicine. There is a learning about both the power and the limits of the mentality - of logic and words. Not an especially good period for writers and communicators. There can be the feeling of the "writer's block". More thought and homework needs to be done when teaching, writing or communicating - as superficial thinking will bring an immediate negative and stern response. The nervous system, intestines, arms and shoulders, lungs need special attention. In many cases people feel little interest in intellectual pursuits. But this transit is not punitive - the purpose is to bring the thinking and communication skills up to par - to strengthen and deepen the mind.

The Spiritual Perspective. The phenomena mentioned above are merely side effects of a very deep and beautiful process that is going on. Order - Divine Order - is being brought to bear on your thought process, writing, ideas and communication faculties. Thinking, speaking and writing are very powerful forces - they are "forces" - energies - vibrations. Thus they have consequences. There is karma attached to them. Error in the mind has karmic consequences. Bad judgement being one of them. Negative or untrue speech and thought is considered a pathology of the mental body. To project these errors to others is to project disease into the collective mental body - it poisons the collective and will manifest at some point (if nothing is done about it) as a physical problem. So, keeping these faculties in order is a high priority for those on the spiritual path. Right now, you are probably reaping the karma of past mental or communication abuses. You are feeling the pain so that you will be forced to make the corrections. Bringing order to the mind is not an easy task. Few will do it unless they are forced to. So, the experiencing of the negative karma becomes the goad - the spur - to bring the necessary corrections. This is a time for honoring truth - for developing a passion for truth - and for learning how to communicate truth as best as possible. Words of themselves can never communicate truth in its entirety, but used properly, they can point a person towards it. The most important thing now is to stop creating new "mental karma" of the negative sort. Under this transit you will learn that it is better to be "silent" and seem "dumb" to others than to speak or write error that contributes more pollution to the collective mental body. Silence is indeed golden.

Transiting Saturn Square Venus

A difficult and long term transit. For about a year now (approx) your love life has been stressed out. (This is so if this transit is to your Natal Chart, not if it is to your Solar Return). The marriage, or current love relationship, or friendships have been tested. If nothing else in the Horoscope helps, there could have been a painful breakup. There is more difficulty in expressing the love feelings - perhaps on an unconscious level. Others perceive you as cold, aloof, separate. You will have to work hard (and it can be hard work) to project warmth and friendliness towards others. Social disappointments force you to take a more realistic perspective on your marriage, love life and friendships. There will be a restructuring of this area along more realistic lines - but it can be painful. Now these re-structurings don't happen all at once - it happens as a process - usually it takes about two years for the full process to happen. But there is much good emerging from this process. Social crisis will show you who your real friends are and who really loves you. This is not a transit for marriage - though other things in the Horoscope can deny this. There is a tendency to feel alone even in a crowd or even when among friends. There is a tendency to feel alienated and unloved. There is a need to learn forgiveness now. But the first law of forgiveness is "sin no more" - and if those who are sinning against you continue their ways - separation is in order. You must rejoice as social reality is revealed to you. From reality you can build a new and healthier social and love life - but if you've been deluded (and this transit will show you if you have) you will only continue in the old pattern. This is a time when you're searching for "enduring love" - love that can stand the test of time. Thus there is undue caution in love - love needs to be tested. But you don't need to do the testing. Events and circumstances will do it. Fear of love or fear of social relationships - undue pessimism about it - can also cause complications in your love life. This is a period for dealing with all these things. On a health level, the kidneys need more attention. Oftentimes this transit brings a conflict between social urges and the career - or love gets stymied because of career duties and obligations. It will be hard work to balance out these urges.

The Spiritual Perspective. Much of what we say above applies here too. Basically, spirit is calling on you to bring "order" and "realism" to your love and social life. To create order out of chaos here. And spirit will supply all the goads and experiences you need in order to achieve this. The pain is not punitive, but revelatory. It shows unrealistic attachments. If love attitudes have been unrealistic, off the mark, un- cosmic, you are now called to revamp this area and create positive and constructive attitudes. You are bringing your "head" to bear on your love life - very necessary these days - but this can be "off-putting" to people - they can perceive it as coldness. As your bring order here, a new and sounder love and social life will start to manifest. One of the main lessons of this transit is that you will learn that you can love, vibrate to love, no matter how you "feel" on the emotional level. Love is an impersonal force that is above the emotional and mental levels. But you will have to work harder, meditate more, exert more spiritual effort and will in order to express this love.

Transiting Saturn Square Mars

A difficult and long term transit. For about a year now (if this is in the natal), physical energy and libido have not been up to par. Your physical limits are being revealed to you. In the mind we can fly to the Moon, run the 3 minute mile, and have 20 orgasms a day - but in actual reality this is not so - and this transit is showing you this. There is a need now to acknowledge present limits and to function from that place. In many cases you can do MORE than you think you can - and this transit will reveal this as well. Your sense of indepen-dence - the ability to act independently - is limited these days. Probably you will have to seek consensus before you act. Often times irrational fears are preventing bold, independent actions - and this is a period for dealing with these fears. Some of the fears might be justified - they are merely common sense - a sense of caution. But some of them are irrational. So you will have to discern between the two. Health can be affected by this transit, but other factors in the Horoscope can deny health problems. The sexual organs need more attention. In general sexual activity needs to be balanced. Neither too much nor too little is good. Your career urges might conflict with your athletic and sexual interests. A stern boss - or career obligations - limits your independence.

The Spiritual Perspective. All the above are the side effects of spirit bringing order and harmony - cosmic order and harmony - to your physical drives, physical passions, and sexual activity. At times like these people tend to experience the karma - the consequences - of the abuse of these faculties, and this experiencing of the karma is the doorway to the healing process. Have we abused the body in the past? Have we leapt into action without forethought? Have we harmed others by our actions? Have we abused our sexual energies? Now we will experience the karmic consequence - and this is the great teacher and healer. We will have opportunity to correct future abuses and have a happier life. There is nothing evil per se in sexual energy, physical passion, physical drives - but there is a "right use" for them. This kind of transit is where we learn their "right use".

Transiting Saturn Square Jupiter

A difficult and long term transit that you feel for about 2 years. But the maximum intensity has been now and this past year. (If this is to the natal.) In many cases this transit brings financial difficulties and actual crisis - but other things in the Horoscope can modify this. You want to expand but you feel blocked and thwarted. Perhaps there is undue fear and pessimism about your financial picture and your financial future. Elders, authorities, bosses, parents (and sometimes the government) seem unfriendly to your financial goals and attitudes. You feel that you can't catch the lucky breaks. Of course earnings will come, but through much more effort and more overcoming of obstacles. Your basic faith in your wealth and affluence is severely tested. In many cases there is a need to tone down the spending. There is a need to manage resources better than before. The cosmos is testing your financial plans, attitudes and behavior. Weakness here will be rooted out. This is a time for being realistic about finances and spending. Expansion plans should be put on hold - and if you do expand be prepared to exert more energy and spend more than you thought you would. It is through periods like these that you really develop your wealth genius. Anyone can prosper when times are good and all factors are cooperating. But it is the bad times that separate the sheep from the goats. The seasoned business person can prosper in good times or in bad - there is just a need for a different strategy. This transit also shows that your religious and philosophical beliefs - your metaphysical view of the world and reality - is also undergoing a reality check. There is gong to be a re-structuring of this area of your life. Crises of faith will lead to a better, more realistic view of the world.

The Spiritual Perspective. Much of what we say above applies here. Jupiter rules our Upper Mental Body - both the personal and the collective. Disorders here have profound effects - both personally and collectively. A philosophical disorder - a false view of the world - a false interpretation of events - can be very harmful to a person. We can cite many examples here - but Ben Laden is a good one. His disorder is in the Upper Mental. Although he has many wonderful virtues and admirable qualities, because of the way that he inter-prets the Koran - the way he interprets Islam - he is ready to kill two thirds of the world's population. Most wars have been merely the manifestation of deep philosophical and religious differences. The recent cold war, was at its heart, a philosophical dispute. Many financial problems - whether they be of excess or lack - also have their origins here. So, once this is understood, we can easily see why it is so important to keep the Upper Mental Body in good condition - to purify it of error or distortion. Disorders in the Upper Mental will also, eventually and in due course, manifest as physical problems - some form of disease. Behind every disease you will find some false belief - some wrong interpretation of events - some impurity in the Upper Mental. So it is under transits such as this, where we will experience the karma of these impurities of the Upper Mental, that we bring it to right order - purge it of error by subjecting it to reality checks. Actually we can't do this, we can only cooperate with a Higher Power and let it have its way. Light will purify this body.

Transiting Saturn Square Saturn

A difficult and long term transit. The normal way that you impose order, discipline and organization in your life is not in synch with the prevailing patterns of the world. Elders, authorities, bosses, parents (and perhaps the government) are not receptive to your management decisions and your sense of reality. Your order could be antagonistic to their order. You will have to make adjustments. Sometimes, an alien and uncomfortable order or discipline is placed on you - very much at odds with the way you would do thing. Though your sense of order can be basically fine - your timing in the implementation could be off - wait a year or two and try again. Often under this transit one feels insecure. More attention needs to be given to the spine, back, knees and teeth.

The Spiritual Perspective. Much of what we say above applies here too. Your "genius" for creating order and organization is not at full voltage, so it is more difficult to do. On a deeper level, what is happening here is that your personal order, the way you set up your life, your personal organization is getting "road tested" to see if it is adequate. This road testing is usually not pleasant, but it has good results. If there are flaws you will know about them and be able to make corrections. Perhaps you designed your life - your order - from an unrealistic perspective. Perhaps you did so "always expecting sunny skies" and when the storms came, you were not prepared. So this is a time for refining and correcting.

Transiting Saturn Square Uranus

A difficult and long term transit. You will feel this about 2 years - the maximum intensity has been for the past year. Your urges for freedom and experimentation in life are thwarted blocked and repressed. Perhaps this blockage is coming from elders, authority figures, bosses or parents. Your need for freedom, your experimen-talism, originality and innovations are perceived to be "rebellious" and threatening to the established order. This can make you even more rebellious. You need to think hard whether it is freedom, or innovation that you want - or just sheer rebellion - doing things that will discomfit the authorities in your life. Doing things that will "stick it to the man" - to use a vernacular phrase. Your freedom loving urges could conflict with your career aspirations as well. You will have to work hard to pursue ambitions in a free and comfortable way. There could be crisis and testing of friendships - alienation from friends nowadays - perhaps a good thing too - for now you learn who your real friends are. It is a time for weeding out the social circle - focusing more on quality rather than quantity. Not an especially great period to market new inventions - take time to perfect them now and release them in a year or so.

The Spiritual Perspective. Your originality, innovations and inventions are getting "road tested" - they are getting a reality check to see how well they perform under real life (and difficult) conditions. It might not be pleasant, but in the end it will be good. It might send you back to the drawing board for a re- design or for improvements. Or, you might pass with flying colors. But only this kind of reality check can show you the true value of what you have created or intend to create.

Transiting Saturn Square Neptune

A difficult and long term transit. Your spiritual ideals - the seemingly highest in you - are being subjected to a painful reality check. Are they really spiritual? Are they true? Are they really worthwhile ideals or are they desires emanating from a lower consciousness? Now you will find out. Really, there is only one way to find out and that is through intense prayer and meditation on the one hand and then through application of these things in the world of practical reality - they must be lived. And here lies the difficulty. Not so easy to apply these high ideals - you are confronted with many obstructions and blockages - some legitimate and some perhaps illegitimate. You will have to sort through these things. Your spiritual faculties of knowing - intuition, psychic gifts, dreams will also be subjected to reality checks - intuition needs verification these days. In many cases this transit highlights a conflict between the worldly, material values and spiritual values - between the urges of career success and the urges of your spirit. Your spiritual values counsel you in one direction while your career urges counsel you in another. Elders, authorities and bosses (perhaps parents) are not sympathetic to your intuitive leadings and spiritual ideals. Your inspired ideas seem impractical in the world - and this may tempt you abandon them. Better to see how you can make them more practical. There is a need to blend the spiritual with the temporal - but the process is explosive and takes hard work. On a health level, you need to take better care of your feet.

The Spiritual Perspective. Much of what we say above applies here too. Spirit and Matter are, in reality, always in harmony, but you will have to do more spiritual work - meditative kinds of work - to perceive it now. Your spirituality, your spiritual powers and faculties, are getting a "reality check" to see how well they perform in everyday reality and life. The testing of these things will actually make them stronger.

Transiting Saturn Square Pluto

A difficult and long term transit. Libido is not up to standard - though other factors in the Horoscope can modify this. On a mundane level you could be struggling with debt. You are paying the price now for irresponsible spending and borrowing. Paying down debt is difficult and borrowing is also difficult. Outside capital is more difficult to access. In many cases, the spouse or partner is having financial difficulties - perhaps crisis - which is affecting you. Tax issues can be a burden. Sexual urges obstruct career progress. Too much focus on career reduces sexual energy and opportunity.

The Spiritual Perspective. Those on a spiritual path find the process of self transformation more difficult - there are stubborn barriers and obstacles to it. The forces of tradition - perhaps elders, authority figures, bosses and parents - oppose your efforts - or find them threatening. Giving birth to the new you could mean career setbacks and being out of favor with the authorities in your life. Are you still willing to transform? Perhaps you will slow it down a bit - perhaps you need to take a less extreme approach. Transformation is not done in a day - you must allow time for the organism (and the world around you) to adjust to it.

Transiting Saturn Square Ascendant

A difficult and long term transit. If this is to the Solar Return it is only valid for the current year. A period to take a lower profile. Your image and appearance is out of synch with tradition, with bosses, parents and elders. Your ego and self esteem is undergoing a reality check. If ego is undeservedly high or unrealistically low - this transit will adjust things. You are feeling your age these days.

The Spiritual Perspective. There is a need to cut back on sensual pleasures - and most will find this difficult. The ego - though not evil per se - needs to be put into right context - it needs to know its place in the scheme of things - an instrument of something much greater and higher. Order needs to come to the ego, and it may not like it. The spiritual person will impose his own order and thus have little need for an "outside" order to come in. But with the unevolved, this usually manifests as some "outside" ordering force.

Transiting Saturn Square Midheaven

A difficult and long term transit. If this is to the Solar Return it is only valid for the current year. The demands of career - the twists and turns of the career - seem to take you away from the career direction you really want to go in. Elders, bosses, authority figures have their ideas of where you should be and where you should go - and it seems contrary to your inner career direction. In many cases your own need for security and safety take you away from your true path. Understand, that sometimes we arrive at our destination in a circuitous path and not directly.

The Spiritual Perspective. Your career and life mission are being subjected to reality checks. How serious are you about your mission? Are you really committed to it or just mouthing nice words? This testing - this subjecting of this area to stresses and opposition - will definitely clarify these things. If you are truly committed you will pass through with flying colors and emerge stronger. If you are not committed you will be led to a different area.

Transiting Saturn Opposition Moon

A difficult and long term transit. It has been going on for about a year and will continue for another year or so. Right now it is most intense. If this is to the Solar Return it is only valid for the current year. Moods are pessimistic and depression is a real danger. Family interests and duties pull you one way while career goals and obligations pull you in the opposite way. Not so easy, these days, to balance the two areas. There could be problems with parents. There are disappointments with family members. Your moods and sentiments are attacked by people in authority, bosses, elders or parents. You feel unsafe about expressing your real moods and feelings. Your sense of emotional harmony doesn't support your career aspirations. If you choose career then you feel emotionally inharmonious. If you choose to be in emotional harmony you harm your career. You have to find the middle way here - and this is what the cosmos is leading you to. Family members are resisting authority now. Management decisions are not in synch with the family. There is a lack of emotional spontaneity these days. Healthwise, the stomach and breasts need more attention. Dietary issues are also more important now.

The Spiritual Perspective. As with the square and the conjunction this transit is about bringing Divine Order to the emotional life - to the Astral Vehicle. Trying to impose a "personal order" will probably not work and only cause repression which will lead to other problems. The prayer should be "Let God's Order, Plan and Process be manifest in my emotional nature". Bringing order to bear into our emotions is probably one of the hardest things a person can do. And probably one of the most important. An uncontrolled Astral Vehicle is a menace to oneself and to others. It is continually - like a machine - generating negative karma. Most people will not do it voluntarily - they need goads in the form of pain or discomfort to get them going - and the cosmos is supplying this now. These are not punishments, only signals and messages. Those who are already working on these things, will see these goads as "revelations from on high" of where more work is needed. They will not experience "suffering".

Transiting Saturn Opposition Sun

A difficult and long term transit. Its been going on for about a year now and will continue for another year. Now, it is at its most intense. There is strong opposition to your will, intent and desires. Overall energy and libido is not up to par. Though you are a star (and nothing and noone can take that from you) elders, authority figures, bosses, parents (perhaps the government) don't think so. Self esteem and self confidence are not what they should be. Creativity is not well received by elders, authorities, bosses and parents. You are not enjoying life as much as usual. A love affair is being tested. There could be disappointments with children. This is a period for taking a low profile and for shining silently. You can shine as you do what is expected of you. You must try to enjoy life as you pick up responsibilities and irksome burdens - these must be seen as part of the joy of life. You will need good discernment between true and false responsibilities. True ones, will help you grow. False ones will only cause suffering and vampirize your energy. Healthwise give more attention to the heart.

The Spiritual Perspective. Much of what we said above applies here too. The spiritual lesson here is two fold. One, Your immortal nature, the God Within is always shining and is not at all affected by opposition, resistance or material conditions. Spirit wants to give you this realization. On the mortal level, it is so easy to shine when surrounded by fawning admirers and sycophants - but when resistance comes, the mortal ego caves in. But for the Permanent Identity none of this is an issue and so the calling here is to arise on to that. The 2nd lesson here is about joy. Properly understood, joy is not dependent on conditions either. It is an impersonal, transpersonal force, available to everyone at any time. It is a force that one tunes into and brings into the world - not something that we get from the world. There are many stories of people who attained this on the battlefield, or as they were being fed to lions. Adversity rather than pleasant circumstances seems the best and fastest way to get there and spirit in its grace is granting this.

Transiting Saturn Opposition Mercury

A difficult and long term transit. Its been going on for about a year now and will continue for another year. If this is to the Solar Return it is only valid for the current year. Now, it is at its most intense. This is a time for deeper, more careful, more thorough thought and communication. Your ideas and your style of presentation are under intense attack or denial by the forces of tradition, bosses, authority figures and perhaps parents. You can not get away with half baked ideas or vague, unproven theories. You must have the facts on your side. The good news is that you are in a period where you can improve your thought process - organize and structure your thinking and communicating - delve deeper into subjects of interest. In many cases this transit produces writer's block. In other cases there is a lack of interest in intellectual pursuits or in talking.

The Spiritual Perspective. The spiritual lesson here, is to make your ideas and logic so compelling, so accurate, so well thought out and organized, that even your enemies must bow down to it. Everyone bows to truth and this should be your objective. That your ideas are getting "reality checked" should be a cause for rejoicing and not sadness - for anything that leads you closer to truth is good - even if unpleasant. Learning goes slower these days. You have to work harder to learn and absorb information. But steady, persistent discipline will eventually pay off.

Transiting Saturn Opposition Venus

A difficult and long term transit. Its been going on for about a year now and will continue for another year. If this is to the Solar Return it is only valid for the current year. Now, it is at its most intense. A very difficult transit for love and romance. Your marriage or current love affair is getting a reality check. Sentiment and emotionalism are being stripped away and you can look at your relationship as it is. Sometimes, this is a shock and a disappointment. But if love is real and true, the relationship will survive. If the relationship is fundamentally flawed, it will probably dissolve. The same kind of thing is going on with friendships. Much more difficult these days to express feelings of love. Oftentimes you feel alienated and alone - though you be in a relationship or group of friends. Singles will probably not marry this period - though other things in the Horoscope can modify this. Love is a wonderful thing, but it also produces duties and responsibilities - burdens that are not always pleasant. Real love carries these burdens willingly - but impure love, balks at it. This too is going on. The social urges pull you in ways that impede your career goals and aspirations. Thus bosses can be displeased with you at this time. But if you devote yourself to career, your social life suffers and a current relationship can go down the tubes - very difficult to please everyone. A current relationship, friendship, or your general social attitudes draws attack from elders, parents and authority figures. Perhaps your love life is merely an act of rebellion and not coming from motives of true love.

The Spiritual Perspective. Much of what we say above applies here too. Your love genius faces resistance and opposition. It might seem that love is stifled, but the intent of this transit is to strengthen it. This is a period for "building your love muscles". Spirit is calling you to consciously generate and project love even though you don't "feel like it". You must do this by an "act of will". You must choose to love even though others are projecting hatred, anger, or rejection towards you. Eventually, you will contact "agape" - the unconditional love at the heart of everything - then you are safe and there is no pain. It is a spiritual axiom that when we lose "human love" we find the real love - our true selves - who we really are.

Transiting Saturn Opposition Mars

A difficult and long term transit. This aspect has been in effect for a year now - and will continue to be in effect for another year (Only if this is to your Natal Chart. If this transit is to your Solar Return it is only in effect for the duration of the Solar Return.). Libido and overall physical energy are not up to par. There is a need to deal with sexual and physical limitations - to face them and act accordingly. One cannot sleep with everyone. And one cannot have sex all day - there are limits. There is a need to re-order, reorganize and re-structure these energies. One will come up against physical limits in the athletic interests as well. There is more inhibition - perhaps fear - in making bold moves, or taking independent actions. Perhaps these will not be well received by the authority figures in your life, parents, bosses, elders or the government. You may be tempted to be openly rebellious against them and that too would be a mistake. Sexual and athletic interests pull you away from career aspirations and could even damage the career. Your sexual and athletic interests - your desire for adventure and independence - are seen as "out of order" by authority figures. Perhaps you need to modify these interests - not give them up - but modify them in a way that is acceptable.

The Spiritual Perspective. "My strength is made perfect in your weakness". "Not by might, not by power, but by my Spirit..." "Those who rely on the Lord shall renew their strength..." These are the things that will be realized and understood under such a transit - the square and the conjunction as well. Perhaps you have been relying on your own strength too much. Spirit wants to show you the real source of strength. Gentle, yet everything and everyone bows before it. It labors not, but mighty works of power are achieved. It neither slumbers nor sleeps, yet it is always at "ease".

Transiting Saturn Opposition Jupiter

A difficult and long term transit - this has been going on for about a year now and will continue for another year or so - though less intensely. (This is only so if this transit is to your Natal Chart, if it is to the Solar Return it is only in effect for the duration of the Solar Return - until your next birthday.) Attaining to wealth goals is difficult and requires much more effort on your part. Earning and business abilities are being tested by the realities of life. Flawed attitudes or practices are highlighted so that you can correct them. There is a need for patience, fortitude, and an "evolutionary" attitude towards wealth these days. Sometimes wealth is enhanced by contracting and cutting back. Sometimes, through cost cutting. There is a need to apply financial discipline and right management to your affairs and many of you will feel that you are trapped by "minutiae" and not able to attend to the real business of wealth building - but this minutiae is important and has important lessons for you. Generally, this is not a time for expanding, but for consolidation. You must put aside ego and image concerns and do what is right financially. Elders, authorities, parents or bosses - perhaps also the forces of tradition in your world - are actively opposing your business or financial plans. If you are to expand and attain to your goals you will have to understand their position and adopt some (not all) of their suggestions. Either that, or you will have to delay expansion plans for another time, when they change their opinions. Students - especially college students - need to work harder at their studies.

The Spiritual Perspective. Your religious and philosophic beliefs are undergoing a reality check - and in many cases this could produce a crisis of faith. You fervently believe in one thing, while actual conditions and events directly contradict. These contradictions will lead to a re-structuring of religious beliefs, more high knowledge and eventually to a deeper faith. But the road is rocky. Students of metaphysics might have problems speaking the word or manifesting their mental treatments. The word is spoken, the treatment is made, but manifestation might take longer than usual. Again, faith is very necessary now.

Transiting Saturn Opposition Saturn

A difficult and long transit. The way you naturally order, organize and manage things is not in synch with the prevailing order of this time. You like to manage things one way, but bosses, authority figures, parents, elders and perhaps the government feel that things should be managed in an opposite way. In the business world, your sense of right order, your management decisions come under attack or criticism by bosses or those who believe in the traditional way of doing things. There are some good points to this transit though - you can enlarge your sense of order and organization by learning from the opposing points of view. Often this shows a conflict of various duties. Your innate sense of duty calls you in one direction, society's sense of duty calls you in another. This is a time to re-think career goals and aspirations as bosses or the authority figures in your life are not supportive. Many will find that they are forced to manage and organize in ways that are uncomfortable or alien to their nature.

The Spiritual Perspective. Saturn is now in its "Full Moon" stage in your life. The order that you planted many years ago - the way you set up your life and affairs - is probably now in "full manifestation". It has a life of its own. You can see and experience the system and organization that you've created. It is full blown - like a billboard. You made your bed and now you're sleeping in it. You can see the good points and the bad points. The strokes of brilliance and the errors. This, of course, is the spiritual purpose here. You might not be able to change things right away - your creation has a momentum and life that you yourself gave it. This is an aspect of the Law of Karma. If you have ordered well, this is a happy transit - a transit of reaping the good that you've sown. But if the order was flawed, you're reaping that too. Later on, once you've digested the mistakes, you can start creating a new order or make improvements on the existing ones.

Transiting Saturn Opposition Uranus

A difficult and long term transit. Its been going on for about a year now and will continue for another year. Now, it is at its most intense. (This is only so if this transit is to your Natal Chart, if it is to the Solar Return it is only in effect for the duration of the Solar Return - until your next birthday.) The forces of tradition, the status quo weigh heavily on you now and you feel very rebellious. You want to break out - to break all barriers to freedom - but there is heavy opposition from parents, elders, bosses and authority figures. Sometimes this transit is showing a conflict with the government or rebellion against the existing order. Your urges to freedom, experimentation and innovation are not well received by those in authority over you or by those who uphold traditional values. There is a need now, to transcend both your personal position and the tradition or bosses position and find the middle way - there is a need to understand both sides of the issue. This is not a time for going it alone. New inventions or innovations are not well received by authorities, parents, elders or bosses. There is great difficulty in making them practical for the present period. Nothing wrong with your inventions or innovations per se, but the timing may not be right. A good time to perfect them. Friendships are being tested these days. Your friends don't meet with the approval of authority figures in your world. Groups and organizations you belong to are probably undergoing crisis and restructuring.

The Spiritual Perspective. Much of what we say above applies here as well. Many lessons are being given here. Perhaps you have been relying overly much on your friends and social connections - your networking skills. From the human perspective there is nothing wrong with this, but from the Divine, it could be a form of "idiolatry". You have placed the power in the wrong place. This doesn't mean that Spirit doesn't want you to have friends - on the contrary - from the spiritual perspective, everyone is your friend - even your opponents. But these things need to be put into perspective. First the Divine, then friendships. Also, your inventions, innovations and experiments are being road tested - given some rough treatment. Stresses are deliberately placed on these things to flush out flaws and to reveal new improvements to be made. If you learn the lessons here this is a most wonderful transit.

Transiting Saturn Opposition Neptune

A difficult and long term transit. Your spiritual ideals, inner guidance, and intuition pull you in one way while career urges and practical concerns pull in exactly the opposite direction. The danger here is that you will choose one over the other and thus negate an important area of your life. You need to find the middle way. In many cases this transit produces a spiritual crisis - the ideals, the intuition, the guidance gets checked by reality - have you been merely dreaming? Fantasizing? Living in cuckoo land? Have the spiritual books, teachers, gurus been speaking truth? Or, are they too, living in cuckoo land? These are some of the issues you face these days. This transit produces the classic conflict between the Ideal and the Real - every Idealist or reformer faces this. Lovely, high flown ideals and visions are contradicted by cold, hard, merciless reality. In meditation you soar to the heights of Unity and Love but when you come down you see death, war, cruelty, despair, poverty. In meditation you are in love with the whole world, but then you go to the supermarket and get angry with a rude clerk or yell at your boyfriend/girlfriend over some trifle. While this is not a pleasant experience it is a necessary one. Bridging these contradictions will lead you to a higher more realistic spiritual position. Spirit needs to be made flesh to be of any use to us. We must make our ideals practical and workable. Intuition and psychic abilities - the dream life too - will be given a reality check. There is a need to apply more scientific thoroughness to these areas. Those who are very career oriented will need to bring some idealism - some spirituality - to their careers.

The Spiritual Perspective. Much of what we say above applies here as well. Nothing can ever oppose something that is truly of the spirit. So this is a time for weeding out what is truly spiritual and what is mortal and human that is hiding behind the spiritual. Also it is good at times to have our spirituality - our faculties and ideals - reality checked. It will lead to overall improvement, the revelation and correction of flaws. Too often we are vague and fuzzy about these things - this is a time for attaining greater clarity. Stay tuned to the spirit - to the Divine - through all this and the clarity and revelation will come - definitely and surely.

Transiting Saturn Opposition Pluto

A difficult and long term transit. Libido is not up to par. Healthwise there can be problems with elimination or with the sexual organs. You may find that you are in a war - a covert, secret, underground war - with authority, authority figures, elders or bosses. You feel that they are unjustly repressing or suppressing you. Your efforts at self transformation stirs the opposition of authority figures in your life. They feel you are undermining them. This could also be a difficult time for borrowing or paying down debt. There are many delays and obstructions to accessing outside capital. There is also a need to be more careful and prudent with debt.

The Spiritual Perspective. If you have abused, overused, or misused the libido - a formidable and precious power - you will find out about it now (also under the square and conjunction aspect). Sexuality is normal for the body - the body is a sexual creature. It is part of the creation which is polarized. Fulfilling the normal sexual appetites of the body is no different from eating, drinking or sleeping. But oftentimes humans "over cultivate" the sexuality. They pervert its true purpose. Perhaps they see it as a form of control or power - or a way to victimize another. And so there are karmic conse- quences under transits such as this. And this is a time for bringing "cosmic order" to this department of life. To establish the sexuality on more cosmic and realistic foundations. For those who have not abused this power this is a time for learning that we achieve our transformation - both personal and on a world level - not by might, not by power (personal power), but by my spirit. Our own personal power to achieve these things is weakened and we are forced (and a good thing too) to rely on the Divine power. The prayer now should be " Thy power not my power, thy plan, not my plan." Since the personal power is weakened now, those on a spiritual path often make long term and significant connections with others on the path - people who will help them.

Transiting Saturn Opposition Ascendant

A difficult and long term transit. Its been going on for about a year now and will continue for another year. (This is only so if this transit is to your Natal Chart, if it is to the Solar Return it is only in effect for the duration of the Solar Return - until your next birthday.) Now, it is at its most intense. The demands of health and work pull you away from attention to your image, appearance and personal needs - the needs for sensual gratification and fulfillment. In many cases, disappointments in love or with friends, lower the self esteem and deplete the vitality. Many people are undergoing a divorce or love breakup under this transit and this brings attack on the self esteem. Your general demeanor, appearance and self concept gets a reality check these days - and perhaps comes under attack by elders, bosses, authority figures, and parents.

The Spiritual Perspective. As with the square aspect, this transit is about bringing a "right order" and "right limits" to the carnal, human ego. This doesn't mean abuse of the body, but only cutting down of excesses which are not good for it. This could be dietary or it could be a need to take a lower profile and learning more humility. None of this is punishment. It is only about bringing the ego in right alignment with its spiritual purpose and function. If the Ego is too bombastic or has overly inflated views of itself, it will not be able to do its job properly. Neither will it be able to do its job if it has "no self esteem". It needs a realistic sense of self esteem.

Transiting Saturn Opposition Midheaven

A difficult and long term transit. Its been going on for about a year now and will continue for another year. (This is only so if this transit is to your Natal Chart, if it is to the Solar Return it is only in effect for the duration of the Solar Return - until your next birthday.) Now, it is at its most intense. Your sense of order and duty pulls you away from career aspirations. Your need to manage and organize your life compels you to put family, domestic or intellectual concerns ahead of the career. There is a need now to focus on re-structuring both the home, domestic life and mental life rather than pursuing career aspirations - but other transits and other aspects in the Horoscope can modify this. Many want to make the family the career. Others want to pursue the career from the home and in emotionally comfortable ways. Others need time to lay the foundations for future career success now, and this requires more internal, subjective work. In many cases there are unusual family burdens placed on the native and these must be dealt with before career issues can be handled.

The Spiritual Perspective. Your spiritual mission is vaster and more profound than you can imagine. A little road testing of it - a little rough treatment - will make it stronger in you. Flaws will be flushed out. Omissions will be corrected. Stress has some good points to it.

It shows weaknesses to be corrected. Also, it is not unusual for the Divine to take you on a "detour" from your apparent mission. For though the human mind can't understand it, there is a training going on for the future. In other words, the detour is also part of the mission.

Transiting Saturn Trine Moon

A happy and long term transit. This transit, which has been going for a year now and will probably go for another, (This is only so if this transit is to your Natal Chart, if it is to the Solar Return it is only in effect for the duration of the Solar Return - until your next birthday.) promotes emotional and domestic stability. The normal order, discipline and organization we need to apply to life - but especially the home life - comes easily. Your feelings and sentiments are supported by the authority figures in your life. Home and career obligations support each other. You find it easy to juggle the two.

The Spiritual Perspective. With this transit spirit is revealing to you that order, discipline, system need not be antagonistic with the emotional life and with the need for emotional harmony. (On an emotional level most people dislike duty, order and system.) In fact, now you see, that a good order actually promotes good emotional health and a stable home life.

Transiting Saturn Trine Sun

A happy and long term transit. This has been going on for a year now and will continue for another year - now it is most intense. (This is only so if this transit is to your Natal Chart, if it is to the Solar Return it is only in effect for the duration of the Solar Return - until your next birthday.) Libido and overall energy is increased. Self esteem and self confidence is realistic yet strong. You have a sound and realistic sense of what you can and can't do. You have the support of elders, authority figures, parents and bosses for your life goals. Career should be going well these days. Relations with children should be good. You attain to your goals through real achievement and in solid, step by step ways. Your creative products are well received by elders, authority figures, parents and bosses. Your creative products are useful, practical and very marketable. Calculated, well hedged speculations will be rewarded, but wild casino like speculations will not be.

The Spiritual Perspective. Sometimes we shine under adversity and sometimes under harmonious conditions - this period it is the latter. From the perspective of your true and immortal nature it is the same. On the human psychological level, of course, the experience is quite different. Under this transit it is more easy for the mortal nature to see the essential harmony between I Am and the Cosmic Order. I can be who I Am and still experience Divine Order and Harmony.

Transiting Saturn Trine Mercury

A happy and long term transit. This has been going on for a year now and will continue for at least another year - though now the transit is most intense. (This is only so if this transit is to your Natal Chart, if it is to the Solar Return it is only in effect for the duration of the Solar Return - until your next birthday.) The mental and intellectual faculties are enhanced - so are the abilities to communicate. Students should do well in their studies. Your ideas and writings are down to earth and practical and well received by elders, authority figures, parents, bosses or the government. Your ideas and writings - your communication abilities - can lead to status and prestige. You are more of a deep thinker these days. You learn subjects thoroughly and easily. You communicate carefully and accurately. Your ideas and writing have credibility. You know how to communicate to traditional type people without giving offense. You find it easy to organize and structure your thought in a coherent way.

The Spiritual Perspective. The Thinking Principle and the Principle of Order are in harmony in you and thus all the things we mention above are just the "natural consequence" of that. Here the Divine is revealing the essential harmony of these two principles. Because this is an "Easy" transit, it is more easy for you to realize this harmony.

Transiting Saturn Trine Venus

A happy and long term transit. Its been going on for about a year now and will continue for another year. Now, it is at its most intense. (This is only so if this transit is to your Natal Chart, if it is to the Solar Return it is only in effect for the duration of the Solar Return - until your next birthday.) The love life is stable and enduring. The duties and responsibilities of love are understood and taken up gladly. Love is both romantic and practical. The love and social urges help to further the career. The lover, partner or friend supports career goals. Elders, authorities, bosses and parents support the current relationship and seem to get on with the lover. For singles, marriage is also a good career move. Often under this transit one is romantically involved with an elder or boss - or perhaps with someone older and more established. Often this transit produces a business partnership as well as a romance.

The Spiritual Perspective. This is a transit of "revelation". Perhaps you thought (as many do) that love and duty were antagonistic - that coming from the Head - the practical side - was not loving or romantic. Now you can see romantic love can include all that - all the practical things - and still be romantic.

Transiting Saturn Trine Mars

A happy and long term transit. If this is to the Solar Return it is only valid for the current year. Libido is enhanced but not overdone. There is good control over both the sex force and over the physical energy. Physical energy is abundant and used very wisely and to best effect. You thrive on exercise and training programs. You take to physical disciplines. You have a realistic perspective on both your sexuality and physical abilities. Bold and independent actions lead to career advancement. Sexual and athletic interests actually support career goals.

The Spiritual Perspective. You have learned the lessons of libido and physical energy and have no need of further testings - for a while, anyway. Since the libido is strengthened now, the challenge is, how will you use this extra energy? Will you use it properly or will you merely create more negative Karma that will have to be dealt with later on?

Transiting Saturn Trine Jupiter

A happy and long term transit. If this is to the Solar Return it is only valid for the current year. A wonderful period for wealth, business and religion and education. Your wealth goals are pursued in realistic ways. You expand your wealth and your business in a gradual evolutionary way. Elders, bosses, authority figures and the government support your wealth goals and provide financial opportunity. You know when to expand and when to pull in your horns. This is a period of "healthy wealth" - stable wealth - stable growth. Your financial judgement now is very sound - conservative, with a long term perspective. This is also a period of religious and philosophical growth. Students are more diligent and thorough. A good period for the disciplined and systematic study of scripture and sacred writings. The mind will absorb them well.

The Spiritual Perspective. The Upper Mental Body - your religious beliefs and metaphysical perspectives on life - is in line with "reality" and experience. Experiences will vindicate your beliefs. Also, spirit is revealing that the principles of expansion and contraction are harmonious and not antagonistic principles. One can be generous and optimistic, but with a sense of realism. One can be generous but in a proportionate way. One can prosper in methodical and healthy ways. In fact, you find that a healthy dose of realism makes your optimism even stronger; that a sense of proportion makes your generosity healthier. There is a good integration of these two principles.

Transiting Saturn Trine Saturn

A happy and long term transit. Your natural and innate sense of order, discipline and organization is very much in synch with the order and organization of the current time. You are in synch with tradition and not in rebellion - though other transits and other factors in the Horoscope can modify this. Bosses, elders, authority figures, parents and even the government approve of the way you manage your life and apply order and discipline to it. In general, if nothing else denies, this is a positive career period for you. You feel more secure about life and about yourself. It is easy to create more security when you need it. Your virtues of patience, practicality and organizational skills are enhanced and strengthened now. Management decisions seem sound and practical.

The Spiritual Perspective. Much of what we say above applies here too. Your innate ability to order and organize your life - and those of other people - is greatly strengthened now. The challenge is, how will you use this extra power? Will you use it properly or will you merely create more Karma to be dealt with later on?

Transiting Saturn Trine Uranus

A happy and long term transit. Your urges for freedom and innovation are supported by the real world - by bosses, elders and authority figures. You easily integrate personal freedom with responsibility and career urges. Your innovations and inventions are very marketable these days - they seem useful and practical. You break barriers but within the tradition. Your particular eccentricities and uniqueness are now "mainstream". Friendships and group activities serve very practical purposes - and also boost the career.

The Spiritual Perspective. Two Principles, generally seen to be opposite and antagonistic, are now in harmony. It is almost as if you experience a revelation from spirit - a new insight into reality. Order and Freedom are generally viewed as opposites. Yet, they were designed to be best friends - complements to each other. A good order grants freedom in many areas. Real freedom MEANS a good order. Originality need not be rebellion, but merely an improvement within the existing order. And a good tradition and conservative perspective will make the originality more sound and useful.

Transiting Saturn Trine Neptune

A happy and long term transit. Your spiritual ideals are not only idealistic but very grounded, practical and useful now. Your inspiration leads to practical results. Likewise with intuition. Intuition is always the most practical thing, but there are times that we don't realize it - now it is clearly recognized. You realize that idealism that is only "up in the air" is useless. Now you know how to make them practical in every day life, in your career, and in worldly life. Artists and creative people will be able to clothe their inspirations in a the best possible form - a good form is as important as a good inspiration. Your ideals and inspirations, your spiritual knowledge and teachings, find favor with elders, authority figures, bosses, parents and corporate type people.

The Spiritual Perspective. This is a period where you can reconcile the Principle of Form (Saturn) and the Principle of the Formless (that which has not yet taken on Form - Neptune). They are two sides of the same coin. The Formless is meant to take on a form. The world of Form that we see around us was once "Formless". That solid object in front of you was once an "abstract dream" in someone's mind. It took on Form by natural and beautiful processes. This is a period where you can more easily see the harmony here.

Transiting Saturn Trine Pluto

A happy and long term transit. Libido is stronger and managed in a realistic way. Sexual urges will be strong but not overdone. The sexual urges and the career are helping each other. There are sexual opportunities at the job, with elders or bosses. Debts will be more easily paid or re- structured in such a way as to be painless. If you have good ideas, elders, authority figures, establishment figures and perhaps parents will back you financially. The earnings of the spouse will be steady and stable. For those on the spiritual path, the efforts at self transformation are supported by the so-called real world - by elders, bosses, authority figures, parents or those involved in your career. You can pursue your transformation process safely and securely. You receive an orderly method for transformation and seem willing to apply it.

The Spiritual Perspective. With libido greatly enhanced now, how will you use this energy? To what end? Will you create a pleasant future with it or more negative Karma? The Divine gives you choice and free will here. How will you use your extraordinary "penetration power" these days? Its up to you.

Transiting Saturn Trine Ascendant

A happy and long term transit. If this is to the Solar Return it is only valid for the current year. Your image and physical appearance is approved of by elders, authority figures, bosses and parents. Your image and personal demeanor will tend to advance the career or bring career opportunity to you. Probably you will dress more conservatively now and dress for success. Disciplined health and exercise regimes are more pleasurable and successful now. Weight loss regimes should go well, if nothing else in the Horoscope denies it.

The Spiritual Perspective. The body readily accepts the "Principle of Order" as this is its nature. The carnal urges are more easily controlled and directed. A good order brings health, beauty and longevity to the body.

Transiting Saturn Trine Midheaven

A happy and long term transit. Its been going on for about a year now and will continue for another year. Now, it is at its most intense. (This is only so if this transit is to your Natal Chart, if it is to the Solar Return it is only in effect for the duration of the Solar Return - until your next birthday.) You have a long term and realistic perspective on your career and life work. You are willing to work towards your career goals patiently and persistently. You succeed gradually - in an evolutionary way - not in a revolutionary way. Patience pays off. Success and advancement comes and is more stable. Elders, bosses, parents and authority figures are helping the career aspirations.

The Spiritual Perspective. Your spiritual mission unfolds before you. You don't need to see the whole picture, only the next few steps. Step by step it is easy to fulfil your destiny. No need to understand everything either. Understanding comes as you travel. The road itself brings the understanding.

Transiting Saturn Sextile Moon

A happy and long term transit. If nothing else in the Horoscope denies, there is emotional stability and domestic tranquillity - and you will have opportunities to establish this more and more in your life. You will have opportunities to integrate family life and career and to pursue career objectives from your emotional comfort zone. You have opportunities to learn how to manage emotions without being victimized by them. It is easier to establish order and organization in the home.

The Spiritual Perspective. The Principle of Order need not be in conflict with the emotional nature. Restriction need not depress us.

Restriction has some good points, which you are seeing now. Right order, the positive use of restriction, can actually improve our moods and feelings.

Transiting Saturn Sextile Sun

A happy and long term transit. A wonderful career aspect. You can be who you are, shine as you normally shine and still advance careerwise. You will have opportunities to combine fun, creativity and your love of children with your career. Libido is strong. Overall energy is good. Your creative products are practical - or can be made practical and useful - and thus they are more marketable to the world. But the main creative product is yourself and this product also seems more marketable.

The Spiritual Perspective. When the natural creativity of the Solar Being is also "ordered" in a correct way - subjected to a positive discipline - great power is generated. There is opportunity for this, this period. Creativity works best when it is harnessed to some practical objective.

Transiting Saturn Sextile Mercury

A happy and long term transit. Its been going on for about a year now and will continue for another year. Now, it is at its most intense. (This is only so if this transit is to your Natal Chart, if it is to the Solar Return it is only in effect for the duration of the Solar Return - until your next birthday.) Opportunities are coming to you that will deepen your mentality, make you able to think more long term, and have your ideas accepted by those in authority over you. You are able to adjust your thinking and ideas to win the favor of authority figures. Intellectual interests can be made to support career goals and aspirations. Deep thought can be pleasurable. Though you might not be the hit of the cocktail party circuit, you will understand your subject more thoroughly.

The Spiritual Perspective. The Principle of Order is helping the Principle of Thinking. Thinking becomes more powerful when it is in "right order" and not random and haphazard. Mental and intellectual disciplines will go well now, if nothing else denies. The intellect works best when it is used for the purposes it was designed for and then "turned off" - it is not meant to be used all the time and for all situations. It needs a discipline which you can more easily apply these days. .

Transiting Saturn Sextile Venus

A happy and long term transit. There will be opportunities for both a happy love life and a happy career. There will be opportunities for enduring and secure love. You will be able to advance your career through social means. You will have the opportunity to enlist elders, authority figures, parents or bosses to aid love and social activities.

The Spiritual Perspective. As with the trine, this is a time where you can learn the essential unity of duty and love. They need not be inharmonious. Seemingly onerous duties CAN be romantic - its up to you. Doing your duty by the beloved is as much an act of love as holding hands in the moonlight.

Transiting Saturn Sextile Mars

A happy and long term transit. Libido and overall energy is strengthened. You have opportunities to blend sexual and athletic interests with career success - to make these two areas co-operate with each other rather than conflict. You have opportunities to make better use - more efficient use - of your physical and sexual energy. Athletes will have opportunity to improve and perfect their style and performance. Physical limits are not necessarily extended now, but existing abilities are improved and enhanced. Bold, courageous and independent actions can win the approval of those in authority over you - bosses, elders, the government or parents. Bold actions - personal independence and courage - boost the career and the overall status in society. Athletic prowess also boosts the status.

The Spiritual Perspective. As with the trine, you have more energy and libido, how will you use it? Constructively or destructively? A right order, a right routine, need not detract from athletic excellence or sexual passion - it can enhance these things.

Transiting Saturn Sextile Jupiter

A happy and long term transit. (If this is to the Natal this transit has been in effect for about a year and will continue to be in effect for another year - but right now it is most intense. If this is to the Solar Return it is only in effect until your next birthday.) You will have opportunities to get the support of elders, authorities, government, parents and bosses to your financial goals. You will have opportunities to expand your horizons in a step by step, structured way. You will find it easy to make budgets and organize your finances. You will be able to see when you need to expand and when you need to consolidate. Right consolidation is the prelude for future expansion. You will be able to expand and prosper without upsetting the prevailing order in your life or in your world. Your religious and philosophical beliefs can win the approval of elders, authorities and parents. Educational and travel opportunities come through parents, elders, bosses, and those in authority over you. Perhaps there will be more travel related to the career.

The Spiritual Perspective. Much of what we say above applies here. Cutting back can lead to expansion. Cutting costs and overhead enhances the bottom line. Expansion can happen in comfortable ways without risk taking or over indulgence.

Transiting Saturn Sextile Saturn

A happy and long term transit. You will have opportunities to enhance your management and organizational skills. Your personal sense of order and security is in synch (or can easily be brought into synch) with the prevailing order in your world. Your organizational skills and sense of discipline is praised by the authority figures in your world - parents, elders, bosses, and those above you in status. Your ability to control your life is increased now.

The Spiritual Perspective. The Saturn force in you - this innate genius - is very much strengthened now and the challenge will be to use this force in a positive way. It will be tempting to try to impose your personal order on things and people as you have more power to do so - but better to discern what the cosmic order is and then apply that.

Transiting Saturn Sextile Uranus

A happy and long term transit. There are opportunities to further your career through innovation and inventions. Your urge for freedom and change can be merged with a successful career. Inventions and innovations can be made practical and useful now. Authority figures, parents and bosses encourage friendships and group activities. Friends are helping the career.

The Spiritual Perspective. As with the Trine, you are getting the spiritual revelation that order and freedom - the new and the old - need not be in conflict. When there is love and cooperation innovations are better and more useful. The old order, the establishment, is more willing to accept these things.

Transiting Saturn Sextile Neptune

A happy and long term transit. You have opportunities to make your ideals reality - to make them practical and useful.. Your spiritual ideals, intuition, and dreams can be career assets now. Spirituality can be a career asset now. You have opportunities to attract power people - authority figures, parents, bosses, elders - to your creative and inspired projects. Overall, intuition and dream life is good and reliable.

The Spiritual Perspective. As with the Trine you receive the revelation that Spirit is not "at war" with society, the establishment, or tradition. All these things emanated from spirit in the first place. So these things exist for a reason. But spirit never stands still, is always bringing in the new and this is the reason for the apparent conflict. Also, this is a period where you can reconcile the Principle of Form (Saturn) and the Principle of the Formless (that which has not yet taken on Form - Neptune). They are two sides of the same coin. The Formless is meant to take on a form. The world of Form that we see around us was once "Formless".

Transiting Saturn Sextile Pluto

A happy and long term transit. Libido is increased. Your ability to focus and concentrate is increased. You will have good opportunities to borrow, or attract outside capital from elders, authority figures, parents bosses or the government. Rather than be a rebel, you have opportunity to mesh your urges for self transformation, renewal, and reinvention with the forces of tradition and authority. You can win their support and cooperation rather than their enmity. A very good period for dealing with tax issues with the government, estates or insurance claims. If nothing else in the Horoscope denies, you should get harmonious and happy results now. Your interests in past lives, life after death and reincarnation can be pursued in a scientific and structured way.

The Spiritual Perspective. Much of what we say above applies here. Time, order, patience need not detract from libido or from efforts at transformation but can actually enhance these things.

Transiting Saturn Sextile Ascendant

A happy and long term transit. If this is to the Solar Return it is only valid for the current year. You will have opportunities to change your image in ways that appeal to elders, authorities and bosses - to dress for success - to take on the image of the status you seek. You will have opportunities to lose weight, to get the body and image in right shape, and to take on disciplined diets or health regimes. The way you look and carry yourself will bring happy career opportunities to you.

The Spiritual Perspective. You have opportunities to apply a conscious order - a right order - to the physical body and its appetites. The body seems responsive to it.

Transiting Saturn Sextile Midheaven

A happy and long term transit. You have opportunities to advance the career through patience and hard work. You have the opportunity to enlist elders, bosses, authority figures and perhaps parents to support the career. Your sense of order and organizations works well to further your career and status.

The Spiritual Perspective. Much of what we say above applies here too. You have help - especially from the established order - to pursue not only your mundane career, but your spiritual mission for this incarnation. These people are actually encouraging you to do it.

TRANSITS OF URANUS

Transits of Uranus like the other transits need to be looked at in two different ways. There is the mundane and the spiritual perspective on it.

On the mundane level, Uranus will bring sudden, dramatic, lightning like change to the affairs of any planet it contacts. These are likes "bolts from the blue" - the action of a lightning strike (which is ruled by Uranus) is very appropriate here. When Uranus makes a transit over any planet, the affairs of that planet will never be the same. Often the changes can be multiple - one after another.

On the mundane level Uranus brings feelings of restlessness, a desire for change, to the affairs of any planet it contacts.

When Uranus is involved in a transit, nothing is ever the way it seems. A dark period can be suddenly and immediately transformed. The spinster can find sudden love. The person in dire financial straits can have a sudden windfall. Surprise and shock are the two keywords that describe Uranus' action.

Uranus's sudden changes can happen in harmonious and relatively comfortable ways - in the cases of the Trine and Sextile. Or in more discordant ways, in the cases of the Square or Opposition.

Uranus will bring a feeling of rebellion too. This is true for everyone to some degree, but will be especially apparent in those already inclined to this - such as teenagers.

From the Spiritual Perspective, Uranus' sudden changes are not about change for the sake of change. They are about liberating a person from a certain kind of bondage. And sometimes these bondages are so strong, that dramatic means are necessary. Uranus does not hesitate to use these kinds of means. If an explosion or earthquake is necessary to liberate someone from a prison - Uranus will happily do it.

Uranus will also bring genius, insight and originality to the affairs of any planet it contacts. A brief flash of insight - a new technology - a new invention - a new way of doing something - will transform industries, and the world, much less the life of just one person.

Genius is considered a great thing - and it is. But there is a down side to it. In the revelation of the new and better, the old ways die or are greatly modified. So, genius has this destructive side to it - though, its intent is not necessarily destructive.

Spirit is showing (through Uranus) a new and better way to deal with a given issue - it is intended to be constructive - but there are destructive consequences. The person who wants social freedom, will probably explode the current marriage or social circle. He or she will attain to social freedom, but with much collateral damage. This is the main challenge of the Uranus transit - to embrace the change, and keep the collateral damage to a minimum.

Transiting Uranus Conjunction Moon

A Neutral and very long term transit. If this transit is to the Natal chart it has been going on for many years and will continue for a few more years. If it is in the Solar Return, it is only in effect until your next birthday. There is an emotional restlessness, a compulsion for change, a need to break out of the controls, duties and tyrannies of the family. A need for emotional freedom. And this is what has been happening. Often there are many moves - multiple moves - as there is a need to constantly upgrade the home. Often there is a kind of nomadic existence where one lives in different places and homes for long periods of time. Even if one doesn't move, there will be multiple and serial renovations, rearrangements and redecorations of the home. Often there are family break ups - divorces or other types of break up with the family and one's past. The main need now - and this is what the Cosmos intends - is to learn emotional stability and equilibrium. Mood changes can be swift and bewildering - both to oneself and to others. Moods can be very high or very low - and often this is mis-diagnosed as a "bi-polar" condition - really it is just the natural effect of Uranus on the Moon transit. Family members can be like this too - not just the native. It is as if all the stability that we expect from the domestic life and from the family is no longer there - family support is no longer reliable - we have to rely on something else - the Higher Power within. By the time this transit is over you will have a new sense of emotional and domestic freedom. But this freedom doesn't come cheap - there are many upheavals in store. One of the main urges here is to get the family connection to be more like a "friendship" - non- committal, free, yet friendly - and eventually this will happen. There is a need under this transit to create a "team spirit" within the family - to have everyone work together towards a common purpose and not just in the pursuit of private agendas. There is a need to create a kind of equality among family members - but since nature herself is hierarchical - this is not so easy to attain. The native will experiment with all kinds of new ways to rear children or to run the domestic life. The native will break with tradition on this score and search, through trial and error, for that which works best. Trial and error often brings new knowledge and insight - and this will happen for you - but when the errors occur, it can be painful. One must stay in a place of consciousness that is above the emotional level - the high mental or spiritual level - to handle this transit properly. Healthwise, the stomach and breasts need more attention.

The Spiritual Perspective. Much of what we say above applies here. The emotional nature needs to learn to cope with change and not be traumatized by it. There is a need to learn emotional equilibrium and to center oneself above the emotions. We are lofty beings who can feel, but we are not the feelings themselves. There is a need to learn emotional detachment, which should not be confused with cruelty or insensitivity. Our compassion comes from a higher and deeper place than the emotional nature. Whether the emotions or moods are very high or very low, we are the beings at the center of them. The emotions are like waves and we are the surfers. This is one of the purposes of this transit - to break the identification with the emotions.

Transiting Uranus Conjunction Sun

A Neutral and very long term transit. If this transit is to the Natal chart it has been going on for many years and will continue for a few more years. If it is in the Solar Return, it is only in effect until your next birthday. Much depends on how you use the energy generated and the kinds of decisions you make. But for sure, this transit brings (and has already brought) major and serial changes in the career, the life focus, and the life direction. Most people have the urge to break with tradition nowadays and explore their bliss in their own way. But this is more than breaking with tradition - it is breaking with the past - a bold exploration into the new, the untried and the untested. This is a very exciting period in your life. Your genius is now very strong. You are unusually innovative and inventive. You apply new solutions or new technologies to your career and your life. You are a rebel to some people, a genius to others; a nomad to some people, and an eccentric to others. Probably there is some truth to all these perspectives. But you need not be concerned. You are exploring your genius and letting it take you where it will - and rest assured it will take you to interesting places if you trust it. You have the support of friends and organizations now. Your scientific, mathematical and astrological abilities are increased. Astrology becomes most important in your life now - perhaps as a tool for making plans and decisions. You shine in groups. You understand the group dynamic as never before in your life. Of course any adventure into the "unknown" is fraught with risks - and so there can be some wild successes and a few crashing failures. You are learning about life and yourself through trial and error - and failure brings as much knowledge as success. Success and stardom (according to your lights) can happen very suddenly these days. Many people are more involved with the media under this transit - in one way or another. Usually this is the electronic media - radio, tv etc. Often there is more involvement with the Internet too. In very old people, this transit can bring a life crisis and some will choose to pass on - but death is still a matter of choice. If they go with the changes they can live many more years.

The Spiritual Perspective. Much of what we say above applies here. This transit is about surrendering to the new, the unknown, the "bornless" (that which is being born in you). It will take you to heights undreamed of, but you will also visit the depths too - but no matter - you are on an adventure. Also this is a period where you take the role of "originator" , "inventor" and "creator". There is often much glamor attached to this - as well there should be - but there is also a price tag. You will learn both these days. The changes happening in your life now are "of the Father", let there be no fear. When barriers are broken - which is what is happening now - you enter into a whole new life with new possibilities.

Transiting Uranus Conjunction Mercury

A Neutral and very long term transit. If this transit is to the Natal chart it has been going on for many years and will continue for a few more years. If it is in the Solar Return, it is only in effect until your next birthday. The mind is being exposed to new and original ideas. You are unusually creative on the intellectual level. You are "hopelessly original" in your thinking these days. You couldn't copy anyone even if you tried. You have a need to think for yourself and to break with all the traditional modes of thinking and communication. This is a time where you will (and have been) acquiring all kinds of new, high tech communication gadgets and equipment. You can be very rebellious in your ideas and in the way you express yourself. Very important to understand the difference between being truly original and merely wanting to "shock" people. The former is creative, the latter is malicious. You will have natural abilities to understand science, mathematics, astronomy and astrology these days. All your former ideas are undergoing radical change. You can change your mind and thinking at the drop of a hat, as new lightning flash like revelations and insights come to you.

The Spiritual Perspective. The intellect and mental faculties are not the enemy to spiritual development as many claim. When it is cleansed and purified - when it functions the way it was intended to function - it is one of the greatest tools a person can have. The intellect was intended to "think from the origin" and to communicate its ideas (the ideas of the origin) to other minds. This is what is happening for you now. The intuitive, the original, the higher invisible laws, need to be "rationalized" so that others can understand them. This makes them useful. Overactive thinking is likely this period. The mind is greatly stimulated. So meditation practice is very important these days. There is a need to turn the mind off when not in use - but it is more difficult to do.

Transiting Uranus Conjunction Venus

A Neutral and very long term transit. If this transit is to the Natal chart it has been going on for many years and will continue for a few more years. If it is in the Solar Return, it is only in effect until your next birthday. A current relationship or marriage has recently gone down the tubes. Perhaps a few relationships have gone down the tubes. Major change and volatility is happening in the love and social life. There is a desire to break all social barriers and restraints - to be free - to explore the social unknown. This is not a great aspect for marriage - generally it denies marriage. If a marriage occurs under this transit it generally doesn't last. The affections become very volatile and changeable. You can be in love one minute and out of the love the next. The love life becomes very unstable. Usually there are serial love affairs. There is great experimentalism in the love and social life. The native learns about love through trial and error. This process brings much new and happy experience - it is quite exhilarating - for one learns much. But the errors can bring much pain. The good news is that the love and social life will be very exciting. Love can happen at any moment in any way. Love happens at "first sight". The native will enter a whole new social sphere.

The Spiritual Perspective. The spiritual lesson here is not to cling to any love or wonderful love experience as there are ever new ones happening. We are not our relationships. We are whole and complete beings, and relationships naturally flow from that. During this transit the Divine is breaking mundane love attachments so that you can find the Real and True Love within. You are that love. Attachments to specific people and situations can obscure this fact and this is why they need to be broken. Once the real and true love is discovered, love relationships happen, they are enjoyed, but from a whole different level and perspective. There is no "bondage" in such relationships.

Transiting Uranus Conjunction Mars

A Neutral and long term transit. If this transit is to the Natal chart it has been going on for many years and will continue for a few more years. If it is in the Solar Return, it is only in effect until your next birthday. Much depends on how you handle this extremely volatile and explosive type of energy. In general this transit brings powerful urges to experiment sexually, to experiment with the physical body, in athletics and in your physical activities. There is a desire to test all physical and sexual limits. Its as if you want to throw out all the rules when it comes to sexuality, athletics and physical limits, and chart your own course. Often this will lead to new sexual highs and athletic excellence - but the road is risky and there can be failures. You thrive on risk these days and the danger is you will overdo it. Physical energy will be very volatile - the highs will be very high but the lows will be ultra low. Athletic ability will also seem more erratic. On good days you will break all records. On bad days you will be below mediocre. A steady consistency is lacking. This is because the cosmos is not so much concerned about performance but more about teaching you about your physical body and sex energy. When your physical energy is ultra high you must be careful not to get violent as this is one of the dangers here. Your aggressive urges will be hard to control. Since you are so sexually experimental - and probably out of the mainstream with your tastes and desires - it is vital that you keep your experiments constructive and not destructive - only you can discern what is what. Many of you will be using new gadgets and mechanical inventions to enhance both sexual and athletic performance. Many will be exploring new high tech drugs, herbs or foods to achieve the same purpose.

The Spiritual Perspective. As we mentioned above, Spirit is helping you to break "physical limits and limitations". Your notions of what your body is, its capacities, its potential, have been shaped by the world around you and the historical experiences of the human race. Much of it is not "really" so and you will see this as time goes on. In truth the body has no capacity to be sick, to be fatigued, to age or to die - all these things are imposed on it by the mortal mind. Change the mind and the body changes. These are some of the adventures and revelations that are awaiting (and which have been happening).

Transiting Uranus Conjunction Jupiter

A Neutral and very long term transit. If this transit is to the Natal chart it has been going on for many years and will continue for a few more years. If it is in the Solar Return, it is only in effect until your next birthday. This transit brings great change to the financial life. Earnings can go sky high for a time but also plummet very low. One has the urge to break with all financial traditions and all financial laws and learn about wealth through trial and error. The Internet and technology boom began in earnest when Uranus and Uranus were conjunct in Aquarius (1997). Millionaires and mega million-aires (even billionaires) were born overnight. The phenomena went against all financial laws and traditions - and much verbiage supported this break. "This is a new economy, a new age - the old rules don't apply." This is the kind of thinking that goes on under this transit. The old no longer applies and I'm in a new era - I'm going my way. Great wealth and wealth opportunities are coming and have been coming. Wealth - substantial wealth - can happen suddenly and unexpectedly. Perhaps new ideas, new technology (sometimes a new invention) come that create wealth for the native. But not wise to forget the traditional laws of finance now - they have not been abrogated. Save and invest some of it. Keep a cool head. This is also a period of great religious and philosophical change, upheaval and excitement. New religious and philosophical ideas are coming to you. Your old beliefs are also seen for what they are - there is more clarity there now. There is a great enlargement of mental horizons. There is much spiritual and metaphysical growth. New prayer and metaphysical techniques come. Very often there is new exposure to Astrology. Science and philosophy are blending into something new in the mind - a new world view that incorporates both. When the philosophical concepts change one can expect much change in many other areas of life as well.

The Spiritual Perspective. Much of what we say above applies here too. Religious and philosophical beliefs - noble and true though they be - are only "forms" of truth. They should point to something deeper - the reality that is beyond name and form. These forms are useful, but they are not "it". Undue attachments to these forms or dogmas can hinder deeper spiritual growth and realization, so the Divine, is breaking your attachments to these things. Once the attachments are broken, you will be able to express or receive truth through all the different forms. Different cultures create different forms - but the essence is the same. When this transit is over, you will be able to use almost any form of truth as it is needed. To a person of one culture you will use his forms, to someone of another culture you will use other forms. The forms will be strictly "convenience" and not passionately held dogmas.

Transiting Uranus Conjunction Saturn

A difficult and long term transit. This can produce all kinds of insecurities and fear. Your notions of reality, order, fundamental facts are being strongly challenged. Your sense of tradition is being challenged and changed. Perhaps you are experiencing attacks on the tradition you were brought up in. If you are someone in authority, there is revolt in the ranks. Your authority is being challenged. Much also depends on what house Saturn is ruling in your Horoscope - that area of life will be undergoing much upheaval and change. The basic lesson here is to take the best of what is new while keeping the best of the tradition. New technology, new innovations, new inventions are changing the way you manage your life and the way you order things. Healthwise give more attention to the spine, knees and teeth. The overall skeletal alignment needs watching now.

The Spiritual Perspective. Much of what we say above applies here too. Your personal order - the way you set up your life - needs changing. Spirit is not doing away with ALL order - many people behave as if this were so. It is only breaking up your attachments to a certain order, a certain way of doing things - fixations and rigidities. It is a transit of revelation. There are many ways to order things. Many ways to do things. But you can't see it if you are attached to one tradition or one way. A person's order is a very important thing and the break up of this order can cause a period of chaos and personal anarchy. But this is temporary. Rest assured, over time, order will be re-established in your life - probably better than before. Also rest assured, if there was any truth, or anything useful, in your old way of doing things it will be preserved and incorporated into your new order.

Transiting Uranus Conjunction Uranus

In the Natal Chart this is a long term transit. A very important transit, but which most people rarely experience. It happens once in 84 years. A major cycle of life has ended and a new one is beginning. One has achieved or experienced the changes one wanted to experience. One has innovated and experimented and now its time for a new sense of freedom. Many choose to leave the body, for greater spiritual freedom and independence that awaits them. But many stay in the body and begin a new cycle, exploring different freedoms - perhaps on the mind and spiritual levels. One starts to make new friends. Old friends have probably passed on and its time to find new ones. In the Solar Return chart, we read this transit differently. It merely strengthens and enhances one's originality, innovativeness and freedom seeking urges.

The Spiritual Perspective. What we wrote above pretty much applies here. The originality is greatly strengthened and there is a need to exercise it.

Transiting Uranus Conjunction Neptune

A Neutral and long term transit. Your spiritual ideals, intuitive guidance and overall spirituality is backed up by science and technology. You begin to see the scientific and lawful side of what you always believed to be "a-rational". Often this transit is showing major changes in your spiritual life - in your spiritual ideas and ideals, in your meditation practice or prayer life, in your teachers and regimes. In many cases the native becomes a spiritual wanderer - an experimenter in spirituality - someone who throws away all teachers, books and traditions and explores the spiritual world on his or her own. Many will use high tech gadgets to enhance their spirituality - things rarely done traditionally - subliminal tapes, fancy lighting devices, sound and magnetic waves, computers etc. The beginner on the path is now going to flit from teacher to teacher, from psychic to psychic, from teaching to teaching - never staying in any one system for too long. The native is gathering facts and wisdom.

The Spiritual Perspective. Much of what we say above applies here too. The Divine is breaking all your attachments - even to your loftiest and highest ideals. Above your Highest Ideal, is the Truth. Ideals (even true ones) derive from the Divine. It is the Divine we must worship and not the ideal. In truth, many of our ideals are of "human origin" and not Divine. And this is a period where we will see what is what. While this is happening a person can feel in a "spiritual chaos" - one can feel that one doesn't know anything. And this too is the work of the Divine. It is healthy sometimes to learn how much we don't know - the depth of our ignorance. Shocking, but healthy. However, there IS a power that "knows it all" and our ignorance will force us to turn to that. This is the purpose of this transit.

Transiting Uranus Conjunction Pluto

A Neutral and long term transit. Much depends on how you handle this very powerful and volatile energy. Your sexual energy is very electric. It can flow unusually strong or crash from over use. Sexual highs will be unusually high, but the lows will be very low. This is a time where you want to experiment sexually - but the experimentalism needs to be kept positive and constructive. You want to break with all sexual taboos, barriers and limits. In general you are more rebellious and self- willed. Your efforts of transformation can succeed very suddenly - out of the blue. New inventions, innovations and scientific discoveries are enhancing both the sex life and your efforts at self transformation. Debts can be paid suddenly and out of the blue. Outside investors or outside capital can come in a flash, when you least expect it. The income of the spouse or partner is volatile - but can go very high now. These financial highs are not consistent but come in spurts. The partner or spouse's generosity with you can also come in spurts and be unusually strong - but difficult to rely or predict when and how these spurts will come or happen.

The Spiritual Perspective. We all have certain limits in sexuality and in our ability to transform ourselves. We feel there is "x" amount that I can do. I have "x" capacity for these things. These limits are being broken now - they were only "thought forms" - and never real. This transit is a revelation of personal power - limitless power - so one must be pure for this or it can lead to all kinds of excess and negative karma. An impure person, ignorant of the law of karma or of spiritual law, who feels and knows he can do anything - can be a menace to society and eventually to him or herself. But for a pure person, this is a wonderful transit. His or her ability to "alchemize" a situation becomes almost unlimited.

Transiting Uranus Conjunction Ascendant

A Neutral and long term transit. If this is to the Solar Return it is only valid for the current year. There is great experimentation happening with the physical body, the image, the dress and your overall personal appearance. You are breaking with tradition, breaking with the past. Many of you are making fashion statements. Many of you are dressing for "shock value" rather than for fashion or aesthetics. This is a period where you constantly tinker with your image and appearance. You are always upgrading - always looking for the ideal - learning about the ideal through constant trial and error. Also, there is a tendency to ignore, or break with, physical limits - the limits of the body are tested to see if they are really "real" - or whether it is some false belief that was entertained.. Also there is usually much travel under this transit - the native is like a nomad now, moving from one place to another and never in any one place for too long. Getting mail becomes a problem as noone can keep up with all your address changes. Yet, it is an exhilarating time - a time of much personal freedom. This is not a very great aspect for serious love - for exactly the same reason. You are footloose and fancy free and don't want any strings tied to you.

The Spiritual Perspective. Much of what we say above applies here too. The Divine is breaking your sense of physical limits. These limits were never real, but only beliefs and thought forms. The body's capacities are really infinite - but the mind imposes limits on it. The body of itself has no capacity to age or be sick. These things come from the mind - personal and mass minds. The body can "fly", Levitate, live on air and spirit, and do all sorts of things. But the mind must be changed in the appropriate way. Most people undergoing this transit won't start levitating, but they will break many previous limitations.

Transiting Uranus Conjunction Midheaven

A Neutral and long term transit. If this is to the Solar Return it is only valid for the current year. This shows many career changes. Serial changes. You are never in one job, or spot for too long. Sometimes this happens within the same company - e.g. someone who is reassigned to different territories frequently - someone who must travel and spend much time in different branch offices or with different customers. Sometimes it shows someone who launches new career paths frequently. In general a career involving the media, the internet, science, technology or astrology is appealing. Often under this transit, these things are important tools in career success. There is a great desire for personal freedom in the career. The native wants to do his or her own thing with minimum of supervision. There is also a desire to experiment careerwise - to experiment with different careers and different jobs. One thing is certain, the native will not stay in the present situation for too long.

The Spiritual Perspective. Uranus on the Midheaven of the Horoscope is its most powerful position. His influence for good or ill is greatly magnified. Much of what we say above applies here. Most of us are constrained in our spiritual mission by unrealistic limits. These limits "seem" logical and realistic but are only "limitations in our own consciousness". Now the Divine, through its grace, is breaking those limits. Sometimes this is disconcerting - for things happen suddenly in a lightning flash way. One needs time to adjust to the "breath taking" change. But when the dust settles we find ourselves looking at infinite vistas of achievement and joy. Often the breaking of these limitations comes from changes going on in governments, society and the world around us. But we are in new and totally different Dharmic circumstances. Under these kinds of transits the spiritual person sees - first hand - the awesome power of the Divine. Nothing obstructs it - no monarchy, no movement, no collective of individuals, no government. It is supreme. All bow before it. The most menacing "bogey man" in your consciousness becomes a docile pussy cat under this transit. But while all these limits are falling away, there can be a period of chaos - let the dust settle and you will see clearly what needs to be done.

Transiting Uranus Square Moon

A difficult and long term transit. If this transit is to the Natal chart it has been going on for many years and will continue for a few more years. If it is in the Solar Return, it is only in effect until your next birthday. Very often it shows sudden and perhaps explosive family breakups, moves, and breaking with the family pattern. The emotional life is volatile. Mood changes are swift and unpredictable. Bi polar forms of behavior manifest. Friends and family don't get along too well. New scientific discoveries, or new innovations - sometimes new fads - disrupt the family and emotional life. The domestic situation is unstable these days. There can be many moves - but not always pleasant ones. The challenge will be to maintain emotional equilibrium through all this - not so easy. One must lift one's energies above the emotional level and function from there. Old habits and emotional patterns are being disrupted and they don't like it. Family members tend to be more rebellious and there is difficulty in maintaining order in the home. Healthwise, give more attention to the stomach and breasts.

The Spiritual Perspective. Sometimes old emotional and family patterns are so rigid, so strong, so firmly held, that it takes drastic measures to change them. So, the Divine, in its grace, supplies the drastic measures. Understand that these changes are necessary and that nothing that is really essential to your mission will be touched.

The Divine Supply of all good will not cease - but your faith will be challenged. By the time this transit is over you will be in a new and better domestic and family situation.

Transiting Uranus Square Sun

A difficult and long term transit. Overall energy and libido can rise very high or fall very low. The will is challenged by friends, new scientific discoveries, and new innovations and fads. Very difficult to maintain your course in life. Sometimes you have to arrive by circuitous routes. There can be many - and disruptive - career changes during this period. Children tend to be more rebellious. Self esteem and self confidence can be challenged by new scientific discoveries, inventions, innovations and fads. The way that you like to shine is challenged by friends and the trends of "modernity". You yourself can feel very rebellious this period - and the danger is that the rebellion will take a destructive rather than constructive course. The challenge will be to rebel in a positive way - by adopting a lifestyle, or career, or creative expression which is truly superior to the old. Creativity will be very strong, but perhaps provocative and rebellious - designed as much for shock value as for genuine creative expression. Your sense of self is being changed in a better way - but patterns that resist get uprooted the hard way. Health wise more care needs to be given to the heart.

The Spiritual Perspective. Your Divine I Am is always expressing its perfect power and destiny; but the way this manifests through your psyche and personality might be distorted by the personal ego. Sometimes the personal ego is so strong that drastic measures are needed and this is being supplied by the Divine now. It might seem that you are making many career changes, but really you are being led to the "right career" that was intended from the beginning. The career - the expression - that your Divine I Am is already doing. Sometimes the lower ego needs to find its right alignment through trying different types of careers and different types of life paths -

through experiment, trial and error, it can arrive at the true career and the true creativity. The Real and Eternal Ego will be untouched throughout this whole transit, but the lower ego can get a battering.

Transiting Uranus Square Mercury

A difficult and long term transit. If this transit is to the Natal chart it has been going on for many years and will continue for a few more years. If it is in the Solar Return, it is only in effect until your next birthday. Your ideas, thoughts, mental processes and communications are being attacked and challenged by new and so-called modern trends - perhaps these are new scientific discoveries, or inventions, or innovations - perhaps they are mere fads. But these are powerful forces. New ideas are kind of forced on you in an inharmonious way. New ideas prevalent in the environment are alien to your normal way of thinking and there is difficulty in understanding them - or difficulty in expressing them properly - hence there can be many arguments and misunderstandings now. Take the time to really digest these new ideas and thoughts - chew on them, until they make sense to you. There is a need to adjust your thinking and communication habits to new scientific or technological advances. Your thought and speech can be very provocative these days. Your mental positions can be seen as erratic. You can switch positions and opinions at the drop of a hat. Healthwise give more attention to the nervous system, intestines and lungs.

The Spiritual Perspective. Much of what we say above applies here too. Basically your thinking - your ideas - need updating and modernization. And since we often don't do things unless we are pushed, the cosmos is supplying the push. It will so challenge your thinking that you will be forced to make the necessary changes. People often get "attached" to their pet ideas - or especially to certain verbal formulations. These attachments served a purpose for a while and now they need to be broken. If you cooperate with the process, it will go much easier. Truth is above every verbal form and is never in an idea. Ideas are useful, but they are not truth. Only when we drop the idea, the word, or verbal formulation can we experience the truth to which these things "point".

Transiting Uranus Square Venus

A difficult and long term transit. If this transit is to the Natal chart it has been going on for many years and will continue for a few more years. If it is in the Solar Return, it is only in effect until your next birthday. Usually it shows the sudden - lightening like - ending of a current love relationship and/or friendship. Divorce often happens under this transit. The love break ups that happen now are breath-taking in their rapidity - stunning and shocking. But the whole social life is now very unstable. Generally (if nothing else denies) this aspect denies marriage. New loves and new friends can come into the picture - also very suddenly - but none of this is very stable. The purpose of this transit is to beak up all the old social patterns so that you are made ready for a new social pattern that is to emerge. The old social patterns have long been in need of changing, but some people don't change unless they are hit over the head. What is behind all this social upheaval are new and modern trends. Often it is one's friends or the organizations that one belongs to. The native is both rebellious and experimental in love - but getting into love affairs from a sense of a rebellion - or merely to experiment - does not usually produce long term good or stability. It does give knowledge and wisdom. This is a period for serial love affairs or serial friendships, neither of which is destined to last very long. One can deal with this by learning unconditional love and granting unconditional freedom. One can learn to enjoy the changes and flow with them.

The Spiritual Perspective. Much of what we say above applies here as well. Love attitudes, love needs and concepts about love, have needed change for quite some time. Perhaps you have resisted these changes and so now the Higher Power supplies the impetus - in the form of shocking and dramatic events. Its almost as if you are forced now to "think out of the box" when it comes to love and romance. Love is inherently and infinite thing - and its hates to be "limited" for too long.

Transiting Uranus Square Mars

A difficult and long term transit. If this transit is to the Natal chart it has been going on for many years and will continue for a few more years. If it is in the Solar Return, it is only in effect until your next birthday. There is perhaps too much sexual experimentation and the wrong kind of sexual experimentation - it can be of a destructive rather than constructive type. The same is true with physical experimentation. The native can be too reckless with the body and all kinds of mishaps can happen. Slow down now, be mindful in your everyday life and especially when exercising or indulging in athletics.

The Spiritual Perspective. Sexual and physical attitudes have needed change for some time. Perhaps you resisted these changes and now the Divine forces you to do what you should have been doing for a long time. These changes will ultimately lead to good - but the process of change can be uncomfortable. Ultimately you will have an enlarged concept of sex and the body - what the body can and cannot do. This transit is leading you to higher knowledge.

Transiting Uranus Square Jupiter

A difficult and long term transit. If this transit is to the Natal chart it has been going on for many years and will continue for a few more years. If it is in the Solar Return, it is only in effect until your next birthday. New inventions or innovations, new technologies and fads, threaten your business or wealth plans. It will be hard work to reconcile your business or wealth ideas with these new trends - but it can be done. Often one feels forced, or coerced to invest in new technologies or inventions before one feels ready. The coercion can often come disguised in your self interest - i.e. "If you don't get this new widget, your business will die" etc. Generally, this is a period of financial instability. People often attain to wealth under this aspect but it is usually unstable wealth. It can disappear as fast as it came. In general, earnings will go to extremes - there will be periods where they are very high - unusually high - or practically absent. When the highs come, don't feel that things will go on this way for ever - set aside capital in a safe place. Invest wisely. When earnings are very low don't feel discouraged - there will be a high coming shortly. Under this transit one needs to be very careful about financial experiments - do a lot of homework first. In religious matters you could experience a crisis of faith. The religious teachings that you were brought up under are attacked or contradicted by new scientific discoveries. You are considered old fashioned, out of date, a fuddy duddy. It will be a challenge to reconcile your religion or philosophical beliefs with modern trends - but with more meditation it can be done.

The Spiritual Perspective. Your religious beliefs, world view and personal religion have needed change and upgrading for some time now. But we don't often do this kind of arduous work unless we are forced to - and so the Higher Power puts you in situations that leave no choice. It is not that these beliefs are "wrong" - some are, some are not. Most probably they need to be understood better, revised and reviewed. Perhaps they need to be given a new and updated form. Also, it is very useful to have our "faith" tested every now and then. If faith is true, it will survive and get even stronger. For some of you, this is a time where you learn that there is NO TRUTH in any mental concept. Truth is always beyond it. So it is useful to destroy even a good thing sometimes, in order to lead you to something better. The more tightly you hold to your beliefs the more traumatic this transit can be. The purpose here is to detach you from concepts - even the high ones. They are useful for communication and can point the way to truth, but are not truth in themselves. The map is a useful tool, but it is not the territory.

Transiting Uranus Square Saturn

A difficult and long term transit. You are in a war now - a war between the old and the new; between tradition and your personal sense of order and new and modern movements in the world. If you are a parent, boss or authority figure, your authority is being challenged. Career can be very unstable these days, and there are likely to be sudden changes. They are not always pleasant - can be shocking, as a matter of fact - but ultimately, when the shock wears off, these changes are good. Healthwise pay more attention to the spine, knees, teeth and skeletal alignment. It would be normal to feel insecure now - to feel that your world is "rocking". But you must find your sense of security in a Higher Power. It is very possible that your management style - the way your order and manage things - the way you discipline yourself and others - will undergo radical change. New and contradictory ideas to the old ways will have to be assimilated and digested - some of them can be incorporated. Some will be discarded.

The Spiritual Perspective. Much of what we say above applies here too. A new order is being created in your life. A new and better one. But before that can happen the old order has to go - the assumptions behind the old order also have to go. And, this is the process that is happening.

Transiting Uranus Square Uranus

A difficult and long term transit. Uranus represents the way you express your originality and innovativeness - where and how you break barriers of tradition. But now your originality and innovativeness is not in synch with the way it is being expressed in the world in these times. For example, perhaps you expressed rebellion and originality in the area of relationships or art. But now, these "originalities" are not in vogue. The world at large is experimenting in finance or religion. If you are in the sciences, your discoveries are not accepted by the scientific community and could meet downright opposition. If you are into Astrology, your originality might not find acceptance within the Astrological community - though it could find acceptance elsewhere. Often this transit over-stimulates your natural originality and innovativeness - perhaps you overdo it and become merely rebellious, in a negative way. Perhaps you "under do it" and have trouble expressing your true originality. Likewise with urges for freedom. It can be overdone or under done under this transit. Finding just the right balance is the challenge now. Believing in your own originality in spite of antagonism and opposition is also a challenge.

The Spiritual Perspective. It is good sometimes to have our originality tested and resisted. This always leads to refinement and improvement - this is the purpose of this transit.

Transiting Uranus Square Neptune

A difficult and long term transit. Your spiritual ideals, dream life and intuition is not in synch with friends, organizations or groups you belong to and with the findings of "modern science". It is possible that they have insights that you're not seeing - and you should work to understand their position. Truth should not be a problem with spirituality. However, it is possible that they have no real truth to offer and thus you must reject their spiritual positions. In the meantime, it is hard to have friends in denial of your own deepest realities and ideals. Love them, be tolerant, but follow your own truth. It is very likely that the scientific denial of this period will be changed to affirmation at a later period as scientific knowledge expands.

The Spiritual Perspective. Your spiritual ideals, your faith, the light that comes to you from above the mind, is getting tested now. Basically a good thing. It gets tested by the highest findings of science and the intellect. Yet, if these things (your ideals and intuition) are so - if they are true - they will survive these tests unscathed - they will actually get stronger. Your ability to receive intuition and higher guidance will also increase, as you have seen the root errors of the opposition. In many cases, the spiritual ideals are deeply in need of change. Usually this happens by evolutionary kind of revelation - but sometimes more drastic measures are called for - and this, the cosmos is supplying. The kind of "disillusionment" that happens now, while not always pleasant, is good. Illusions should be destroyed. Only truth should remain.

Transiting Uranus Square Pluto

A difficult and long term transit. In the Natal Chart this has been going on for some years. And though it is only in effect in the current year of the Solar Return - it has appeared in past Solar Returns and will appear in future ones. This could be a period of sexual rebellion - undue sexual experimentation of the destructive kind. Sexual experiments are likely to turn awry. Libido can be unusually high or unusually low. There is a strong need now to keep sexual experiments positive and constructive. Sexual preferences and desires change like the wind. There could be problems with debt. If nothing else denies there could have been a sudden death of someone close. Your efforts at personal transformation are not in synch with current modes of scientific thought - or perhaps they are seen as anti-modern. The income of the partner or spouse is highly unstable - it can be wildly high or wildly low - difficult to rely on his or her earnings - or to make any kind of long range plans based on this.

The Spiritual Perspective. Sexual attitudes have needed change for a long time, but perhaps you resisted it - not unusual. We prefer the status quo until some event or series of events forces change. So, now you are being forced to make the changes that should have been made a long time ago. This is the purpose of this transit. The same is happening with your urges of self transformation and re- invention.

You need to take a new tack, a new approach.

Transiting Uranus Square Ascendant

A difficult and long term transit. If this transit is to the Natal chart it has been going on for many years and will continue for a few more years. If it is in the Solar Return, it is only in effect until your next birthday. Right now it is most intense as the aspect is exact. Upheavals and sudden changes in either the home, the career, the family life and relationship impact negatively on self esteem and self confidence. They produce sudden changes in your image, body and personality that you may not have planned. They take you away from personal needs and the pursuit of personal pleasure.

The Spiritual Perspective. Your self concept - your opinions about yourself, your body, image and appearance - have needed change for a long time. But you procrastinated. Now you are forced to make these changes. Changes in the self concept, in the understanding of the body, will inevitably (as a side effect) impact on your personal appearance and overall "look". You will now "re-define" your personality whether you like it or not, whether you want to or not.

Transiting Uranus Square Midheaven

A difficult but very exciting career transit. If this transit is to the Natal chart it has been going on for many years and will continue for a few more years. If it is in the Solar Return, it is only in effect until your next birthday. You are unusually experimental with the career. You change jobs and even career paths at the drop of a hat - sometimes involuntarily. You are being guided to a new and better career path - but the bumps on the way can be stressful. In many cases this transit shows major upheavals with parents, elders and bosses. They seem unpredictable. They change their attitudes towards you in a trice. You never know when they will explode. This is another reason for the job and career instability. Your career aspirations are being tested these days. Perhaps they are unrealistic

- either too high or too low. Perhaps you are not in your proper life expression.

The Spiritual Perspective. Much of what we say above applies here too. Sometimes we get stuck in a career path that is not right for us. We stay with it out of insecurity. So now the cosmos has to do dramatic things to bring you to your true career path and your true lifework. If you are already in your true life work the cosmos will show you new ways of doing it - it will enhance your flexibility. Often this takes the form of some new invention or technology that makes the old way of doing things obsolete.

Transiting Uranus Opposition Moon

A difficult and long term transit if it is to the Natal Horoscope. It has been going on for some years. In the Solar Return it is only in effect for the current year. You find it difficult to integrate modern trends (or fads) into your daily domestic life, emotional life and family relationships. It is difficult to maintain a team spirit with the family. Family relationships and domestic arrangements are highly unstable these days. There could be many moves - a nomadic existence. Sometimes the native doesn't officially move, but lives in different places for prolonged periods. Often there are many redecorations of the existing home - the native is trying to constantly upgrade the home and family situation. There is also a great feeling of emotional instability. One doesn't know where one will live next and for how long one will live there. Difficult to make long range domestic plans. There could be many shakeups in the family under this transit. Often the family relationship will break up. But it is painful. On the one hand you are lured by freedom from irksome domestic or family demands, but on the other hand the family connections are still strong. You are being led, perhaps unpleasantly and grudgingly to greater emotional and domestic freedom. A new family and domestic pattern will eventually emerge, but for now it seems like chaos. Under this transit there can be many mood changes - astonishingly swift. People can see you as "temperamental" or volatile. Very important now to cultivate inner peace and emotional equilibrium - it is perhaps your most important project. You must see yourself as someone who is "above the emotions" - you have them, but they are not you - you are the being "that feels", but you are not the feeling.

The Spiritual Perspective. For a long time you have had a need to break old emotional and family patterns. Perhaps you have been stuck in a rut and routine. You procrastinated. Now the Higher Power forces these changes on you - for your ultimate benefit. You might not see the benefits immediately, but in hind sight you will. The emotional instability that you feel is only a side effect of the action of a Higher Power. The Archangel of the Presence is troubling the waters. Out of this chaos a new order will emerge. You are being led to your true destiny.

Transiting Uranus Opposition Sun

A difficult and long term transit. These trends have been in effect for some years and will continue for a few more years. New and modern trends - perhaps new scientific findings - challenge the way you approach life, and make it more difficult for you to shine and maintain your self esteem. The way you like to shine is challenged by outside events or faddish trends. This could effect self esteem, personal creativity or your children. Often, because you are "not in style" there could be multiple career changes and adjustments to make. The best way to handle this transit is to take what is positive and useful from the new trend or fad and integrate it into your selfhood and personality - or to your career. A classic example of this transit is what happened to the silent film stars when new technology came out that allowed talk in films. Major stars of the old era were suddenly passe - out of work. They couldn't make the transition to the new medium. You are facing a similar situation in your life now - you can either adapt or choose another (and perhaps more satisfying) career.

The Spiritual Perspective. For a long time there has been a need to make changes in the direction of your life in general - in your career and life purposes - in the way that you shine - in your personal creativity. Perhaps you procrastinated. Perhaps you resisted. Now the cosmos sort of forces these changes on you. Sometimes you feel that you are "jumping off a cliff" - you are jumping into the unknown. But the unknown is also lawful - just as lawful as the known is. Underneath are the "everlasting arms". Often this transit shows important changes with the children (if you have them - or with those who are "like" children to you). They too have needed to make important changes, and now is the time.

Transiting Uranus Opposition Mercury

A difficult and long term transit - especially if it is to the Natal Chart. It has been going on for some years now and will continue for some more years. In the Solar Return this transit is only in effect for the current year. Much sudden and dramatic change is going on in your mentality and thought process - also to the way you communicate. On one level, new scientific advances or modern trends and fads (some of which could be sheer nonsense) challenge your thinking and ideas. Your normal thought patterns are not in vogue and perhaps even attacked. You are also challenged to change the way you communicate. And, this might not be pleasant or easy to adjust to. For example, the Internet changed the way people communicated and advertised. It changed traditional journalism. Perhaps you were used to communicating by letter, now you must use e-mail or some other unfamiliar medium. New trends could make your normal speech, your humor etc. "politically incorrect". On a health level you must watch the nervous system, lungs and intestines. The nervous system is likely to be hyper these days and learning the art of relaxation will be a big help.

The Spiritual Perspective. For a long time you've needed to make changes in your thinking - in the ideas that you hold and in your intellectual interests in general. But few of us make laborious changes unless we are forced to - so this is the purpose of this transit. The mental body is getting "upgraded" with new ideas, new ways to communicate, and new interests. Old fixed ideas will have to go or be modified. The mental body will become more "flexible" and better after this transit - but in the meantime it can be uncomfortable. Instead of a harmonious, evolutionary kind of change, there will be sudden shocks - sudden exposure to new ideas and new scientific discoveries. You are getting just the "right prodding" that will produce the changes needed. A passion for "truth" will be a guiding light now.

Transiting Uranus Opposition Venus

A difficult and long term transit. If this transit is to the Natal Chart this has been going on for some years now. And, it will continue for a few more years. Now the influence is most powerful. If this transit is in the Solar Return it is only in effect for the current year. This transit tends to de-stabilize the love and social life. Marrieds tend to divorce under these transits (if nothing else denies). There can be changes of affection that happen swiftly and suddenly. These changes of affection can occur with you or with the partner. Friendships too can dissolve suddenly. Here's what's happening. Your love nature, attitudes and relationships are being opposed and de-stabilized by modern trends, fads, innovations and perhaps new scientific discoveries. New technology can also be a factor. These new social trends or fads can be good or merely public manias that will not last long, but nevertheless they put stress on your love and social attitudes - they seem diametrically opposed to your perspective on these things. You feel a love relationship should be conducted in a certain way, but modern trends dictate otherwise. Or perhaps, there is tendency to experiment in love that doesn't work out for you. The main spiritual lesson now is to sit loose to love; to flow with the changes. A current relationship can last if you allow a lot of space for yourself and the lover. You must allow the maximum freedom. Long term social plans are difficult to make now as you don't know who you will be with or if you will be with anyone. You don't know where you stand with a current love from day to day - perhaps even from moment to moment. Sudden eruptions of displeasure are common. But sudden eruptions of love are also common. You don't know how long either will last. Its as if you are forced into social experiments and innovations whether you like it or not.

The Spiritual Perspective. Much of the phenomena here is similar to what happens with the square aspect. For a long time there has been a need to make important changes to the social life, the love life, and the social attitudes in general. But, in general, we are loathe to make these changes as it "rocks the boat" and disturbs a tenuous status quo. So now, the Higher Power forces the changes that should have been made long ago. This happens in the form of shocking outside events. There is a restlesness in love - vague dissatisfactions. Affections are unstable and can change at the drop of a hat. The social, romantic and marital status quo, is over with. Committed marriages can survive (mostly they don't) but the ground rules will change dramatically. Even the best of marriages and friendships will get tested.

Transiting Uranus Opposition Mars

A difficult and long term transit. If this transit is to the Natal Chart this has been going on for some years now. And, it will continue for a few more years. If this is to the Solar Return, it is only in effect for the current year - until your next birthday. You could be tempted to risky sexual or physical experimentation. The urge to test the physical limits needs to be kept in reasonable bounds and with a concern for safety. Sexual and athletic interests interfere with social interests - or with groups that you belong to. Sexual issues can complicate a friendship. Your sexual and athletic interests conflict with what is new and modern in your world. You find it more difficult to adjust to groups and organizations as your desire for independent action and self sufficiency seems to conflict with the interest of the group. The mental life - the life of the mind - opposes your physical life - the life of the body and senses. Its as if you are forced to choose between one or the other. The values of the mind - coolness, calmness, objectivity, non-reactivity etc. do not sit well with your desires for action and adventure. You will be making radical changes to your exercise or athletic regime. Keep in mind that new is not necessarily better - sometimes it is and sometimes it isn't. New innovations in your world may not be to your liking and could provoke argument and warfare on your end. In a woman's chart this transit shows that the men in her life could be more volatile and unpredictable.

The Spiritual Perspective. Sex and the use of power are perhaps the most dynamic forces available to a person. They spring from life itself - from the life power. Without the procreative urge and the ability to "defend oneself" life is impossible. Because of the power of these urges, there is much confusion and misinformation about these things. Wherever you see great power, you will also see great controversy. For a long time you've needed to make changes in your attitudes to these things. Perhaps you've been muddled or confused. Perhaps you held attitudes that were hurting yourself or others. Few of us make changes unless we are pushed and so the Higher Power supplies the push in the form of painful events, or upheavals. If you cooperate with the process instead of resisting, things will go easier for you. A passion for truth will be a great help now.

Transiting Uranus Opposition Jupiter

A difficult and long term transit. If this is to the Natal Horoscope these trends have been going on for some time and will continue for a few more years. Now the effect is most powerful. If this is to the

Solar Return Horoscope the effect is only for the current year. Basically this transit is producing great financial instability. Major and long term changes are happening to the financial life and to the wealth attitudes as well. There will be other sudden and long term changes happening, but this will depend on what Jupiter rules in your chart. There could be sudden financial losses or a sudden change in the financial picture that causes you to change your investments, strategy, planning or even the way you earn your money. Financial planning is very difficult now as you don't know what will happen or what you will have from day to day. Finances can be a wild roller coaster ride now with very high ups and terrible, devastating downs. This is not punishment, but only the Universe's way of making you change - of getting you out of uncomfortable financial patterns that you've been locked into. Eventually you will be led to a new sense of financial freedom. Perhaps you've been prospering in a business, but haven't really been enjoying it. Perhaps you deserve better but are afraid to launch out into deep waters - now you are being shoved - perhaps uncomfortably - into the deeper waters. How these things happen can vary. But usually it comes from new social, scientific or technological trends that oppose your current financial thinking or situation. If you can remember the fear that occurred in Old Economy companies with the advent of the Internet you get a feeling of what I mean. So many things were rendered obsolete. When TV became popular, radio companies were very threatened - many faced crises. They were forced into changes. But this transit also effects other things in your life. Namely, your religious and philosophical beliefs - your view of the world - your personal religion - your perspective on the meaning of life. Again, the modus operandi can be new scientific discoveries or technological innovations. Perhaps your world view was conditioned in ways that predated these discoveries and now must be updated, revised or even discarded. Your religious notion are challenged by new and modern social trends - some of which can be good and some of which can be merely "fads". It doesn't matter, you are forced to adapt your outlook to accommodate these trends. In many cases, the native experiences a "crisis of faith" as outer events seem to contradict deeply held religious or philosophical principles. That which is true will survive. That which is not true will get discarded.

The Spiritual Perspective. Much of what we said above applies here. It is good that old, fixated beliefs - religious or financial - get challenged and even broken. As long as a person is in a little hovel, he or she can't see the sun and the sky. But destroy the hovel, and a whole new world, with new opportunities, is revealed. This is what is happening now. None of what is happening should be considered punishment - really it is "liberation". This transit need not be painful if you understand what is going on. But if you are attached to your hovel, it can be "traumatic".

Transiting Uranus Opposition Saturn

A difficult and long term transit that has been going on for many years now, but now it is most powerful. The personal order that you have established in your life - your "rock like" securities - are now being challenged by new and modern forces. These can take the form of new scientific discoveries, new technologies, or rebellious type people or forces. If you are an adult and in authority, your authority is challenged - you are dealing with rebellion in the ranks. Your management style is questioned and opposed. Management decisions are second guessed. This is a classic conflict between the new and the old. Your time tested beliefs might need some revision these days. They may not be all bad, but perhaps they need some updating and now is the time that it is happening. There would be a natural tendency for you to "over control" and micro manage these days - but don't be provoked into rash behavior. New scientific breakthroughs or technologies, or the forces of "modernism" challenge your notions of order - these can seem to create dis-order or chaos in your life. But understand, that this is only temporary. Out of this seeming disorder and chaos, a new and probably better order will emerge. Perhaps you were on a career path that was based on certain fundamental assumptions about business or the world - well, now, new technologies or changes in the world - undermine those assumptions. Parents, elders, authority figures, bosses are experiencing major changes and disruptions in their lives and by the time this transit is over (in a few more years) a new and different power structure will be in effect. If you feel insecure these days, it would be natural. Adapt to the changes that are positive and constructive and leave the rest alone. Some changes really are improvements and some are not - discern between the two and take appropriate action.

The Spiritual Perspective. Much of what we say above applies here. One of the spiritual agendas here is to "test" your present order - the way you have set up your life. If it is basically sound, founded on cosmic principles and spiritual law, the order will survive and thrive. It will get even stronger. Your management ability - your organizational abilities will all be enhanced - for these, like muscles, get exercised. But if your notions of reality, your personal order, has been amiss, faulty, untrue - the Higher Power is doing you a favor by destroying it. You will build something better in its place. You will make the improvements that need to be made. Since Saturn also relates to a person's mission in life - the Dharma - this transit will destroy false notions about your mission and reveal the new and better ones.

Transiting Uranus Opposition Uranus

A difficult and long term transit. Uranus represents our personal needs to innovate, invent and express our originality - to break with barriers in ourselves or in the world. With this transit, the way you do these things is not in synch with the innovations and trends of the times. The trends of modern innovation, invention and originality is in opposition to the way you do it. You may find, during this period (and this has been going on for a while) that the things and conditions you rebelled against are now in style. Or that there is rebellion against your rebellion. A backlash. A karmic kickback. The same tactics you used - the same slogans - the same arguments - are now being used on you. Or, you may find that in this time of your life you must embrace all the things that you rebelled against at one time - that what you rebelled against is now "the new, the modern, the avant garde". Spirit loves irony, and in this case it is very educational. This is a time to review your notions of what in the world needs changing - perhaps the world doesn't need changing, only your consciousness needs changing. Your personal originality needs review, questioning, upgrading and perfecting. Previous scientific knowledge (that seemed true to you for much of your life) is now contradicted by new scientific findings. Your notions of what friendship is, gets challenged by new knowledge. New friends come into your life who are perhaps not in synch with your old friends. There is tension among your friends. The new that you worked so hard to establish all these years is now "old hat" - not new, but something established and something that now needs "changing".

The Spiritual Perspective. Much of what we say above applies here too.

Transiting Uranus Opposition Neptune

A difficult and long term transit. Whether this is in the Natal or Solar Return Horoscope, these trends have been going on for many years and will continue for a few more years. On a worldly level this transit shows the natural conflict that exists between spirituality and secular science. They are worlds apart and see things completely differently. On a personal level, your spiritual ideals, intuition, inner guidance is being opposed - perhaps coming under attack - by modern science, new technological developments, and modern trends and fads. Perhaps even your friends (or professional organizations you belong to) are also opposing these things. But this opposition is only the mask for what is really going on - major and abrupt changes in your spiritual life and spiritual ideals. The opposition that you feel will only intensify your spirituality - it won't stop it. But you may be doing a lot of experimenting in this area. Perhaps you run from Guru to Guru, psychic to psychic, channel to channel, teaching to teaching, technique to technique. You can't seem to settle into one practice and stick with it. Just because a technique is new and modern, doesn't automatically make it good. Intuition needs much verification this period. To succeed spiritually there is a need for great faith and confidence and this seems lacking. Your own scientific tendencies tend to cast deadly doubts here, which on the subtle level of spiritual phenomena can be major obstructions. Long term, you are going to have to be able to see the scientific basis behind spiritual phenomena and your own inner experience and practice. There are also many other changes going on in your life - but this will depend on what Neptune rules in your Horoscope.

The Spiritual Perspective. Much of what we say above applies here. Your spiritual ideals have needed strengthening, refining and adjusting for quite a long time. Perhaps you accepted these ideals "uncritically". Perhaps you were lacking in certain "nuances" here. So now the cosmos supplies the goad for this updating. Also it is good at times to have your ideals "road tested" - subjected to some rough treatment and stress. The same is true with your spiritual practice and regime. The road testing will strengthen your practice - your concentration - your commitment. Here the road testing comes from science and new technologies - the forces of "modernism" challenge the eternal verities. Your commitment, your passion for truth, will carry you through this and you will get even stronger.

Transiting Uranus Opposition Pluto

A long term and difficult aspect. In the Natal chart (if this aspect is to the Natal) this has been going on for some years now and will continue for some more years. In the Solar Return Chart this transit is only in effect for this year - but keep in mind, that this aspect is likely to manifest in future Solar Returns too. In general the sexual urges are erratic - sometimes very strong and sometimes nil. Sexual experience fluctuates erratically - sometimes reaching the peaks and sometimes the depths. Spirit is changing your sexual attitudes and beliefs - changing them to a more positive approach. It is these wild experiences (out of the norm) that bring the new knowledge to you. There is much sexual experimentation going on in your life and not all of it is positive or happy - but how else will you learn? Nothing wrong with sexual experimentation so long as it is constructive and kept positive. But it will be difficult to keep it positive. You are expressing your rebellion through sexual means. This aspect affects finances - especially when it comes to other people's money, outside investors, partners, and people or companies that you borrow from. Credit can come easily at times or not at all. The income of the spouse or partner is very erratic and you don't know where he or she stands from day to day. Debt should be carefully watched. The urge to self transform undergoes many erratic ups and downs. It doesn't come easily. Your understanding of death, birth, life after death, reincarnation is undergoing radical change.

The Spiritual Perspective. The sexuality, sexual attitudes, and all the areas of life that Pluto rules in your personal Horoscope need upgrading, modernization and change. This is not punishment, but intended as "improvement". But since we rarely make important change unless we are pushed or goaded, the cosmos is supplying this goad now - probably in the form of crises. Attitudes to debt or other people's money - attitudes to death and life after death - are also being modernized and updated. And because the attitudes are being changed, the events that happen on the physical plane are merely reflecting these changes.

Transiting Uranus Opposition Ascendant

A difficult and long term transit. In the Natal Horoscope this transit has been in effect for many years now. In the Solar Return it is only in effect for the current year. Many changes - and abrupt, sudden changes - can cause much change in your image and self concept. Also, the reverse is also true - your constant experimentation with your image - the constant changes of your self concept - cause many changes in your love and social life. Very understandable - we attract according to who we are. As we change our relationships change. If you are changing all the time - not yet settled on a self image - relationships will constantly change. The spouse, partner or current love is also making dramatic personal changes. The whole love life is undergoing change. A current relationship is in crisis.

The Spiritual Perspective. Your self concept - your self image - has needed updating for quite a long time and now spirit supplies the "push" for you to do this - a push that you cannot ignore. Have you been eating improperly? Impurities in the body will come up for cleansing. Are you holding concepts about yourself that are no longer true? These will get shattered. Perhaps you believed that your body was a "thing", now you will learn that it is really a dynamic energy system. Perhaps you thought you were just a mortal, now you will learn that you are much more than that. Many other adjustments to the image and self concept will also happen. When the Divine is through with you, you will have a totally new self image.

Transiting Uranus Opposition Midheaven

A difficult and long term transit. If this transit is to the Natal Horoscope, it has been going on for some years now and will continue for some more years. If this is in the Solar Return Horoscope, this transit is only in effect for the year. Basically, emotional-domestic instability, or uncontrollable intellectual curiosity obstruct or negatively impact on your career or career goals. Public or social status can also be affected here. Usually there are many moves under this transit and this could impact on the career. Family upheavals and crisis - the breaking of old family patterns also distract one for the career. There is a need now for emotional equilibrium. But no question the domestic and emotional life is more exciting than the career. Parents or parent figures are experiencing life changing kinds of events.

The Spiritual Perspective. This transit will be most powerful on those who are in careers that are not suitable for them, or not in line with their spiritual mission in life. It is good that these careers sink into oblivion. Sometimes we find out what we are supposed to do, through a long series of "trial and error" experiments. We learn what we want by learning what we don't want. Sometimes, this transit will show that a new stage in the life work is manifesting. An old stage is over with. If a person is doing his or her spiritual mission, they will now do the same things, but in different ways - perhaps more modernistic ways - i.e. if a person has been lecturing to groups on a physical level, now he or she might do it electronically - over the internet or through conference calling. There is a need to update and modernize the approach to the life work - and spirit will provide the goad to do it.

Transiting Uranus Trine Moon

A happy and long term transit. If this transit is to the Natal Horoscope it has been going on for many years now, but now it is most powerful. If it is to the Solar Return Horoscope this transit is only in effect this year. Your emotional life, domestic life and family situation is happy and full of pleasant change. Family life - that most routine and drab thing - is now one of the most exciting areas of your life. Probably there will be moves - perhaps multiple moves - but each one will be better than the previous one. You are seeing ways to combine the need for freedom with a stable home base. New technology is brought into the home - big ticket gadgets come to you. New innovations enhance the family life. There is a sense of a "team spirit" in the family - the family activities are seen as "group activities". Family members are experimental and open to new and innovative things and methods. Your emotional life and family situation is seen as "up to date" and "modern". But often what seems like the most modern is really the most ancient, with some new clothes. You can understand the highest scientific principles in an intuitive way - you can feel them. The truths of astrology are also felt on a gut level now - not so much with the intellect but with the feelings. Very unlikely that you will be stuck in some emotional rut now - not with all the happy and exciting change going on.

The Spiritual Perspective. We often think that excitement, change, originality - the awe and wonder and power of life - is "somewhere else" - in some exotic or romantic locale. We think that new scientific discoveries have to happen in the laboratory or observatory; that the discoveries and actions that will ultimately change the world happen in the Senate or White House or in plush executive offices. The revelation of this transit, is that all of this is here-now. It is present with us, in our so-called drab and ordinary daily life - in the domestic chores - in our most intimate surroundings; in our commonplace moods and feelings; in our relations with family members. One dream can bring revelation that will change the world. All of the excitement we could ever want is veiled in the common place things. And we see this, they cease to become common place. The Divine is lifting the veil of the common place to reveal the kingdom of heaven. No common place action can ever be the same from moment to moment. All is new and different when we see with the right eyes. There is no more excitement or joy in the world than exists right here in your home, in your kitchen or back yard. Major dramas are happening all around us if we could but see. And this vision is the gift of this transit.

Transiting Uranus Trine Sun

A happy and long term transit - this is so whether it is to the Natal or to the Solar Return. It has been going on for some years now and will continue for a few more years. Now, the effect is strongest. This is a period of much change, innovation and experimentation - but mostly of the happy sort. You explore your personal creativity and experiment with it in various ways. You are very original now, and if nothing else denies, your originality is accepted by the world. Modern trends, fads, scientific or technological discoveries boost your self esteem and sense of star quality - and tend to enhance your personal creativity. You are a unique and original being who shines in a unique and original way. Life is interesting and exciting these days. There will be career changes but mostly for the better. There will be a continuous upgrading and updating of the career and life work.

The Spiritual Perspective. Basically this transit reveals the essential harmony between your true being and the science, technology, experimentation that is going on in the world. Its as if these forces are merely "validating" what you are and how you express yourself.

Transiting Uranus Trine Mercury

A happy and long term transit. If this transit is to the Natal Horoscope it has been going on for many years now, but now it is most powerful. If it is to the Solar Return Horoscope this transit is only in effect this year. Your ideas, thought processes, and style of communication is very well received by scientists, techies, friends and organizations that you belong to. The media is also receptive to your thoughts and ideas. Your mind is very original these days. You have constant revelation on many subjects - especially science, astronomy, mathematics, and astrology. A very fertile and creative period.

The Spiritual Perspective. Being original need not make us rebel-lious or argumentative. It can be a smooth, harmonious flow of energy from the source - the origin. This is the revelation of this transit. True originality happens quietly, in silence - the result of originality can create quite a fuss later on - but the essence is in silence and peace. The health of the mental body is important to each person - more important than most realize as yet. Scientific knowledge - true science - astronomy and astrology supplement gaps in the mental body. The mental body would not be complete without these things. And so the cosmos is giving a "vitamin transfusion" into the mental body these days. Also, science and technology are "validating" (confirming) your ideas and thinking these days.

Transiting Uranus Trine Venus

A happy and long term transit that has been going on for some years (especially if this transit is to the Natal). In the Solar Return Horoscope, this transit is only in effect for the current year. Love is exciting and happy. Never dull. There is constant change and excitement and the changes are pleasant. You feel a sense of anticipation in social situations - what new and exciting person am I going to meet today? Friends are helping you to manifest your fondest love and social hopes and wishes. Friends like to play cupid. Love can happen for you at any time. You frequently have very happy romantic surprises. You are experimental in love, but in positive and happy ways. You have love experiences that are out of the ordinary and beyond your expectations. Your sense of beauty, style and fashion is unusually original these days.

The Spiritual Perspective. Basically this transit is a revelation of the essential harmony between love and change, love and experimentation, love and freedom. Real and true friends are not a distraction to romantic love, but actually enhance it. It is also the way that Spirit "rewards" you for having correct love and social attitudes.

Transiting Uranus Trine Mars

A happy and long term transit. If this is in the Natal chart, you've been feeling the effects of this for many years. If this is in the Solar Return, it is only in effect for the current year. Your physical energy is being stimulated and enhanced. High technology and innovations enable you to maximize physical energy, enhance athletic and sexual performance and explore new avenues of physical and sexual expression. There is much sexual experimentation in your life and it leads to positive and happy results. Athletes will often perform at "personal bests" under this transit. Under this transit people "test" their physical limits. They discover these limits to be purely imaginary - and break through them with ease.

The Spiritual Perspective. Much of what we say above applies here too. As with the conjunction, the Cosmos is showing you that your physical limits, your notions of your body and its capacities are not set in stone. The Body is much, much, more than we think it is and can do much, much more. So this is a period of revelation on this score. Since this is a harmonious transit, the revelations come with harmony and tend to be happy.

Transiting Uranus Trine Jupiter

A happy and long term transit that has been going on for many years and will continue for many more years. New technology, new social changes, new inventions are having a positive impact on your wealth and wealth goals. You have an innate ability to integrate these things into your financial life. Astrology is also a powerful tool for wealth. New friends and groups you belong to are supportive of financial goals - and perhaps very instrumental in their achievement. You have new and original ideas of how to expand and prosper. There are many and sudden financial changes in your life, but they are positive - you go from glory to glory on the financial level. The financial life now is very exciting in a positive way. Any good thing can happen at any time. Manna can fall from heaven when you need it. The good happens outside the limits of your conscious and logical mind. Your religious and philosophical beliefs get reinforcement from the findings of modern science and from astrology. Your friends and the groups you belong to also support your world view and religious beliefs. This bolsters basic faith - and when faith is bolstered, the sky is the limit in your life.

The Spiritual Perspective. Much of what we say above applies here as well. This transit is really about the revelation of the natural harmony of two spiritual principles. You find it easy to adjust and adapt to positive changes in science and technology. Change has become your friend and not your enemy. You have learned to embrace it and not to fear it. It enhances both your prosperity and your religious and philosophical beliefs.

Transiting Uranus Trine Saturn

A happy and long term transit - whether it is to the Natal or Solar Return Horoscopes. These trends have been going on for some years now and will continue for some more years. Now the effect is strongest. Modern trends, fads, styles, scientific or technological discoveries aid and assist you in creating order, structure and security in your life. These also assist you in your management style. Your sense of tradition - your perception of reality - is supported by modern trends and science. New technology comes to you that helps you become more organized and manage your time more efficiently. There will be many (and happy) career changes as you constantly upgrade and update to better and better positions and situations.

The Spiritual Perspective. This transit is really about a spiritual revelation of a harmony that most people don't think exists. Tradition, conservatism and the urge to the New are seen as essentially antagonistic. Modernity and tradition likewise. Originality tends to be "anti traditional" for most people. But now you will see how they were meant to operate - how they were designed to operate - by the Higher Power. Innovation is meant to solve problems that tradition hasn't yet figured out. Eventually these solutions will become "part" of the tradition. One need not rebel violently to change tradition, one only needs to invent the better mouse trap.

Transiting Uranus Trine Uranus

A happy and long term transit. This transit can only occur in the Natal Horoscope and has been going on for some years now. Your sense of originality - and the way you express freedom from limits - is very much in synch with modern trends, fads and styles. Your understanding of science and technology is in synch with current modes of understanding. You find it much easier to break barriers now - to invent and innovate. Your personal fondest hopes and wishes are supported by friends and by modern scientific trends and inventions. Its as if certain of your fondest hopes and wishes needed new science or undreamed of technologies to make them happen. You are able to make changes in an easier way. You can innovate and experiment with less opposition.

The Spiritual Perspective. With your originality and scientific mind greatly strengthened, the challenge here is about how you will use these gifts. Will it be positive and constructive or destructive? Right now - if nothing else in the Horoscope denies - the Higher Power gives you a "blank check".

Transiting Uranus Trine Neptune

A happy and long term transit. In the Natal this has been going on for some years now and will continue for some more years. In the Solar Return it is only in effect for the current year - but future Solar Returns are likely to have this aspect too. Your spiritual ideals and spiritual regime is undergoing constant growth and change. You are very creative in this area. Your changes lead to greater and greater results. Its as if you are playing with the Spirit in a positive way - experimenting - learning and growing. (More likely, the Spirit is playing with you - but you feel that you are dong the playing.) New technology or scientific discoveries are aiding your spiritual life and helping you to manifest your ideals and dreams. Friends and organizations you belong to are also fostering spiritual development and the manifestation of your highest spiritual ideals. During this period you will see that there is no conflict between real science and real spiritual knowledge. They go hand in hand. Those in the fields of science and technology will have much revelation in their field. Perhaps they will dream of new inventions or new innovations. Perhaps they will have new scientific information "revealed" to them either through dreams or through "chance" occurrences. Your idealism is very strong now and more likely to manifest if nothing else in the Horoscope denies it.

The Spiritual Perspective. Much of what we said above applies here too. Spirituality is merely a science that secularists haven't yet grasped. But a science it is. The virtues espoused by spiritual teachings - the character traits that one should cultivate - have a deep scientific basis. Faith which secular science rejects, is also scientific. So this transit is about seeing these connections. What happens on the material plane are merely side effects of these very important revelations.

Transiting Uranus Trine Pluto

A happy and long term transit that has been going on for many years now, but now it is most powerful. If this transit is in the Solar Return it is only in effect for the coming year. Future Solar Returns however are likely to have this aspect too. This a period where sexuality is enhanced through constructive experimentation. New ways, new attitudes enhance both the joy and understanding of sex. If nothing else denies, the spouse or partner is prospering - perhaps in sudden ways - and is wildly generous with you - also in sudden and unexpected ways. Debts can be paid suddenly too. Your efforts at reformation and personal transformation - your efforts to give birth to the ideal you and to rid yourself of old effete concepts, emotional and behavior patterns- are enhanced by new techniques, new technology and new scientific discoveries. You can expect much sudden illumination - lightning flashes of insight - into death, rebirth, reincarnation, life after death and the like.

The Spiritual Perspective. This transit is really about choices. Libido is greatly strengthened. This can be squandered in prodigal and wasteful ways - the Divine sort of gives you a blank check - or this same energy can be used for personal transformation - the reinvention of your self. Probably the middle way is best.

Transiting Uranus Trine Midheaven

A happy and long term transit, especially if this is to the Natal Chart. In the Solar Return it is only in effect for the current year. In the Natal it has been going on for some years and will continue for a few more years. This is a time for making positive changes to the career and career aspirations. These changes are happening and they are harmonious to you. Many will break out of career ruts now. Many will change jobs within their company (many times) or take work with a new company (many times). Many will change their actual career path in a fundamental way. Its as if you are constantly upgrading your career. Career experiments are more likely to pay off now (if nothing else in the chart denies). Friends and networking boost the career. Fondest career hopes and wishes are coming to pass.

The Spiritual Perspective. A very happy transit here. Many people feel blocked from pursuing their true mission in life because of a "lack of wherewithal" or skills. But this transit reveals that all the forces of science and technology are at your disposal when you are in line with your true Destiny. With new insights into your mission and a new perspective on it, you can see original and innovative solutions that weren't there before.

Transiting Uranus Sextile Moon

A happy and long term transit. In the Solar Return it is only valid this year. You have opportunities to make home and family life more interesting and exciting - to innovate in these areas in positive and happy ways. Experiments at home go well. There will be opportunities to inculcate a team spirit at home and to install high tech gadgets in the home. Moves could happen, and if nothing else denies, they are happy. If you have been stuck in an emotional rut this is a period to break loose.

The Spiritual Perspective. The Cosmos is giving you a glimpse of how ITS ideas can transform your daily life and domestic routine. A little innovation and originality applied to your present situation will transform it.

Transiting Uranus Sextile Sun

A happy and long term transit. In the Solar Return it is only valid this year. You have many opportunities to be creative, innovative and experimental and these seem happy. Scientific gadgets or new technologies are there (if you want it) that will enhance your creativity, self esteem and entertainment pleasure. It is as if all the inventive genius in the Cosmos is busily at work bringing you joy and fun in life. This is also a good health aspect.

The Spiritual Perspective. It is under transits such as these that a person discovers that the Divine is not at war with your Ego. You are a light and were made to shine. This is the Divine Will. This is how we were created. But "letting light shine" and sort of "making it shine" are two different things. One is a natural consequence of being, the other is the machination of a mortal ego.

Transiting Uranus Sextile Mercury

A happy and long term transit. In the Solar Return it is only valid this year. You are more able to absorb new scientific truths, discoveries or technological developments. High tech is aiding you in your communications - and perhaps there will be opportunities to employ high tech in your communication. Your thinking - your thought process - and ideas are pretty much in synch with modern trends, fads and scientific opinion - and if not, you have the opportunity to create better synchronicity. The thinking and speech will tend to be more original these days.

The Spiritual Perspective. The heavens are working on your mind to give you new and better ideas. This is a period for "intellectual breakthroughs". Every intellectual conundrum that you face is already solved in heaven. The answer is known. You just have to open up to it - and this is what's happening. A new idea can totally transform a person - even though nothing material has changed. The mind is changed and that is enough. Material change will then become inevitable.

Transiting Uranus Sextile Venus

A happy and long term transit. In the Solar Return it is only valid this year. There will be opportunities for freer, less restrictive relationships. Love will be more exciting and happy love and social opportunities can come out of the blue when you least expect it. Friends may play cupid. Love opportunities can come as you are involved with organizations and group activities.

The Spiritual Perspective. Change, originality and excitement need not conflict with human love. It can enhance human love as is the case now. Too often, when love is good, we try to hold that pattern of good. But now you can see that there is no need to hold any specific pattern, you can flow with change and love will even improve. Nor do you need to run after new lovers. Sometimes, the same love can be so different day to day as to be "like" something new.

Transiting Uranus Sextile Mars

A happy and long term transit. In the Solar Return it is only valid this year. Physical energy and libido is enhanced. There will be opportunities for constructive sexual and athletic experimentation and innovation. There will be opportunities for breaking physical, athletic and sexual limits.

The Spiritual Perspective. Much of what we say applies here as well. Libido and physical energy are increased and it becomes an issue of how you will use it.

Transiting Uranus Sextile Jupiter

A happy and long term transit. In the Solar Return it is only valid this year. In general prosperity is boosted. You will have opportunities to employ your own original ideas to your financial life - to enjoy more freedom in finance. You will also have opportunities to employ new technology or scientific discoveries to your financial life - and with good results. Financial experiments (if nothing else denies) are likely to be happy. You will also have opportunities to upgrade and update your religious and philosophical beliefs. New philosophical insights and revelations are coming to you.

The Spiritual Perspective. Though not as strong as the trine or conjunction, this transit brings harmony between your religious and philosophical beliefs and your originality and scientific under-standing. If you look hard enough you will see that real science is validating your religious and philosophical beliefs. Also, though a correct belief system is a wonderful thing, when it is scientifically established it becomes stronger and more wonderful.

Transiting Uranus Sextile Saturn

A happy and long term transit. You will have opportunities to exper-iment with your management style and with the way you order and discipline yourself. Perhaps new technology comes that assists you in taking control over your life. The way you exercise authority will not create rebellion these days. You are likely to attract bosses who allow more freedom. Parents and authority figures in general are allowing more freedom.

The Spiritual Perspective. As with the trine, this transit is really about a spiritual revelation of a harmony that most people don't think exists. Tradition, conservatism and the urge to the New are seen as essentially antagonistic. Modernity and tradition likewise. Originality tends to be "anti traditional" for most people. But now you will see how they were meant to operate - how they were designed to operate - by the Higher Power. Innovation is meant to solve problems that tradition hasn't yet figured out. Eventually these solutions will become "part" of the tradition. One need not rebel violently to change tradition, one only needs to invent the better mouse trap. Because this is a sextile, the transit is showing that you have "opportunity" for this revelation. It is there for you if you want it.

Transiting Uranus Sextile Uranus

A happy and long term transit. This only happens in the Natal Chart and has been going on for some years now. Your urges to be free, original and to break barriers are very much in synch with modern trends, fads, and scientific knowledge. Your inventions and innovations are in synch with the times - and friends are supportive in these endeavors.

The Spiritual Perspective. With your originality greatly strengthened, the question now is "how will you use it?"

Transiting Uranus Sextile Neptune

A happy and long term transit. It is more significant in the Natal chart and has been going on for some years. In the Solar Return chart, this is only reinforcing the basic tendency of the Solar Return - but since this is a long term transit - you can have this aspect for a few more Solar Returns. Your spiritual ideals are in synch with modern trends, fads and scientific thinking. You have scientific support for your ideals, intuitions, dreams and hunches. Your spirituality is trendy these days. You might have a dream of some insight or idea and then a week or month later see it in some scientific journal.

The Spiritual Perspective. A with the trine, this transit is about revelation of harmony that most people don't see. Spirituality is merely a science that secularists haven't yet grasped. But a science it is. The virtues espoused by spiritual teachings - the character traits that one should cultivate - have a deep scientific basis. Faith which secular science rejects, is also scientific. So this transit is about seeing these connections. What happens on the material plane are merely side effects of these very important revelations. This transit brings opportunity to experience these revelations.

Transiting Uranus Sextile Pluto

A happy and long term transit. There will be opportunities for sexual experimentation and it will tend to be positive. You have opportunities to make important and benefic changes to your sexuality and sexual attitudes. The income of the spouse or partner benefits from new technology or from positive experimentation. The partner is enjoying more financial freedom these days. New scientific discoveries and new technology enable you to explore the deeper things of life - death and rebirth, personal transformation, past lives and life after death.

The Spiritual Perspective. Libido (if nothing else is denying) is stronger now - how will you use this powerful energy? Will it be wasted in the pursuit of lust or will it be used for personal transformation and healing? Perhaps you will do a little bit of both.

Transiting Uranus Sextile Ascendant

A happy and long term transit. In the Solar Return it is only valid this year. You have opportunities to experiment with your image and appearance and upgrade it to the way you like it. Modern scientific or technological discoveries are available to help your image.

The Spiritual Perspective. In theory a person has total dominion over the body and all its functions. But few of us (because of karmic conditions) ever exercise this dominion. Under this transit the innate dominion is strengthened. You have more power to make the dramatic changes that you have been longing to make.

Transiting Uranus Sextile Midheaven

A happy and long term transit. In the Solar Return it is only valid this year. There will be opportunities to enlist the support of friends and organizations towards your career goals. Technological advances boost the career. The forces of "modernity" help the career. There will be opportunities to upgrade the career and to make positive and happy changes.

The Spiritual Perspective. The Heavenly forces are working to give you more freedom in your life work and mission. The solution to your career conundrums already exists in heaven, and now you have the opportunity to see them. You probably don't have to change your life path too dramatically, but just apply a little innovation, a little technology, a new twist to what you are already doing.

TRANSITS OF NEPTUNE

All the planets are essentially spiritual, but Neptune is the most spiritual of all of them. Its whole purpose is to bring transcendent energy to any planet it contacts - and to the affairs of life ruled by the planet. Where the Sun brings light and illumination, the Moon feeling, Mercury ideas, Mars constructive or destructive actions, Saturn order, Uranus, the breaking of barriers - Neptune brings transcendence.

Neptune is not interested in solving problems in the mundane, natural ways. How dull! How boring! How terrifyingly mundane! Neptune likes to solve problems in the ways of the super-natural. Now if people are not on a spiritual path, these solutions can seem very "illusionary or delusionary" - and for them they are. But not so for the one on the spiritual path. Neptune lifts them "above the world" where the problem exists, to the world where there are no problems. Sometimes, this mere elevation is enough to solve a problem. And sometimes, the living in the spiritual world reveals solutions that can be applied in the material world.

Neptune refines, sensitizes and spiritualizes any planet it contacts. It brings the quality of intuition and inspiration to the planet.

Since Neptune's energies are very high - not of this world - its stressful transits can lead to a lot of turmoil and confusion. Deception will often happen under these kinds of transits - but not a conscious deception - wilful and malicious (those will usually come from negative Mercury transits), but from a mistranslation or misinterpretation of very high kinds of ideas. A person has an idea for some very beautiful and altruistic enterprise, but in the communication of it to others, the full import doesn't come across - and there is deception. The best way to illustrate this negative side of Neptune is to draw from recent history. Millions and millions of people were deceived by the high blown rhetoric and high, ultra high ideals,

288

espoused by the communists. The pull was so irresistible that at one time, there was no serious intellectual who was not a Marxist - and its pull is strong even now. Neptune, revealed, very high ideals, but which were not workable on the earth. The human condition at its current state of evolution couldn't handle it. The ideals were merely masks through which very sinister and negative forces were able to work - to hide themselves as they worked.

How often have we been bedazzled by a glamorous beauty (male or female) - attributed all kinds of high attainments to him or her - all kinds of virtues - only to find that they were never real. Beneath the facade of high glamor was a very plain, and perhaps sub-normal in many respects, individual.

But Neptune never sets out to deceive. Human cupidity steps into the picture and does the deceiving.

These are the challenges of Neptune. But Neptune's ideals are real on their level. The challenge is manifesting them on the earth in a proper way. But at least Neptune shows us where we must go.

Neptune will bring the urge to transcend - to rise above conditions - to any planet that it contacts. This is a wonderful thing, but if a person doesn't know the correct way to transcend - through spiritual discipline and practice - Neptune will seem to bring the false and destructive ways - drugs or alcohol.

In Kabbalah Neptune is related to the sphere of Kether, the Crown - the Primordial Will of the Divine. So, spiritually speaking, Neptune will bring a revelation of the Divine Will to any planets (and to all the affairs ruled by the planet) that it contacts. This revelation is sure, over time, to have huge consequences in that department of life. The person will start to become more idealistic in these matters. All sorts of disillusionment might come too - for the Divine Will, shines its light very brightly and things - good and bad - are revealed for what they are.

We must stress here, that the disillusionments that come are not coming from Neptune - the Divine Will - the Divine Will never sets out to deceive us - but they come from our departures from this will

- which are now clearly illumined and which can't be escaped.

Certainly the Divine Will is not about murder, mayhem, theft, adultery, or doing harm to others - either on the physical or psychological levels - and these things are revealed to us as Neptune holds the torch to the given planet.

Neptune's job is to elevate the affairs governed by the planet that it contacts into their "original purity and perfection" - before human thinking mis-qualified the energy.

Transiting Neptune Conjunction Moon

A Neutral transit. If this transit is to your Natal Horoscope it has been going on for many years now and will continue for some years in the future. Now it is most intense as the aspect is exact. If this transit is to your Solar Return Horoscope it is only in effect this year. For those on the spiritual path this is a most wonderful and illuminating transit. New and higher spiritual energies are coming into the being - through the subconscious and the dream life. The native will be prophesying - seeing clearly into the future. The native will receive revelation into the past - both the personal past and the most distant past. The native will recall past lives and understand the whole sweep of human evolution. Probably, the native will be in contact with exalted spiritual beings on another dimension. The inner life is very rich and satisfying now. New spiritual powers are being awakened. But there is a downside here too - the emotional sensitivities are greatly magnified. The native recoils - can be in actual physical pain - from negative voice tones, inharmonious thoughts from others, body language and the like. In many cases family members will also become hyper-sensitive as well. Thus there is a need for more emotional harmony - more care in the kind of energy that is emanated towards others - especially the family. This hyper-sensitivity can be very painful if one is around the wrong types of people. The native is more reclusive and solitary for this reason. For one who is not on the spiritual path, this transit can be very negative. It produces hypersensitivity, but with none of the positive benefits that come with it. There is much emotional confusion now. The native doesn't know how to handle the influx of spiritual energy coming into the subconscious. Often drug and alcohol abuse can develop because of this. Often the native becomes unusually psychic but because the subconscious is not purified, he or she sees into the lower astral realms - and this can be very shocking. There can be nightmares and the like. Those not on the spiritual path should seek the guidance of gurus and enlightened ones now - as only these people can explain what is happening. This is the time to embark on a spiritual path.

The Spiritual Perspective. Much of what we say above applies here. The Divine is spiritualizing and refining the emotional nature, the family and domestic life. The light of the Divine is shining on these things bringing much revelation. Revelation is just that - the light is turned on and we see truly what is going on. No more sweeping things under the rug. No more hiding from unpleasant realities. Thus, many scandalous and uncomfortable things are brought out in this light. And family scandals are likely to happen here. But this is not the intent of this transit - it is not a punitive thing. There is a cleansing and refining going on - and the debris - as well as the good - gets revealed. The light of truth is a wonderful thing - for in this light of truth - you will know the next steps to take with your emotional, family and domestic situation. Spiritual guidance will often come through women under this transit - especially if this is a man's chart. In a woman's chart, she herself is likely to start "channeling" and "prophesying".

Transiting Neptune Conjunction Sun

A Neutral and long term transit. This transit has been going on for many years now but now it is most intense. You are coming under very powerful and intense spiritual energies. Much depends on how you use these energies. Most of the time there is an intense urge to "transcend" present reality. The native gets glimpses - either in dreams, soul remembrances, intuitions or just feelings - of a grander, happier universe where none of the present limitations exist. Nothing on the physical plane can compare to this. Physical reality - the present life - seems so tawdry and cheap compared to these grand visions. The soul "falls in love" with these realms. So there is an urge to return there. Those on a spiritual path will enter these realms in the correct way - through prayer, meditation and spiritual discipline. These natives will bring down wonderful spiritual energies - either artistically, creatively or philosophically. It can also manifest as spiritual works - i.e. spiritual, supernatural powers, more involvement with charities, ministries and working for the spiritual upliftment of mankind. Many will opt for a spiritual career under these transits - even if up to now they have been heavily materialistic. Many who have never been on a spiritual path will enter the path now. The idealism is very strong now. The world dismisses these people as "dreamers or hallucinatory" as they live in a world that is so radically different from the "world as it is". So there is a sort of "disconnect" with the world and the worldly minded. The native will have to learn to be "in the world but not of it". The native will have to learn how to handle "matter is fact" kinds of people in the most compassionate and harmonious way. Basically, the law of "live and let live" applies. Often this transit can lead to drug and alcohol abuse - especially in cases where the native has not learned the correct ways to transcend. And, if the mind is not purified, these energies can be "misinterpreted" by the mortal intellect and distorted in hideous ways. This can lead to illusions and delusions - being involved in false causes or causes that purport to be humanitarian but which are not. A delicate transit. The energies need to be handled "just so". Everyone under this transit will be thinking of their spiritual mission and purpose in this life.

The Spiritual Perspective. Much of what we say above applies here as well. The Divine Immortal in you - your Solar Consciousness - is always "one with the Father" - but now you can really feel it and experience it strongly. This is a time for "surrendering the personal will" to the Will of the Father. You find it easy to do this. And if done sincerely, you don't need to worry about anything else. The most interesting things will start to happen. You will be led into your true destiny for this life.

Transiting Neptune Conjunction Mercury

A Neutral and long term transit - especially if this is to the Natal Horoscope. In the Natal Horoscope, these trends have been going on for some years now and will continue for a few more years. In the Solar Return Horoscope it is only in effect for the current year. You are in a period of life where you are blending logic and intuition. The psychic abilities will be very much enhanced. You will know things instantly without thinking, but working to "rationalize" that which you know. The intellect will be involved with explaining spiritual intuitions or truths in a logical way. This is a period where sacred studies go very well. The Mind can grasp spiritual truths - the truths that are "between the lines" of books, scripture or even in mundane literature. Its as if the mind looks at where the writing "comes from" and not so much as to what is actually written. Intellectually, the native will be drawn to poetry, fine art, spiritually oriented studies, channeled writings, prophecies and the like. On a worldly level, this transit can create problems and interesting adventures. For the native is reading or hearing "behind the word" and could not be attentive to the actualities of what is being said or written. Thus there can be more miscommunication these days. The lawyer said "x", but you only heard that he had a fight with his wife the night before - so you missed "x". Creative writers will be unusually inspired and creative now. Mental workers, likewise. Thoughts will flow as in a musical composition. There will be a natural rhythm and flow to the thought. There will be a tendency to be "dreamy" in the normal workaday world and this should be guarded against. In the world, be attentive and alert. Let the dreams happen at home while in your in meditation or private revery.

The Spiritual Perspective. Much of what we say above applies here as well. The Divine is working to spiritualize and refine your thought process and ideas - to elevate them. And all the other phenomena described above are merely side effects. You are becoming a "mouth piece" for the Divine. Its thoughts will become your thoughts, its word, your word. It has a message that it wants you to communicate to the world.

Transiting Neptune Conjunction Venus

A Neutral and long term transit. If you are an artist you are particularly inspired these days. Your sense of beauty is unusually refined. You see vistas of beauty and love that most people never dream about. This is a time in your life when you are reading (or writing) poetry; where the fine arts are more interesting. Artists will find that their creations are being "channeled" by higher beings. In many cases, ideal love manifests - the highest ideal you can think of. In general, the love ideals are very high. Love is spiritual these days. Anything less than "sainthood" is unlikely to interest you very much. Love brings you closer to god. Love is probably your religion. If this transit receives good support, the love life will be unusually happy. Important spiritual friendships will be made. You will learn to love more fully and completely and in a spiritual way. But if this transit receives stressful aspects, there can be much disappointment and self deception in love. The lover or partner was never those things that you projected on to him or her - and so disappointment was inevitable. In general, this is a transit for "fantasy romance". A time for "casting all of one's love burdens on the God within" and letting that handle the love and social life.

The Spiritual Perspective. Much of what we say above applies here as well. Your love nature and attitudes - your aesthetic sensibilities as well - are being refined, elevated and spiritualized. All the other phenomena are merely side effects of this. The Divine is calling you to express its ideas though the arts and in your social relationships.

Eventually love will become "impersonal" under this transit. You love everybody, but its really a Higher Power loving through you. And, this force has a dramatic healing impact on others and the world. Under these kinds of influences you discover that you ARE love - this is your nature and your essence - there is no effort in loving, because you love in the same way that a bird sings - its just natural self expression.

Transiting Neptune Conjunction Mars

A Neutral and long term transit - especially if it is to the Natal Horoscope. It has been going on for many years and will likely continue for a few more years. In the Solar Return the transit is only in effect for the current year (and will probably just reinforce the tendencies of the Solar Return Chart.) New and intense spiritual energies are coming into your sex life, your physical body, and your athletic interests. Instead of rough and tumble sports you will be drawn to more spiritual types of movements - dance, yoga, tai chi, eurythmy and the like. This transit will also transform the sexuality, uplifting and spiritualizing it. Sex will become (and this is the purpose of the transit) more of a sacrament, a form of prayer, a spiritual experience, rather than just a mere animal function. The spiritual aspects of sex are being revealed to you. On a mundane level the native will find it easier to translate spiritual ideals into action. The native will put spiritual teachings into practice. A good period for practicing Karma Yoga. The body will become more refined under this transit as well - the native will experience psychic and spiritual energies "right in the flesh". This is a period for developing psychometric abilities and clair-sentience. The native will have the power to hold an object and know its entire history and the character of its owner. The native needs to be more careful and mindful on the physical plane as there is a tendency to get "dreamy" there.

The Spiritual Perspective. Much of what we say above applies here

as well. The Divine is elevating, spiritualizing and refining the most "animal" of the functions - sex and physical activity. All the other phenomena described above are merely side effects of this process. Our so-called "animal" functions are really Divine in their essence. They show the activity of spiritual principles in their densest form - on the instinctual level. This is a time where you will have realization of these things. Realization will change the whole vibration of these activities and make them "sacred".

Transiting Neptune Conjunction Jupiter

A happy and long term transit. If this transit is to the Natal Horoscope, its been going on for many years now and will continue for many more years. Now, it is at its most intense as the aspect is exact. If this transit is to your Solar Return Horoscope, it is only in effect this year. This is a most spiritual and idealistic period in your life. Religious experience is leading you to mystical and transcendental experience. Your religious and philosophical beliefs are being illuminated. You are learning religious and philosophical truths in the real way - by interior revelation and direct experience - not from books or lectures. You are learning that God is the one and only source of supply - the source of all wealth. Intuition, dreams, psychics and gurus guide the financial life and this guidance is worth more than many years of hard labor. You are having visions of unlimited success - unlimited wealth. Only remember that you can't take the whole manifestation all at once - you need to let this vision unfold gradually. In general you are more idealistic about wealth and finances - you use your resources for good. You are more generous and charitable these days. The spiritual laws of affluence are being revealed to you - and this is an ongoing process. This is a time for casting all your financial burdens, cares and goals upon the Spirit and letting that have its way. Big wealth can come to you if you allow it in spirit's way and not your own. Spirit desires your wealth - and in better ways - more fervently than you do.

The Spiritual Perspective. Much of what we say above applies here as well. It is not just finance that is getting elevated and spiritualized - it is also happening in your religious life. You are seeing the "interior reason " - the original experience and revelation - that is behind all your religious practices. Your religion - whatever it is - becomes more alive now. The purpose of religion is to help people to make "God Contact" - which you are getting right now. But once this aim is achieved, religion might take other forms. Much of the rote nature of it can be dispensed with, but you keep what is real and true.

Transiting Neptune Conjunction Saturn

A Neutral and long term transit both in the Natal Horoscope and in the Solar Return. These trends have been going on for many years and will continue for a few more years. Your sense of "reality" and practicality is becoming more spiritualized - this is the purpose of the transit. This is the lesson to be learned here. You will see, that what you think of as "hard and real" - or some "hard and fast law" is only a thought form or image in your mind. A deeply held belief. Change the belief and your reality is changed. Create a new image and you have a new reality. Saturn represents a person's notions of "worldly order", but now you will see that there is a "spiritual order" that supersedes that. And, you are being asked to align your sense of 'worldly order" with the already existing spiritual order of things. Your sense of order and organization will not be destroyed only refined and expanded. It will be put to its true purpose to manifest the Divine Plan (perhaps not your personal plan) on the earth. Many under this transit will become managers or adminis-trators in spiritual or charitable type organizations. Discipline will be applied with more compassion and understanding. Limits (though always necessary in the world) will be understood for what they are - self imposed things that enable us to focus and concentrate better. You will have a greater ability to make spiritual ideals (often airy and abstract things) tangible and real these days. You will have a natural ability to make them "practical and useful" both to your self and others. But while this process is going on (and it is a gradual process and doesn't happen overnight) you might feel as if you've lost "control" over your life. That it is harder to get into your normal routine and regime. That you can't manage yourself or others. You might feel fearful and insecure as your old notions of reality and routine get dissolved. But rest assured, a new order is in process of manifestation. And this is what the transit is all about.

The Spiritual Perspective. What we say above applies here as well. Your personal order - the way you set up your life - must now be aligned with the Spiritual Order - the Divine Will. Before this happens the light of revelation will shine on these things - your errors will be clearly seen (but also your good points). In this light it will be very easy to set up a new and more spiritual order in your life.

Transiting Neptune Conjunction Uranus

A Neutral and long term transit - also a very rare transit. This is a very spiritual transit. Your understanding of science and technology is being spiritualized. You are seeing that all science all knowledge comes from the Higher Power and that what you call "scientific method" is only a way of validation. You are experiencing much scientific and spiritual revelation these days. Scientific knowledge, new inventions and innovations come to you in dreams and hunches - not through the "reasoning out" process. Your spiritual ideals could make you more rebellious these days - the dichotomy between the ideal and actual conditions is seen very starkly. Spiritually you are seeing that there is no real conflict between science and spirituality - science and mystical experience. You are being given new inventions and innovations from a higher source in order to improve the lot of humanity.

The Spiritual Perspective. Much of what we say above applies here

too. The Divine is the true and actual source of all new inventions, technologies and so-called scientific breakthroughs. This is something that is clearly seen under this transit. Your scientific mind and attitudes, which in many cases, has been an obstruction to the Divine, is now being spiritualized, elevated and refined. Awesome spiritual power is flooding into your scientific mind - and things will happen. You will also see - eventually - the unity between true science and true mysticism and spirituality. They are two sides of a coin.

Transiting Neptune Conjunction Neptune

A Neutral and long term transit. In the Natal chart it could happen in childhood, but never again in the life. And, when it happens it will only reinforce the spiritual and idealistic tendencies of the Natal Chart. The same is true in the Solar Return. It will only reinforce the spiritual and idealistic tendencies of the Solar Return Horoscope.

The Spiritual Perspective. What we say above applies here. The spirituality, the intuition, the innate idealism, the urge and power to transcend are merely strengthened for a time.

Transiting Neptune Conjunction Pluto

A Neutral and long term transit that has been going on for many years and will continue for many more years. This transit will not happen in the Natal Horoscope - not for people born in the 20th or 21st centuries - or for anyone likely to read this report - though dramatic changes in longevity could change this. It is a powerful transit. The sexuality is being spiritualized and many other levels of the sex experience are being revealed to you. New insights on meditation and concentration are being given to you. Your urges to personal transformation are being spiritualized and you will rely much less on "material things" in this process - i.e. drugs, surgery, hormones, clothing etc. You simply must allow a Higher Power to effect the transformation. This is a time for the "born again" experience. You are being reborn in spirit. Its as if you die to every-thing you once knew and are reborn on a higher level. You will not necessarily depart from this world, but you will function in it as a whole new being and in a whole new way with a whole new attitude. The spouse or partner will prosper by intuitive means and not necessarily from hard work. The spouse or partner will prosper through dreams, visions, channeled messages from other dimen-sions and the like. In the early stages of this transit, the spouse or partner could be very confused in financial matters. Perhaps there will be loss due to unrealistic dreams or decisions. But as time goes on, the spirit will prosper directly. The spouse is learning that there is ONE and ONLY ONE source of supply and one must seek one's "fortune" there. If the Divine grants prosperity than nothing in the universe can prevent it - but if it is withheld from there, then there is nothing that can create it. There is a need now (and it will happen) for the spouse or partner to learn the spiritual laws of supply. This is also a period of other types of revelation - there will be revelation on reincarnation, and the life after death experience.

The Spiritual Perspective. Much of what we say above applies here as well. The divine is refining, elevating and spiritualizing your sexuality, your understanding of life and death and past lives. Many functions of the body which are considered "gross, disgusting" - i.e. sex, death, the process of decay and putrefaction, bowel elimination and the like - are now revealed to be "Divine Functions" - essentially holy. These are laws of the universe operating through the lowest instinctual levels. Without bowel movements we die. Without sex, the race cannot survive. Elimination is a survival mechanism. So all these functions are not only going to be understood better, but also "raised in vibration" by your new understanding and insight. This is the way that the Divine "alchemicalizes" gross matter. We still do the same things but with a whole different attitude and perspective - so the actions are different in "quality" - in vibration. They evoke different feelings and responses in us.

Transiting Neptune Conjunction Ascendant

A Neutral and long term transit - especially if it is to the Natal Horoscope. In the Solar Return chart it is only in effect for the current year. The physical body is becoming more refined and spiritualized. It will become more sensitive to finer vibrations - a mixed blessing. On the one hand, the native will feel positive energies more keenly - but this applies to the negative energies as well. If the native is around negative people or negative situations the pain and discomfort will be very keen. The native will have to take special measures to be around only the most uplifting and positive people. Thus there will be a limit on many social activities. The native will have to be more selective in these matters. The native is called upon to learn many spiritual lessons. He or she will see that much of what he or she feels comes from outside vibration. If you sit next to someone with a heart condition you will feel it as your own - even though its not yours. Thus there is need to sharply discern the vibrations that one picks up. One must become almost impersonal to the body. The other spiritual lesson is that the body ONLY exists to do the will of the Higher Power. When it is rightly aligned with this power all will be well and health will be good. But sickness can come from misalignment, If the native is in inharmonious environments there will be many temptations to drug and alcohol abuse - or to other kinds of addictions. This is because the native seeks to relieve the pain of the increased sensitivity. But if the native is rightly aligned and takes proper precautions (does more psychic hygiene) there will be great beauty and glamor in the image. The native will have great power over the body. Positive thoughts will impact on the body instantly and in dramatic ways. The native will be able to "adopt any image" he or she chooses - to sculpt the body through thought, prayer and meditation. The native's movements will be fluid, graceful and poetic - poetry in motion - music made manifest in the form and movement. Dancing will be an interesting hobby these days. Also yoga, tai chi, eurythmics and the like. The native will manifest a "supernatural beauty", rather than just a "natural beauty".

The Spiritual Perspective. Pretty much everything mentioned above applies here. The Divine is spiritualizing and elevating the vibrations of the body and all the other phenomena are merely side effects of this.

Transiting Neptune Conjunction Midheaven

A Neutral and long term transit. (This transit has been happening for some years now and will go on for a few more years - but now it is most intense.) For those on a spiritual path and who know their life path, this is a most wonderful and successful transit. You see your spiritual mission and are doing it. Your spiritual mission can seem very worldly - but underneath the worldliness is a higher agenda. You are working for a purpose that transcends you, your business and your status. You are more concerned with your "spiritual status" and evolutionary growth than with your worldly status. You will meet spiritual people of high status - gurus, mystics, channels etc. Some of these meetings can be on the physical plane, but some can also be on the inner planes as you pray and meditate. You are very idealistic now. For those not on a spiritual path, this can be a difficult and confusing time. You feel fed up with what the world calls success - you feel empty inside about it. It all seems so meaningless. Your spiritual values conflict with the values of a successful career. You are in the midst of a career shift these past few years. You are going to apply spiritual values to your career. You will try to marry your spiritual urges with your work in the world - not always an easy thing to do. This is a time for more involvement in charities, ministries and volunteer work for causes that you believe in.

The Spiritual Perspective. Pretty much everything mentioned above applies here as well. The light of revelation is shining on your life mission and purpose. This is revealing your true purpose and true career. It is also revealing where you have gone amiss in the past as well. But this is impersonal and not punitive. With the light you will be able to see what you have to do and where you have to go.

Transiting Neptune Square Moon

A difficult and long term transit. If this is to the Natal chart, this transit has been going on for many years now and will continue for many more years. Now, it is at its most intense as the aspect is exact. If this is in the Solar Return chart, it is only in effect for one year. Spiritual energies - very high ones - are coming into the subconscious but moods, emotions and feelings - the normal sentiments are probably mis-interpreting them. Your normal moods and feelings - your past conditioning - is out of synch with the spiritual guidance and energy coming in. Spirit is urging you to re-evaluate your domestic life and your emotional patterns. The dream life, intuition and spiritual teachings one receives need much verification - it may not mean what you think it does. Because of this mis-interpretation there can be a mis-placed idealism. One can become a pawn in political or power schemes that masquerade under idealistic pretenses. In many cases, there are nightmares and doom and gloom types of dreams. Drug and alcohol abuse is more likely now - both in the self and with family members. Family members idealism can also be misplaced or misdirected. Even in cases where the spiritual energies are interpreted correctly, there is difficulty in applying them to family and everyday affairs. It is not unusual for spiritual teachings to contradict how we feel - our everyday sentiments - and this is happening now. Spirit is calling you to transcend your past conditioning. The advice of a real guru is invaluable these days.

The Spiritual Perspective. There is a need to elevate, refine and spiritualize your emotional nature - emotional habit patterns, moods and reactions - also your family situation. There is a need to raise its tone and vibration. Frequently this can be hard work - perhaps the hardest, at times, that any person can do. Few, therefore, undertake this voluntarily. They need a goad - a push. And, this the Divine is supplying now. Many people have high spiritual ideals - but they are "abstract" and disconnected from the everyday affairs of life. Their ideals are high, but emotionally they are subject to all sorts of impurities - they can be filled with anger, resentment, negative moods, intolerance etc. The Divine is now shining the light of revelation on these things, so that action will be taken. Probably it is not pleasant. Often times this "light of revelation" brings out family scandals or shameful incidents from one's own past. This is part of the cleansing process. Our spirituality must become so strong that our emotional nature is transformed by it. This is a time for "casting all family burdens on the Divine" and letting that handle things. Those already on a spiritual path - and who are sincere about it - will have little trouble with this transit. For they will already be in harmony with it.

Transiting Neptune Square Sun

A difficult and long term transit. (This transit has been going on for a number of years and will continue for a few more years - but now it is most intense.) Though you are in essence a "light of the world" you might feel that your personal sense of self - of self esteem and self confidence - is out of synch with the spiritual values prevalent at this time. Perhaps your sense of self esteem is based on "materiality" - how much money you have, what you have been able to achieve, your worldly status, the clubs you belong to or the friends that you have - and these false assumptions are getting tested now. There is the most contradictory and confusing feeling that your will and purpose is "out of synch", not aligned with God's Will and purpose. And this will take much meditation and prayer to straighten out. This conflict can weaken self confidence. Your personal creativity is strong, but seems out of synch with the spiritual values of this time. You should just continue with it as the tide will turn in a few years.

The Spiritual Perspective. There is a need to elevate, refine and spiritualize your life purpose and sense of self. On its level, the Divine I Am, that you are is never out of synch with the "father". But on a psychological level, your concept of I Am, your personal under-standing of I Am, might be out of synch. And so a realignment is necessary. For those of you already on a path, this transit will bring both testing of your sense of "I Am" and revelation. The light of revelation will shine on your ego structure. You will see the flaws, the errors, the shameful things that you have done - but also the good. This light of revelation is strictly "impersonal" - it just shines light on the area, so that you can see what's going on. Also it is good that your ego structure gets tested by spiritual forces. It leads to greater understanding and a realization that the Divine Will for another - for a another, person, group, culture or organization could be different than the Divine Will for you. On a certain level it is all "one will and one mind". But the expression could be different for different individuals.

Transiting Neptune Square Mercury

A difficult and long term transit - especially in the Natal. In the Natal chart this trend had been going on for some years now and will continue for some more years. In the Solar Return it is only in effect for the current year and will basically reinforce the tendencies of the Solar Return chart. (These tendencies are already there in the chart, regardless of this transit.) The mental process, the ideas, the logic and modes of communication are becoming intensely spiritualized, but rather than as a natural, harmonious process (which it is supposed to be) it happens through shocks or conflicts. Perhaps you are exposed to spiritual teachings that totally conflict with your ideas and habitual thoughts. Perhaps you have spiritual experiences that also conflict with these things. The mind feels confused by it all. How can it be? How will I explain it? But given time and more meditation you will eventually be able to absorb and integrate these energies into the intellect. One of the problems with this process (and it is a long term process) is that you will feel that you are living in two "worlds" at the same time - the dream world and the actual world. You might feel that you are having "hallucinations" - though in reality you are looking into the spiritual world. You need to exercise special care while driving or doing mundane tasks. Always be mindful and focused on what you are doing in the world. Observe the spiritual visions, but keep focused on the task at hand. Your thoughts can seem jumbles these days - as there were no coherence or order to them. Logical thinking is more difficult. Why is this happening to you the "hard way"? Due to past karma. Perhaps you were overly materialistic in your thinking and now very strong measures are needed. Usually this transit will lead to more spiritual study and the search for answers. And the search will inevitably lead to the cure. In many cases, natural psychic abilities will suddenly become more active - and it takes time to integrate these things into the psyche and mentality.

The Spiritual Perspective. Much of what we say above applies here as well. Your thinking and ideas need to be refined, spiritualized and elevated. They need to come into better alignment with the Divine Will in you. Right now, they seem out of synch. But few undertake this labor - and it can be labor - without some goading - and this transit provides the goad. You can make things easier on yourself by cooperating with the process rather than fighting it. Pray to the Divine that it enter your thought process, cleanse it of error, and grant it illumination. Offer the mind (the intellect) as a sacrifice to the Divine and let it have its way there. Often, under this aspect, one is exposed to spiritual teachings that say "the mind is the enemy" - setting up a conflict between the mind and the spirit. But these things are not so. The mind is not the enemy - it is the error in the mind that creates the problems. The mind has its role and purpose in the spiritual life - and a very important one.

Transiting Neptune Square Venus

A difficult and long term transit. If this is in the Natal chart it has been going on for many years now and will continue for some more years. If this is in the Solar Return it is only valid for the current year. This transit creates complications and difficulties in the love and social life. The way you relate, your current relationships, your needs and goals in love, are not "in synch" with the spiritual fads and trends of the times. There is a need now - the Cosmos is forcing this - to create harmony between your notions of romance and your notions of spiritual love. It seems to you that they are "different things" - and in a sense you are right. Romantic love is usually personal and based on sensual factors - it is based on an object of love. Spiritual love needs no object and no sensation - it just is. Yet, romantic love is often the doorway to learn about spiritual love. And spiritual love often leads to romantic love. But while this reconciliation is taking place there can be many contradictions and conflicts here. Your spiritual ideals can pull you one way, while romance and the social life pulls you in another. Spirit is going to bring about important changes in your social life - to make it more harmonious with itself. These changes can appear to be uncomfortable, but the end result will be good - a more spiritual relationship and a more spiritual social life. Many will feel that their current romance or current relationship doesn't have the "seal of approval" from spirit - and this will create some "subtle, unnameable" dissatisfaction. It feels like an itch that can't be scratched. Often there will be difficulties in integrating unconditional spiritual love into the current romantic love. There can be much confusion on the love front these days. But there will also be much spiritual revelation thrown on it.

The Spiritual Perspective. Much of what we say above applies here. The Divine, through its zodiacal servants, is elevating, refining, and spiritualizing your love and social life. The whole tone and vibration is to be raised to a new level. And, all the phenomena described above are merely side effects of this process. The discomforts you feel stems from your own inner resistance and attachment. You can ease this by cooperating with the process rather than fighting it. When the light of revelation shines on our love life and love attitudes it can be very unpleasant. Our ideas of love and how we actually function in love are often miles apart. But this unpleasantness can lead to positive change - and this is the purpose. There can be love scandals

- both personal and with the partner or lover. Everything gets revealed these days. But past these scandals, lies redemption - you can change your ways, your thinking and attitudes.

Transiting Neptune Square Mars

A difficult and long term transit. If this is to the Solar Return it is only valid for the current year. You have high dreams and high spiritual ideals, but find it difficult to put them into practice - difficult to act on them. Your urges for physical action - sex, athletics, exercise - conflict with your spiritual ideals and teachings. You can feel the conflict of the spirit with the body. "The spirit is willing but the flesh is weak" is a scripture you can relate to these days. "When I would do good, I do evil" is another one. The urges of the body conflict with the urges of the spirit. The spirit counsels patience and love - but the body is hasty and impatient. The spirit says, "let things happen" but the body tries to "make things happen "- by brute force. Sometimes there is a feeling that the ideals are so high that they are "physically unattainable" and one gives up on them. The body is undergoing a refinement and spiritualization these days and one must be patient with the process. Many people feel dreamy, ungrounded and spaced out on the physical plane - thus this is not a time to add more problems by taking drugs or alcohol. Generally, this is a period for "mindfulness" and "attention" on the physical plane - especially when driving, exercising, or doing strenuous kinds of work.

The Spiritual Perspective. The Divine wants to refine the physical body, elevate the sexuality and refine it - elevate its vibration to make it more sublime. But the process can be uncomfortable. The body and its habits resist and so there is discomfort involved. There is nothing inherently wrong with any of these things - they are merely normal animal functions. But when approached in a certain way, with a certain attitude, they can be lifted up from mere animal functions into something much higher and powerful. This is the spiritual intent. You can make it easier by cooperating instead of fighting. The body is a temple of the most high. When we exercise or indulge in sports, it is really Spirit doing these things through us. When we make love it is the God and the Goddess mating. These attitudes will get you through this transit much easier.

Transiting Neptune Square Jupiter

A difficult and long term transit. Your urges for wealth are in conflict with spiritual ideals and inner guidance. Ideals and guidance seem to weaken your urges for wealth. Your religious and philosophical beliefs come under assault from spiritual people, spiritual forces and even your own mystical experiences. There is a need (not easy) for reconciling the conflicts. Financial and business judgement might not be realistic these days and it is good to do more homework on important financial decisions.

The Spiritual Perspective. There is a need to refine, elevate and spiritualize your religious and philosophical beliefs - your personal religion - your outlook on life. The Divine does this by the "magic of light" - through interior revelation. This light reveals many religious pathologies that many of us are prone to. It is not usually pleasant. Religion itself (whichever one you follow) is basically a wonderful and important thing - it's the abuses of it that are revealed now. In this light you can see errors and make the corrections. Financial attitudes are also getting refined and elevated. The light of revelation shines on those things too - where is the true source of supply? What to do really believe about supply? How do you behave with money? Is there greed? Is there irresponsibility? Are your behaviors hurtful? All these things are shown for what they are, the underlying errors are revealed, and you will be able to make corrections - to bring your financial life more in line with the Divine Will.

Transiting Neptune Square Saturn

A difficult and long term transit. The way you normally manage your life, organize yourself and order your environment is attacked by spiritual people, idealistic types of people and even by your own sense of idealism. Your sense of security and tradition is considered "unspiritual" in the climate of these times. You find it difficult to be practical and spiritual at the same time. Practical decisions - especially important ones - need more homework. Your sense of order and reality is being changed the hard way.

The Spiritual Perspective. Your sense of order - your sense of reality upon which you base your life - needs to be elevated and refined. It needs to come into more alignment with spiritual truth. But perhaps you are resisting this and so the process can be unpleasant. If you cooperate with the process it will go much easier. There is a need to base your "personal order" around spiritual truth and the spiritual order and not vice versa. You have to adapt to the Divine and not the other way around.

Transiting Neptune Square Uranus

A difficult and long term transit - this is so whether it is in the Natal or Solar Return Horoscopes. It has been going on for many years and will continue for many more years. Your normal urges for freedom, innovation, experimentation and rebelliousness against the norm are not in synch with the spiritual values of the time. Your spiritual values, urges and disciplines conflict with your need to be free. The spiritual lesson here is that freedom - real freedom - only comes when you give up your personal free will. Indulging in your personal ideas of what freedom is could impede your spiritual progress and ideals. Other issues are also highlighted these days. Mystical experience - things that transcend the mind, contradict strongly with your scientific understanding of things. Now you must expand your understanding of science to include this kind of phenomena - and the process may not be comfortable.

The Spiritual Perspective. Much of what we say above applies here

as well. The light of revelation is now shining on your scientific knowledge, understanding and attitudes. For astrologers, it is shining on their astrological studies and understanding as well. This can be quite unsettling as basic assumptions get tested. Science and originality -though wonderful things - are not independent. They too serve the Divine - and if not, they will be brought into line.

Transiting Neptune Square Neptune

A difficult and long term transit that only happens in the Natal Chart. And, it generally happens when the native is in the 40's. Usually this shows a spiritual crisis - a crisis in your ideals. The pursuit of your highest ideals of spirituality have now led you to a place far removed from what is was originally. The pursuit of your ideals has led you into things that seem "unspiritual" to you - that conflict with your original notions of spirituality. A part of you feels that it wants to get "back on track" but doesn't know how. And it will take much meditation to see the way. Idealistic organizations and causes that you believed in now seem to contradict your notions of spirituality - you seem disillusioned with them. This is a time for reviewing your notions of spirituality _ deepening and widening your ideals so that they embrace all the contradictions. When you started out, your spirituality and ideals was perhaps vague - you went after them blindly and perhaps haphazardly. By now you are aware of what is involved in these things and not as naive as you once were - will you continue? Will you abandon your ideals? Will you pursue them in a different way? This is up to you. You are in a period for re-thinking these matters.

The Spiritual Perspective. What we said above applies here too.

Transiting Neptune Square Pluto

A difficult and long term transit. If this is in the Natal Chart these trends have been going on for many years now and will continue for many more years. This is true even in the Solar Return Chart. You've had this aspect for a number of Solar Returns and will likely have it for many more. Your sexual urges and preferences are not in synch with spiritual values and ideals of the times. Perhaps you are made to feel that these things are "unspiritual". This could be a period of sexual confusion. The basis of your sexuality is questioned. Everyone has a desire to reinvent the self - to give birth to the person that he or she wants to be. These are legitimate and lawful urges, but now they are being challenged by the spirituality of the times - the spiritual teachings that are being given out at the moment. You are forced to re-think what you plan to be and the methods by which you will achieve this. Meditation could be more difficult this period - the ability to focus is not as strong. On the mundane level, there is a need to be more careful of debt as there is unrealistic thinking happening. There would be a tendency to either borrow too much or not enough when the circumstances call for it.

The Spiritual Perspective. Much of what we say above applies here as well. Deep and secret processes in your nature are getting elevated, refined and spiritualized. The light of revelation is shining on the "underworld" of your psyche - and this underworld is much vaster and perhaps much more "vicious" than anything you read about in the world. You can understand now why mafia people or terrorists are the way they are. These motivations lie within all of us, on very deep levels. Though these things are difficult to face - if it is happening to you, it means that you are ready to face it. This light of revelation is impersonal and not punitive, and though it reveals many "underworldly things" it also reveals the way out. Your new perspective will be a big help. Often, there are sexual or financial scandals under this transit as this is part of the "revelatory process". Spiritually oriented people will understand death and decay more - how sacred these things are. Death is part of life. It is part of Nature's continual "recycling program". When death comes it is the great "liberator" - an angel of light and not of darkness. Another spiritual agenda that is happening is the elevation of many of the so called animalistic functions of which we all partake - emptying the bowels - the process of elimination - sexuality - a woman's menstrual flow. The tendency is to view these things with some "disgust", or in the case of sex with excess lust. Now it is seen for what it truly is, and since our attitude towards these things are changed, the vibrations are changed. Indulging in these things - in natural ways - will no longer "degrade" the consciousness. In fact, it will now bring healing and light, where once it brought darkness and degradation.

Transiting Neptune Square Ascendant

A difficult and long term transit - especially if this is in the Natal Chart. In the Natal Chart this transit has been going on for some years now and will continue for some more years. In the Solar Return this transit is only valid for the current year. The spiritual climate of the times - the spiritual teachings being given out - appear to conflict with the image you want to create, the way you dress, and the way you accessorize. (You might like to wear fur, while the spiritual ideals of the times, disapprove of fur - this is just an example.) The body can become hypersensitive to spiritual and psychic energies in an unpleasant way. Very important to be mindful in your every day activities - such as when you drive or do your chores. Keep both feet on the ground. Self esteem and self confidence will be challenged by the spiritual ideals and teachings of the times.

The Spiritual Perspective. There was a need to refine the body, to spiritualize it, for a long time. Perhaps you've procrastinated - now you are pushed into it in perhaps unpleasant ways. These are the goads that are needed to get us to do what we have long needed to do. The vibrations of the physical body are going to be raised and all the other phenomena described above are merely side effects of this.

Transiting Neptune Square Midheaven

A difficult and long term transit if this is in the Natal Chart. It has been going on for some years now and will continue for some more years. In the Solar Return Chart it is only valid for the current year. Your career path - your life work - your mission in life - appears to conflict with the spiritual ideals, trends and teachings of the times. You may have embarked on your career from altruistic motives, but now you are forced to question them. Objectives that you once considered to be lofty and worthy seem out of synch with current spiritual trends. Reviewing your career objectives now will be a healthy thing. Clarity will happen eventually. Also it is spiritually useful to stay with something you believe in though the trends of the times are not in synch. One develops strength and character. Dross is purged from the mind. One does what is right, though the glory is not there.

The Spiritual Perspective. The Divine is refining and elevating your mundane work in the world - your career. Perhaps you've "gotten off track" and it is going to push you back on track - to the work that you came here to do. The Divine does this through "interior revelation". Are you in this line of work for money? To prove something? From human psychological urges? To get back at your parents or some authority figure? Or are you doing it from the only motive that's worth anything - because this is what you were born to do - your duty to life and to the world. Career setbacks (and sometimes scandals) are educational now and not punitive - these are all part of the revelation process.

Transiting Neptune Opposition Moon

A difficult and long term transit that has been going on for many years now, but now it is most powerful. Those who are on a spiritual path will have to work hard to discern what is true intuition and true spiritual guidance and what is merely a mood or feeling. You seem emotionally unreceptive to your intuition, spiritual guidance or highest spiritual ideals. You are not in the "mood" for spiritual teachings. Family members oppose spirituality. And, family duties and obligations seem to take you away from spirituality and your deepest ideals. In many cases, the spiritual ongoing (the most important thing in your life) will force a separation from the family. The values of each have become so far out of synch that keeping it together is impossible. In other cases, the values of home and family will temporarily stop the spiritual growth or ongoing. It is a time of crisis and choice. Keeping both urges together will be hard work as you will feel that neither is satisfied. Family members are dissatisfied with the attention you give to your ideals, meditations, or studies. While your spiritual urges are unsatisfied when you spend time on family issues. This conflict is faced by many on the path - and on a deeper level, is actually part of the path. Whichever choice is made leads to growth and learning. Dream life at this time needs much verification - much can be unrealistic or distorted by the subconscious. If this is in the Solar Return it is only valid for the current year - until your next birthday.

The Spiritual Perspective. Much of what we say above applies here as well. The emotional life is being elevated, refined and raised in vibration - but its not a smooth process. There is much personal and perhaps family resistance. It is more difficult to see the spirituality in the mundane affairs of life. It is also more difficult to see how spiritual truths can be applied to the mundane affairs of life. Deeply held emotional patterns resist the spirit. A rhythmic alternation between mundane family affairs and the spiritual practice might be a good idea now.

Transiting Neptune Opposition Sun

A difficult and long term transit. Whether this is to the Natal or Solar Return, this transit has been going on for many years and will continue for many more years. Your ego, self esteem and urge to shine is opposed by the spiritual forces of the times. The ideals being espoused these days are not in synch with the way you like to shine. What you want to do in your heart - something that is holy and real - is portrayed as unspiritual - perhaps you feel it is unspiritual or selfish. These things that you want to do will require more patience - there's nothing wrong with them per se, only the timing is off. This could be a period of confusion and self doubt as you are not sure that your life goals are in synch with the Divine. This is a good period to attain clarity in these matters - and this is the whole purpose of the transit. The struggle to produce harmony with the spiritual forces can often lead to unrealistic idealism or to goals out of synch with reality. Know that the Divine gave you the desires of your heart, but manifestation will happen in its own timing. Stop trying so hard to make others believe you are spiritual, and just be spiritual - listen to the promptings of the Divine in your own heart.

The Spiritual Perspective. It is a wonderful thing, at times, to be exposed to spiritual teachings that conflict with what "we want to hear" - with what we like to do - and that even challenge our ego and self esteem. If this is handled correctly it will lead to a "synthesis" of both positions. Your spirituality will grow in subtle ways and so will your sense of self - of I am. Hold both positions in your mind and watch as a "third position" manifests. This position will incorporate both of the others. Under these kinds of transits it is not unusual for the devout and sincere minister to be exposed to teachings that attack organized religion and ministry; or for the artist or poet to be exposed to teachings that attack these things. Since both ministry and art - and the spiritual teachings - are all coming from spirit, there is a need to gain "higher ground" here. And this is the purpose of this transit.

Transiting Neptune Opposition Mercury

A difficult and long term transit if this is to the Natal Chart. If this is to the Solar Return it is only in effect for the current year. In the Natal Chart these trends have been going on for some years and will continue for some more years. The spiritual forces, teachings, and overall climate completely contradicts the way you think, talk, communicate - also your ideas. You mistrust your own logic and thought process. You feel that your thinking is not realistic or perhaps it is too "materialistic". Now, some doubt of the mortal intellect is a good thing. The Wisdom of God is foolishness in the eyes of man and vice versa. You are apt to be in intellectual conflict with spiritual teachings being given out at this time. You feel that these things violate your intellect. But this is only on the surface. In truth, the spiritual teachings never violate the intellect - they are very rational - but the intellect must be elevated and trained in order to see this. This is a period of spiritualizing the thought processes. The end result will be very good, but while its happening, the old thought patterns feel threatened and confused. There will tend to be many intellectual objections of spiritual teachings - also many arguments and intellectual conflicts with these things. But out of all this new clarity and perception will come. Your intellect is not evil or bad - it is only being put in right perspective. It is to be used and not abused.

The Spiritual Perspective. Much of what we say above applies here. The Divine is elevating and spiritualizing the thought process. Habitual ways of thinking - the ideas that you hold - are being challenged by spiritual truths. Intuition will often contradict logic. One is often exposed to teachings that say "the mind is the enemy" or that "thinking is very dangerous". But since the mind - the intellect - is a Divine Principle, and itself is a manifestation of spirit - obviously there is a need for "higher ground" and deeper under-standing. This is the purpose of this transit.

Transiting Neptune Opposition Venus

A difficult and long term transit - especially if this is to the Natal Horoscope. In the Solar Return this transit is only in effect for the current year. In the Natal Chart, these trends have been going on for many years and will continue for some more years. Now it is most intense as the aspect is exact. Your social and romantic attitudes are being challenged and opposed by the spiritual forces, teachings, and ideals of the time. Its as if you are made to feel that your romantic and social notions are not spiritual and that they must be elevated. Perhaps they are spiritual and idealistic, but this is a period for spiritualizing these things even further. The spiritual teachings of the times could alienate you from friends and loved ones. Sometimes (and this is especially true for those on the spiritual path) your attempt to spiritualize your love life, marriage and social life could lead you to unrealistic idealism. Sometimes there is a feeling of vague dissatisfaction as if "there has to be something more to love than what I'm manifesting". Sometimes the love ideals of a given time are not your love ideals. These love challenges should be welcomed as it will give you opportunity to refine and exalt your love life and love ideals. If there are weaknesses there, they will be revealed now.

The Spiritual Perspective. Much of what we say above applies here as well. Spiritual love - the unconditional love of the Divine - challenges your personal sense of love - your human and romantic ideas and attachments. Your love nature is being elevated and refined now, and it could be unpleasant at times. Often under this kind of transit you will feel a "chemistry" with a person, but the person is not in your Destiny. And often, you will be led to people where you feel "no chemistry" but something deeper - and you are required to love them or be involved with them. Your aesthetic sense will be challenged as well. Perhaps your aesthetics are attached to certain things or people or styles. Spirit will show you that real beauty comes from above and is not to be identified with any specific object, person, or sense of style. These things may indeed be beautiful - but they are not the source of beauty. Beauty is a wonderful thing, but we are to worship and honor the source more than the shadow.

Transiting Neptune Opposition Mars

A difficult and long term transit. If this is to the Natal chart these trends have been going on for many years now and will continue for many more years. But now the effects are most intense as the aspect is exact. If this is to the Solar Return it is only in effect for the current year. The spiritual forces, ideals and teachings of the current period oppose your normal sexuality, sexual attitudes, desire for independence and the innate courage. Courage and independence can falter due to self doubts about the Divine Will and the spiritual realities of life. Some of this self doubt is a good thing. You have to work hard to align your independence and courageous actions with the Higher Power. Should I go off on my own just now? Should I take this action? Are my sexual urges and desires in line with the Divine Will? These are healthy questions. But until you resolve them, there can be delays. The normal forcefulness of the nature is not there. Athletic performance (unless other things deny) can suffer. The Mars Principle in you believes that many problems can be solved by direct and forceful action. But now these kinds of solutions are called into question - and rightly so. Many of the situations you face now cannot be solved in this way. The grace of a Higher Power - Spiritual type solutions - are necessary. Once these are attained, direct action will be successful. This is a period for spiritualizing the sexual nature. Nothing wrong with it per se, but it needs to be elevated to a higher vibration. Until this is achieved, there can be many sexual misadventures - subtle dissatisfactions - a vague unease about your current sexuality and enjoyment. It is also a time for elevating and spiritualizing your physical body and actions. Normally this should happen in harmonious and happy ways, but these days it can happen through challenges and problems. These problems are the spirit's call to you to align your physical body and physical actions with it. Very important now to practice mindfulness and awareness in everyday life - when you drive, when you exercise or do physical labor.

The Spiritual Perspective. What we say above applies here as well.

Transiting Neptune Opposition Jupiter
A difficult and long term transit, especially if it is in the Natal Chart.

In the Solar Return it is only valid for the current year. Financial judgement can be unrealistic right now and more homework needs to be done. Optimism can be boundless and unrealistic. Financial goals are larger than life. Financial intuition is strong but needs verification. Your tendency is to glimpse into the Infinite and this is basically good, but the manifestation is always finite. Be aware of your present capacity. Often, this transit shows the classic conflict between mystical, inner experience and the religion and philosophy we were raised with. One seems to contradict the other. In truth there is no contradiction as mystical experience tends to lead to institutional religious practices and vice versa. Intuition can seem to contradict your personal world view and personal philosophy of life. In many cases the spiritual forces on the planet (ministers, channels, psychics, gurus etc) are channeling things that seem to contradict your religious and philosophical beliefs. Don't reject either out of hand - just give these matters more thought. You will see the resolution.

The Spiritual Perspective. What we say above applies here as well. Your personal philosophy of life and your religious beliefs are getting elevated and refined. Sometimes elevation is best achieved through harmonious revelations, and sometimes - as in the case with deeply held, passionate beliefs - through challenge and stressful situations. Truth will withstand any kind of stress. But falsehood will not. And this is the purpose of the transit. Often under this kind of transit, it is not just your religious beliefs that get tested, but the way you worship - your techniques and practices.

Transiting Neptune Opposition Saturn

A difficult and long term transit. In the Natal Chart these tendencies have been going on for many years now and will continue for many more. In the Solar Return it is only in effect for the current year. Though the end result of this aspect will be very good, it can feel weird while it is going on. Basically, your notions of "reality" of security and how it is attained, is being challenged by the spiritual forces, ideals and teachings of the times. Your sense of reality - the fundamental axioms upon which you base your life - are not "bad" per se - only limited and incomplete. There is much more to it than you can presently comprehend. Spirit is revealing new things to you with its own brand of "tough love". When fundamental axioms and belief systems are challenged there is usually anger, fear and uncertainty. Intuition is guiding you in ways that seem "far out - "dreamland" - not trustworthy. But in the end you will find that it is trustworthy, especially if it is a real intuition. When the transit is over you will have a more spiritual perspective on reality. You will see that your present reality - though it seems real - is only the end product of a long chain of causation - which began in what you call "fantasy". Your present reality was once a fantasy in your mind. Your future reality will be built on today's fantasies. Spirit is offering you things that seem "too good to be true" - and therefore they are true. But much discernment is needed - and this too is being trained. There are forces that will try to manipulate your dreams and ideals against your own best interest. From a health perspective more attention needs to be given to the spine, knees, teeth and overall skeletal alignment.

The Spiritual Perspective. Much of what we say above applies here too. The Divine wants you to modify your priorities in life - to modify your "personal order" - the way that you have ordered your life. In this case it happens through challenges and tests - because, deeply ingrained things need to be changed.

Transiting Neptune Opposition Uranus

A difficult and long term transit. In the Natal Chart this transit has been going on for years and you've been feeling it - now it is most powerful. In the Solar Return chart this aspect is only in effect this year (technically) but in all probability you have had this aspect in past years and will continue to have it in future Solar Returns too.

This is a classic conflict between Science and Spirituality. They seem to contradict in your mind. Spiritual teachings that you hear or are exposed to completely contradict your scientific understanding of the universe. Spiritual ideals conflict with scientific knowledge. Your urge towards freedom and to experiment and innovate in life are opposed by spiritual teachings, teachers, swamis, gurus or ministers. New discoveries that you make - new technologies that interest you - could be seen as "immoral" or unspiritual.

The Spiritual Perspective. Your job now is to bridge the two opposites mentioned above - to see the essential unity between science and spiritual phenomena and ideals. Real Science comes from the Spirit. The action of Spirit is always the truth. Science and scientific verification come afterwards. It is harder for you to take the "leap of faith" so necessary for spiritual success as your rational, scientific mind resists. Science only deals with the natural world and is completely superseded by the "super natural" power of the Spirit. Spirit is urging you go "above your mind" - but its not so easy.

Transiting Neptune Opposition Neptune

A Neutral and long term transit. This can only occur in the Natal Chart and usually happens very late in life. Your spiritual life, ideals and practices which were mere seeds when you were born have now come to fruition. You can see them writ large - in banner headlines - in the world and in your environment. Much of it is good. Much of it is mere delusion and you can see it very clearly now. Ideals that you thought would "save the world", "rescue the planet", "bring peace on Earth" and make "heaven manifest" will do no such thing. True there are improvements in life, but also many unintended consequences. Spiritual ideals might need more re-thinking and refinement. You are seeing the spiritual meaning of your life. Your innate spirituality is very strong now.

The Spiritual Perspective. Much of what we say above applies here

as well. The time is coming where you have to go more inward and refine your spirituality and spiritual ideals. There is nothing more "disillusioning" than obtaining your desires - or manifesting your spiritual ideals. Yes, there is a brief euphoria, but after a while one asks "is that all there is?"

Transiting Neptune Opposition Pluto

A difficult and long term transit that has been going on for many years now - it will continue for many more years - though right now it is most intense. (This is so both in the Natal or Solar Return Charts.) Your sexuality pulls you one way while your spiritual ideals and intuition pull you in another - both these urges are very powerful and it is difficult to deny either one. One feels that sexuality is counter to God's will. Or perhaps one is allured by a relationship that really is counter to one's highest ideals - perhaps it is with a married person, or with the spouse of a dear friend. One is torn between these two urges. Often there are sexual or financial scandals under this transit. The urges to prosper others or to pay down debt are also clouded and confused these days. Perhaps your plans might run counter to your own ideals - though they seem practical and doable at the moment. Your urges to transform, reinvent yourself and resurrect yourself seem to go counter to your own ideals and spiritual guidance. You need to be careful not to deceive yourself. Those involved with estates or inheritance need to take special precautions against deception. All the facts need to be checked out, nothing is as it seems. There are other agendas going on that you may not be aware of. This may not be the right time to be exploring past lives, reincarnation or life after death. Real spirituality calls you to other studies.

The Spiritual Perspective. Much of what we say above applies here too. The sexual nature and the underworld in yourself (and probably in the world) is being elevated, refined and spiritualized. The light of revelation is shining on these things, and its probably not a pretty sight. But look deeper. Let the light do its perfect work. None of these things are evil per se. But perhaps there has been an "over cultivation" of things. Something that is just normal and natural has been given over-emphasis or been expressed in imbalanced ways.

Transiting Neptune Opposition Ascendant

A difficult and long term transit - especially if this is in the Natal Chart. These trends have been going on for many years now and will continue for some more years. But now, since the aspect is exact, the effects are most intense. In the Solar Return chart this transit is only in effect for the current year. Your body, image and urges to personal pleasure are challenged and opposed by the spiritual ideals, teachings and trends of the times. There is a feeling that urges to personal pleasure are unspiritual - or that the Divine frowns on this. Nothing could be further from the truth, but getting clearer on these matters will bear much fruit. This is a time for spiritualizing the body - for refining it and making it more sensitive to higher vibrations. It is a time for balancing the spiritual and the other worldly with your physical needs and drives. We are all spiritual in essence, but we are incarnate in a body that is of the animal kingdom. Under this transit we can really see how strong the body-animalistic pulls are in us. You have difficulty accepting the spiritual teachings of the time because of ego reasons. And yet, you need to understand that true spirituality is not making war on your ego - so don't feel so threatened. The ego is merely being put in right perspective. On a more mundane level, you could feel "unglamourous" as the glamor crowd idealizes an image that is opposite of yours. There's nothing wrong with you per se, you are only "out of style" for a while.

The Spiritual Perspective. What we say above applies here as well.

Transiting Neptune Opposition Midheaven

A difficult and long term transit. If this is to the Natal Chart these trends have been going on for some years and will continue for some more years. In the Solar Return these trends are only in effect for the current year. Your career path and outer aspirations are not in synch - are actually facing opposition - from the spiritual forces, trends and teachings of the time. Your career seems to be "unspiritual" or "unidealistic" by these evaluations. But look again, it might not be so. This is a time for spiritualizing and elevating your career. This doesn't necessarily mean that you leave it but, perhaps you will pursue it in a more idealistic way. Perhaps you will make idealistic types of change to it or pursue it in a more spiritual way. Usually this aspect happens with Neptune in either the 3rd or 4th Houses. Thus the challenge to the career can come from siblings or because you are spiritualizing your thought process. New ideas, more spiritual type ideas will naturally change your perspective on the career. The challenges to the career can also come from family members - the ideals of family members - or through new emotional sensitivities that you are developing. Family obligations can seem more spiritual than a mere career. Though what is happening can seem uncomfortable, in the end this will be a good thing. Your career and outer aspirations will be balanced, with your spiritual ideals - but through challenges. Almost by force and coercion rather than by natural evolution. Spiritually we grow in two ways - either through a harmonious expansion of the consciousness or through difficult situations that are placed before us. This is a time of growing through the overcoming of difficult situations.

The Spiritual Perspective. What we say above applies here too.

Transiting Neptune Trine Moon

A happy and long term transit. In the Natal chart this has been going on for some years and will continue for some more years. Now the energy is most intense as the aspect is exact. In the Solar Return chart, this transit is only in effect for the current year. You are unusually creative and inspired now. Emotional sensitivity is strong. You are receptive to spiritual forces and to spiritual teachings. The dream life is active and prophetic. Psychic abilities are developing and growing. Family members are becoming more spiritual and idealistic. You find it easy to incorporate spiritual values into the every day domestic life. The prevailing spiritual energies, teachings and trends (and these are always shifting) are helping you to create harmony in your home and in your emotions. You have great ability to manifest your ideal domestic life now.

The Spiritual Perspective. Under this transit "spiritual realization" is much easier to attain - it happens quite naturally. Theory and idealism is one thing. Knowledge is another. Striving is still another thing. But realization and attainment is something else. This comes when you "feel" what you have been striving for as a "present reality" - when it becomes "real" to you - when you start to "function from that reality". True realization changes behavior. When the spiritual force has come to the "Moon Level" - the emotional nature - it is not only the emotions that change, but actual behavior.

Transiting Neptune Trine Sun

A happy and long term transit that has been going on for many years and will continue for some more years. Now it is most intense. It is a time when you can live out your ideals. Great spiritual revelation and guidance is helping you towards your goals, and your purpose in life. Spiritual guidance is also helping Healthwise and in areas of self esteem. You can shine without compromising your spiritual values. This is also a very creative time - an inspired time - artistic creations are unusually inspired. Meditation and spiritual practices go very well. You are a star in the spiritual and artistic realms these days.

The Spiritual Perspective. The Divine Immortal is always in alignment with the "will of the Father" but sometimes it is more difficult to experience it. Now, experiencing it is very easy - natural and normal. Spirit is inspiring you to be more creative in your life - this can be in the field of artistic creation or in the creation of physical babies. Much depends on your age and stage in life. Young women under these aspects often dream of babies. Spirit is announcing a new creation. Also, it becomes much easier now to transcend yourself - to enter into your deepest identity in the unmanifest - in the world beyond name and form. No matter how much you have attained in life - no matter how high your opinion of yourself is - the truth about you is much greater than anything you can imagine.

Transiting Neptune Trine Mercury

A happy and long term transit. In the Natal Chart these trends have been going on for many years now and will continue for some more years. In the Solar Return Chart, this transit is only in effect for the coming year. The energies are more intense now as the aspect is very exact. The spiritual forces, energies, teachings and trends are serving to expand your thought processes, communication abilities and ideas. You absorb spiritual information easily. Your literary tastes are inclined to the mystical, poetical and metaphysical. You are very inspired communicator and teacher now. Your speech has a musical flowing quality - so does your writing. Your ideas and thought process is becoming spiritualized but in a harmonious way. Your mind is growing wings. You have a unique ability to under-stand scripture and other sacred writings these days. You are learning to hear not only what is said (or written) but the place of consciousness from which these things come. Your intuitve powers are unusually strong. Spirit is elevating the mind in harmonious and ways.

The Spiritual Perspective. Everything we say above applies here as well. Under this kind of a transit (if nothing else is denying" you can see that intuition and logic need not be in conflict, but actually cooperate with each other. The mind (the intellect) takes its right place in the scheme of things. It explains the wordless intuition in a logical way. It makes logical plans to carry out the Divine Will.

Transiting Neptune Trine Venus

A happy and long term transit. If this transit is to the Natal chart, this has been going on for many years and will continue for some more years. If this is in the Solar Return chart it is only in effect for this year. This transit shows a refining of the love and social life. The native is attracting spiritually and creatively oriented friends and lovers. The native is realizing the highest love ideals. The native is able to love - to stay in that vibration - regardless of circumstances (unless other transits deny). The native is unusually creative and very inspired. If the native is not involved in personal creativity, then he or she will be more appreciative of the fine arts - the aesthetic sense is much more developed these days. The native very glamor oriented either personally or through the social circle. The love life is being guided by intuition and often by psychics, gurus, ministers, channels and the like. The native has many dreams of love. Dreaming will be more lucid. The dream life will be highly active. The native will receive much artistic inspiration in dreams too.

The Spiritual Perspective. The love nature readily and easily receives the inspiration of spirit and so many exalted love and aesthetic experiences are happening.

Transiting Neptune Trine Mars

A happy and long term transit that has been going on for many years and will continue for some more years. Now it is most intense. If this is in the Solar Return it is only in effect this year. The actions tend to be inspired. Actions tend to come from intuition rather than overly planned out - though other things in the Horoscope can deny this. Spiritual Ideals are translated into actions. Movements will be more graceful and rhythmic these days. The tastes in sports and exercise regimes will be more artistic and spiritual - yoga, tai chi, eurythmy are preferable to vigorous type exercise. Ballet, dance, figure skating will be preferable to hard contact sports. Sex will be more spiritualized. Fantasy will play a bigger role - a positive role - in sexual activity than before.

The Spiritual Perspective. Much of what we say above applies here. Since the sexual and physical nature is more receptive to the spiritual energies - to the Divine Will and Plan - these experiences will become very elevated now. This is a time for "in my flesh I will see God" - for spiritual realization in the present body consciousness. The Divine is there in the cells, in the most instinctual functions - like sex. This realization will undoubtedly transform the sexual act into "something else" - something more than has been previously conceived.

Transiting Neptune Trine Jupiter

A happy and long term transit. Its been going on for many years now and will continue for a few more years. But now it is most intense as the aspects is exact. If this is in the Solar Return it is only in effect this year. This is a very spiritual and idealistic period in your life. Your urges to wealth and wealth activities are not just personal but serve a higher social and spiritual good. You are prospering in a way that improves the entire world. You can be idealistic and become wealthy - there is no contradiction now. The intuition and spiritual guidance not only leads to greater religious and philosophical clarity, but to increased wealth as well. Intuition creates luck nowadays and the intuition seems very good. Often, under this transit people have huge financial dreams - one feels that there is no limit to one's earnings abilities or to what one can achieve. Spiritual teachings, teachers, channels and gurus are all supporting wealth goals.

The Spiritual Perspective. Much of what we say above applies here as well. Wealth and spirituality are not in contradiction but in harmony. Often people experience conflicts between religion and their spiritual ideals and experience. But now, personal spiritual experience, will validate your religious beliefs - it will illumine them. The spiritual teachings of the period will also tend to validate your personal religious beliefs.

Transiting Neptune Trine Saturn

A happy and long term transit. Its been going on for many years now and will continue for a few more years. (Even if this is in the Solar Return, this transit has been appearing in past Solar Returns and will appear in one or two future ones.) But now it is most intense as the aspect is exact. You have the best of both worlds these days - spirituality, an inner life, intuition and a worldly life - a career in the world. Your sense of reality and practicality is supported by the spiritual forces of the times. For you (and this is a wonderful position to be in) the most practical values are also the most spiritual. Your spiritual life and growth is enhanced through handling the everyday concerns of the real world. Your highest career aspirations are also spirit's aspirations for you. Intuition is guiding your management decisions and your career path. Important career information comes to you in dreams, intuition and through psychics, channels and gurus. Though you've got your nose to the grindstone, you are manifesting a higher, loftier plan. You have the ability to be fair but also compassionate - to be just and loving. The right and practical thing to do is also the most loving in many cases. Spirit is helping you to take charge of your life and to organize it in a proper way.

The Spiritual Perspective. There is really no conflict between the "tangible" and the "spiritual" - there is an orderly manifestation and de-manifestation process in life. The most tangible of realities was once a "fantasy" in someone's mind and eventually will return to the plane of spirit. The world began in the spiritual realm and will return there someday. New worlds are constantly being born. This is a transit for realizing the essential harmony between "matter and spirit".

Transiting Neptune Trine Uranus

A happy and long term transit - whether this is to the Natal or Solar Return Chart. These energies have been going on for some years now and will continue for some more years. Now, because the aspect is exact, the energies are most intense. You are original and inspired. Your urges for freedom and innovation are supported by the spiritual trends, teachings and energies of the time. Your originality is awesome now - inspired from on high. Your innovative ideas are likely to benefit all of humanity - and even future generations. You are seeing clearly that there is no real conflict between real science and real spirituality - they are two sides of a coin. New ideas for inventions (and even scientific breakthroughs) are coming to you and these are inspired by the spirit. Your urge for freedom is not something personal but what God wants for you. Your understanding of science, mathematics, astrology, astronomy and technology is being deepened and aided by spiritual forces and teachings. All these subjects have a spiritual basis, which you are seeing right now. They are laws of the Creator and not contrary to Him. Properly understood, when you study science or mathematics you are studying the mind and laws of the Creator. There is a strong mystical aspect to these so-called worldly and secular subjects.

The Spiritual Perspective. Much of what we say above applies here as well. This transit is about the revelation that science and spirituality are not in conflict. They are two sides of a coin. Spiritual revelation, and the way to it, is a science. Scientific discoveries come from spiritual revelation.

Transiting Neptune Trine Neptune

A happy and long term transit. This can only occur in the Natal chart and only happens once every 50 years or so. Your innate spirituality and idealism - your unique take on it - your unique approach - is very much in synch with the spiritual trends and teachings of the times. If nothing else in the Horoscope denies, you are very comfortable with your spirituality. This is a period of happy and harmonious spiritual growth and development.

The Spiritual Perspective. What we say above applies here as well.

Transiting Neptune Trine Pluto

A happy and long term transit. Whether this occurs in the Natal or Solar Return Chart, it has been going on for many years, only now it is most intense as the aspect is exact. Your urge to transform yourself, to reinvent yourself, to become the person that you want to be, is being supported by the spiritual forces, trends and teachings of the times. New spiritual ways and techniques for transformation are being revealed to you. Your sexuality is being spiritualized and enhanced. The vibrations of the sexual act are being lifted up from mere animal functions into something that is sacred, sublime, and healing. The sexual act is inspired. Imagination and fantasy can either exalt or demean it - but probably now it is exalting it. There is something very spiritual about working to prosper others and you are seeing this now. As you prosper others you prosper yourself. The financial intuition of the partner is very strong these days and right on target (if nothing else in the chart is denying). You are losing your fears of death as spirit (and spiritual teachings and teachers) are showing you the truth. Those on a spiritual path will have opportunities to transcend death itself and see what lies beyond. The transcendence of death can happen harmoniously or inharmoniously - now the tendency will be toward the harmonious way. The deeper mysteries of life are being revealed to you through dreams, intuition and through spiritual teachers, channels and psychics.

The Spiritual Perspective. Much of what we say above applies here as well. This transit is about the revelation of the Divine Presence in the underworld of your life - it is there even in the "hell spaces" and is the deeper reality of those spaces. It is there in your sexual urge, in the bowel movement, in the intestines, in the processes of death and decay going on around you and within you. Such a revelation is bound to change your attitudes to these things and this is the purpose of the transit.

Transiting Neptune Trine Ascendant

A happy and long term transit. If this is in the Solar Return it is only in effect this year. Intuition guides you on how to dress and create your personal image. There is much glamor to the image these days. The body is more sensitive and responsive to vibrations. You are more able to adapt any look you desire. You are more able to connect up to the source in a physical way. This transit favors spiritual types of regimes such as hatha yoga, eurythmy, tai chi etc. Meditation and spiritual study will do much to improve the body and appearance.

The Spiritual Perspective. Much of what we say above applies here too. It is a transit of realization that the Divine abides in your body. Underneath the self image and personal story is a Divinity carrying out a specific plan and purpose. You "personal image" is nothing more than a "creation" - a vehicle - through which it can express its purpose, and you build your image based on that. The person who is destined to play in the NFL will need a certain type of body. The person destined to be in the arts or an intellectual will need a different kind of body. Spirit will now mold your body according to its purposes.

Transiting Neptune Trine Midheaven

A happy and long term transit. If this is to the Natal Chart, these trends have been going on for some years now and will continue for some more years. In the Solar Return Horoscope this transit is only in effect for the coming year and will only reinforce the already existing tendencies of the Solar Return Chart. Your spiritual ideals, spiritual regimes and overall spiritual orientation is actually helping your career. You are more able to integrate these ideals and practices in your outer work. In many cases, the native will pursue a more spiritually oriented career. Career guidance - and very helpful guidance - is coming from astrologers, psychic, channels, ministers and through dreams and intuitions. What is especially happy here is that you are shown that your highest career aspirations have the blessing of the spiritual forces of the universe. You are not going it alone here, but powerful forces are helping out and guiding. Your career aspirations are very much in line with the Divine Will. In many cases important career contacts will happen at spiritual retreats, church, ashram or meditation seminar - also as you involve yourself in charitable and altruistic goals.

The Spiritual Perspective. Much of what we say above applies here too. Many of you are realizing that your mundane "work in the world" has a deeper agenda behind it. Underneath all the so-called success and failure, a Higher Plan, is being carried through. Many will get revelation about their spiritual mission for this life under this kind of a transit. The true meaning of your work in the world is being revealed.

Transiting Neptune Sextile Moon

A happy and long term transit - especially if it is in the Natal Chart. In the Solar Return chart it is only in effect for the current year. In the Natal Chart this transit has been going on for some years now and will continue for some more years. You will have opportunities (and encouragement) to apply spiritual principles to the daily domestic life, to spiritualize the home and family relationships. There will be opportunities to develop the spiritual and psychic faculties and to get a spiritual perspective on your past. Your ability to interpret dreams (and your dream life in general) will be enhanced. Family members will have opportunities to enter a spiritual path or to otherwise enhance their spiritual interests.

The Spiritual Perspective. There will be many opportunities for spiritual realization now - to feel the spirit as a living reality on an "emotional level" - but it is up to you take them.

Transiting Neptune Sextile Sun

A happy and long term transit - whether it is in the Natal or Solar Return Chart. You will have opportunities to expand your sense of self and to transcend your ego - to see yourself from a higher and larger perspective. You will be able to see yourself through heaven's eyes. You will have opportunities to develop your spiritual interests and incorporate them into your life goals - your creativity. Children will have opportunities to develop their spirituality. Spiritual insights and teachings will enhance the sex life, athletic interests, and overall vitality.

The Spiritual Perspective. We are all much more than even our loftiest concept of ourselves. In essence we are "beyond name and form". This is a period where you will have opportunities to experience this.

Transiting Neptune Sextile Mercury

A happy and long term transit. If this it to the Natal Chart it has been going on for many years now and will continue for many more years. If this is to the Solar Return, it is only in effect for the current year. You have opportunities to spiritualize your mind and your mental interests. Opportunities for spiritual study are coming. The intellect will become more intuitive - being able to arrive at correct conclusions through leaps of logic. A very wonderful aspect for spiritual teachers, creative writers, musicians, poets and students of scripture. Spiritual reality transcends the intellect, but now you are in a period where you can more easily understand these things with the intellect. A wonderful aspect for philosophers, hermeticists and Jnana yogis.

The Spiritual Perspective. Much of what we say above applies here as well. It is easy, under this kind of a transit, to understand the purpose of the intellect - to make concrete plans to execute to the Divine Will and to "rationalize" the intuition - and often to communicate it to others.

Transiting Neptune Sextile Venus

A happy and long term transit. You will have (and have had in the past few years) opportunities to spiritualize your love and social life - to elevate it to another plane. You have opportunities to meet new and creative-spiritual type friends. Perhaps you will have a romance with one of these people. Spirit and intuition is guiding your love life. Love is very idealistic. Personal creativity is very inspired. The fine arts call to you - either in a creative way or as an appreciator of them.

The Spiritual Perspective. What we say above applies here as well. If you take the opportunities offered there will be many exalted love and aesthetic experiences - beyond your present concepts of these things.

Transiting Neptune Sextile Mars

A happy and long term transit. You will have opportunities to take positive action on your ideals - to apply your spiritual principles and ideals in the world. Spiritual insights will enhance your courage, independence, athletic ability and sexuality. If this is in the Natal Chart these energies have been going on for some years now. In the Solar Return, this transit is only in effect for the current year.

The Spiritual Perspective. There will be opportunities to realize the Divine in the "flesh" - in the musculature and sexual activity. All these activities are essentially Divine. If you take these opportunities, you can expect more "rarified" sexual and physical experiences.

Transiting Neptune Sextile Jupiter

A happy and long term transit. In the Natal Chart these tendencies have been going on for some years now and will continue for some more years. In the Solar Return this transit is only in effect for the current year. You will have many opportunities to spiritualize your personal philosophy of life and to view it impersonally from a higher level. This higher perspective will, of itself, therapize many errors. When we are on the ground we form certain concepts and beliefs and they seem right from that perspective. When we view the same terrain from the air we get a much larger perspective and this of itself will modify our concepts. There will also be opportunities to develop the financial intuition and to learn the spiritual principles of wealth and supply. The financial intuition will grow. A good prosperity aspect. You will have opportunities to apply your spiritual ideals to your financial life and to manifest your ideal of prosperity.

The Spiritual Perspective. Much of what we say above applies here. This transit is a revelation about the true harmony of mysticism and direct experience with the Divine and organized religion. There is no real conflict. Religions and their practices arose from the spiritual experience - the mysticism - of a few people. Religion has its root in the mystical. Under this kind of a transit, personal spiritual experience can lead you to embrace "the religion of your fathers" rather than reject it.

Transiting Neptune Sextile Saturn

A happy and long term transit, whether it occurs in the Natal or the Solar Return. These trends have been going on for many years and will continue for some more years. You have many opportunities to manifest - make practical - high spiritual ideals and personal inspiration. Managers with this aspect will discover that intuition and spiritual guidance is aiding them in their efforts. The role of intuition in mundane affairs is more recognized. Your personal sense of order - your sense of the realities of life - get support from spiritual sources - psychics, spiritual channels, dreams, astrologers and the like. You are seeing that a stable material life is also highly spiritual - that spirituality and material concerns need not contradict each other.

The Spiritual Perspective. Much of what we said above applies here. There are opportunities to realize the essential unity of spirit and matter and thus the intense "practicality" of the Spirit in the life of the world - in the career, in your use of power, in the way you organize your life.

Transiting Neptune Sextile Uranus

A happy and long term transit, regardless of whether it is in the Natal or Solar Return chart. It has been going on for some years and will continue for some more years. You have opportunities to manifest your highest ideals of freedom and innovation now. There are also opportunities to spiritualize your scientific and techno-logical knowledge - to use these things for higher purposes. Astrologers will take a more spiritual approach to their craft - as will astronomers and mathematicians. You also have opportunities to make spiritual types of friends.

The Spiritual Perspective. Much of what we say above applies here too. Science and the Divine Reality are not really in contradiction. Science is "one way" of knowing and understanding this reality. Scientific break throughs come from the Divine - and its intermedi-aries.

Transiting Neptune Sextile Neptune

A happy and long term transit, whether it is in the Natal or Solar Return Charts. Your now innate spirituality - your particular approach - is in synch with the spiritual energies, teachings and trends of the times. This will tend to bring opportunities to deepen these things - to joining spiritual type groups and organizations. Your highest ideals are in synch with the idealism of the times and thus have more possibility of manifestation.

The Spiritual Perspective. Much of what we say above applies here too. The spiritual nature is greatly strengthened now.

Transiting Neptune Sextile Pluto

A happy and long term transit. If this is to the Natal Horoscope, these trends have been going on for many, many years. This is a long term transit in the Solar Return too as you will tend to have this configuration for many more Solar Returns (and if you had it for a few past ones too.) The effect here is not "dramatic" but kind of gradual. Little by little, you discover that Higher Forces, Invisible Forces, are aiding you in your efforts at self transformation. The aid is offered, but it is up to you to take it and use it. Little by little your sex life and sexual attitudes are being elevated, spiritualized, raised up to a higher level. There are many opportunities to discover the spiritual aspects of sexuality. The partner will prosper now through spiritual means - through inner guidance, intuition, dreams and the counsel of astrologers, psychic, gurus, ministers and the like. The spiritual laws of affluence are offered to the spouse or partner - he or she will have the opportunity an encouragement to learn them and apply them. There will also be many opportunities for spiritual revelation on issues involving past lives, life after death and reincarnation.

The Spiritual Perspective. What we say above applies here too. Spirit is granting opportunity in all these areas - but you have free will to take it or leave it.

Transiting Neptune Sextile Ascendant

A happy and long term transit. In the Natal Chart this has been going on for some years now and will continue for some more years. In the Solar Return this transit is only in effect for the current year. You will have opportunities to refine and spiritualize the physical body - through meditation, yoga, tai chi and other spiritual regimes. There will also be many opportunities to glamorize the body and image and to make it more amenable to your will and mind. When you see view your body and personality from a Higher Level, you will have a clearer picture of it and be more able to make the desired changed. It is merely a thought form.

The Spiritual Perspective. Much of what we say above applies here. Spirit itself will create the proper image and keep the body in order if we let it. You seem more amenable to this now. Often we just need to "get out of its way".

Transiting Neptune Sextile Midheaven

A happy and long term transit. If this is to the Natal Chart its been going on for some years now and will continue for a few more years. In the Solar Return chart this is only in effect for the current year. You have opportunities and encouragement to further your career by joining spiritual groups, getting involved in idealistic causes, charities and ministries. The spiritual trends in the world are aiding your career aspirations. Psychics, astrologer, gurus, channels, and spiritually oriented people are aiding the career and have helpful guidance. Dreams and intuition are also very much involved with the career and life work and have much revelation for the native.

The Spiritual Perspective. There was never a time when you were not doing the will of the Divine. There was never a time when you were not fulfilling your spiritual mission. But now the Divine is granting opportunity to "consciously cooperate" with and "consciously understand" your mission.

TRANSITS OF PLUTO

Transits of Pluto, as with other other transits, must also be looked at in two different ways - from a mundane and from a spiritual perspective.

On the mundane level Pluto brings crisis - death or near death experiences. Encounters and brushes with death and dissolution. The mighty forces of the underworld are in contact with the affairs of life ruled by the planet that Pluto contacts. If there are vulnerabilities in these affairs - either on a structural or attitudinal level - rest assured that they will be revealed and the end result will be a correction in one way or another. He will bring transformation, transfiguration, and re-invention to any planet that he contacts.

Pluto's transits last a long time and so he does a thorough job.

Pluto rules estates, inheritance and other people's money. So he will bring these kinds of opportunities to any planet that he contacts. Thus if Pluto contacts Mercury, there can be an inheritance of intellectual property. If he contacts Venus the inheritance can be money, jewelry, or art objects and the like. If he contacts Jupiter the legacy will most likely be money.

Pluto rules taxes too. And if his transit impacts on a financial planet or House - tax issues will be important in the financial decisions making.

Pluto not only brings physical transformation, but also psychological transformation in the affairs of life governed by the planet.

The transformation that Pluto brings go deeper than the cosmetic changes of Venus or the breaking of barriers of Uranus - it brings deep, fundamental change. Pluto is not interested in covering an old face with makeup and lipstick. It wants to rebuild a whole new face.

Pluto rules sex, which is perhaps the greatest transforming power that we know. The sexual force creates new bodies - on various levels of existence, not just the physical. The sex force is very intense and penetrating - hence the association with Pluto. So any planet that Pluto contacts is going to become "sexier", filled with more libido than usual - and this can happen on various levels. If Pluto is contacting Mercury, the mind, the speech, the thought process becomes charged with sexual energy and power - the person's voice will radiate sex appeal. The thinking will be more on sex. The mind becomes a sexual organ as much as the actual organ.

On a spiritual level, Pluto is seen as the "renewer". He is the "resurrection flame". But before he can resurrect a given area of life, there has to be death. There is no resurrection without death. If we understand things deeper, we find that death doesn't really exist as we understand it. Only unreal things can die. That which was created by the Divine never dies - it only takes on new forms. A given masterpiece might die, but the principle of beauty never dies and will re-incarnate in another masterpiece. Only that which is unreal can die, and this is Pluto's function. He destroys the unreal and gives a new form to the essence. He rules death and rebirth.

Death and Birth are twins, linked at the hip. In truth we can never separate them. Whenever you see a birth, there is also a death. Whenever death occurs there is always a birth. When a soul incarnates on the Earth we say he is "born" but at the same time the soul incurred a spiritual death - it died as a spiritual being. When a person dies, he dies to the things of earth but is born as a spiritual being - he is like a baby in a new world. A year ends - it died. But simultaneously another year is born. The New Moon is death of an old lunar cycle and the birth of a new one. Some seers see death and birth happening every moment. An old "moment" dies, but a new "now" is born. Life is an eternal series of beginnings and endings - births and deaths.

So, from the spiritual perspective, Pluto is bringing death, but simultaneously bringing a new birth as well. For the new birth to happen, the old has to die.

Whenever you have creation, you also have destruction. If I build a new home, it means the destruction of trees, a certain landscape or form, and mineral and iron deposits within the earth. The natural wildlife of the area will be relocated.

So Pluto is really bringing resurrection and renewal to any area that he contacts - but one must be spiritually aware to handle the prelude - the death. Also Pluto will bring complete instructions on how one is to renew and resurrect the given area of life. He does the work, but he teaches, so that the spiritual person can be a conscious co-rebirther.

Pluto's forces are intense, deep and penetrating. Only masters who have already conquered death, can escape these forces. (They don't really escape them but channel them in proper ways.)

Transiting Pluto Conjunction Moon

A Neutral and long term transit if this is to the Natal Horoscope. In the Solar Return these trends are only in effect for the current year. In the Natal Horoscope these trends and energies have been going on for some years now and will continue for some more years. But now, because the transit is exact, the energies are most powerful. This transit is bringing emotional, family and domestic transformation into your life. And, this is happening on many, many levels. On the purely mundane level there will be moves or major renovations of the home. These are not cosmetic types of renovation either - but deep things. It can involve the tearing down of walls, the ripping up of pipes, plumbing and wiring - to be replaced with new materials. If you are a renter, the landlord might be doing these kinds of things. Sometimes (but many things can modify or deny this) there is a death in the family. This is a time for confronting the deepest of the deep emotional patterns and cleansing them. The emotional and overall psychic energies are very intense now. The voltage is high. A mere irritation can come out as tantrum or sound like anger to someone else. You often don't realize the intensity of the energy you project and will have to consciously work to soften it. Because of this intense psychic energy you are manifesting your desires very quickly. If these desires be good and in line with the Higher Self, this is a happy period. For you are pretty much having your way in life and at home. But if these desires be impure, you are manifesting those too - along with all the karma these bring. Very important now to keep the thoughts and emotions at their highest and most benign level. Violent feelings now can beget violent events (this always happens, but now much quicker.) Power urges will beget stormy power struggles. The most constructive use of the energy and power at your disposal is to go into deep introspection - to rid yourself of addictions (be they substance, food, or emotional patterns and behaviors) - you have a special power to do this now. This is a good period for depth psychology or depth meditation. You have the opportunity to be reborn again on the emotional level. During this period you will be made aware of the deepest origins of your moods and feelings. Memories of early childhood, long buried, will make themselves known. Unresolved issues will come up for resolution. You are doing a major emotional house cleaning these days. Just as physical impurities often collect in the body and then get discharged either through de-tox or what is called "sickness" (sickness is nothing more than nature's method of detoxing the body) so too the emotional nature can collect impurities - and these too get eliminated either through conscious de-toxification or through emotional "illnesses" that force these things to the surface. When you understand what's going on, you will be able to cooperate with the process and not be too alarmed. A discharging of impurities is taking place and on very deep levels. As this transit progresses you will see very clearly how you have created your own reality and circumstances and once this is seen, you can uncreate them and create something new and better and more to your liking. In a man's chart these dramas will probably objectify in the women in his life. In a woman's chart it will manifest in herself. Usually this transit brings an "emotional separation" from family members. This needn't be a break with the family (though this often happens) but relating to them in a different way and from a more conscious place in you. Emotional chains and bondages are being broken. Healthwise there is a need to give more attention to diet, the stomach and the breasts.

The Spiritual Perspective. You have always been a magician. You have always created your reality whether it be pleasing or unpleasing. But you did so unconsciously. Now you are to become conscious of it and exercise the power in a constructive way both for yourself and for others. You are no longer to be the "victim" of your moods and passions, but the director and controller of them - your rightful and true destiny.

Transiting Pluto Conjunction Sun

A Neutral and long term transit - this is so whether it occurs in the Natal or Solar Return Horoscope. (You will have this aspect in future Solar Returns and have probably had them in past ones.) Now, because the transit is most exact the energy is most intense. You have an intensity and power these days that is simply superhuman. You have a wonderful ability to focus on anything and achieve it. You are a star these days - getting your way in life (unless other factors are denying this) or focused on getting your way in life. You have a special ability to do what you really want to do without compromise. This is not a time for taking a job or choosing a career merely for money or convenience - but for the love of the thing in itself. Libido is very strong now. The opposite sex takes notice. Obstructions to your will and to the things that you love are being removed. Sometimes in dramatic ways. In many cases, because of this intense power, there are career changes. The native will either take a different approach to the present career or change it entirely. You are in no mood for compromise or consensus politics. You are a person of power and you are learning of this. (As the Centurion said " for I too am a man of authority, I say to one come and he comes, I say to one go and he goes..." Power struggles don't scare you these days and this brings about one of the challenges of this transit. You may be too quick to get involved in this when perhaps there are other ways to achieve the same end. This transit can bring a death of a male in your life or a near death experience - but many, many other things in the Horoscope can deny this. But certainly you are confronting death more - either psychologically, or in your career and aspirations. The fear of death has prevented you from doing many things that you love to do - it has obstructed the true desire of your heart - and so it must be dealt with. If you are sure of what you want in life, this is the time to go for it.

The Spiritual Perspective. This is a time for rooting out of the ego any impurities, false concepts, false identifications. A time for identifying with who you really are and who you have always been - an immortal being of light, untrammeled, free, living in Divine Ease and fulfilling your destiny.

Transiting Pluto Conjunction Mercury

A Neutral and very long term transit. This has been in effect for many years and will continue to be in effect for many more. This is a time for completely transforming your intellectual life, your mental interests, your thinking, rationality and communication abilities. The mind is being transformed and renewed. But before the renewal, the rebirth, can occur, the old has to die - and this is what is going on. Old logic, old ideas, old ways of communicating are being rooted out and dying. These will be replaced by new and better ones. It is a painstaking process that requires time. This is a time when your intellectual faculties are becoming more powerful. You have good ability to concentrate and learn. The mind is being deepened. Your intellectual interests will be pruned and you will focus only on those that are really important. You will learn less subjects, but penetrate more deeply into the subjects that you do study. Your mind is like a laser beam now. You have the power to sway masses of people with your ideas and communication. Your words can be very cutting these days - you need to be careful about this. Though you may not realize it, they have a tremendous impact on others. Keep thoughts and words positive and constructive. Better not to talk at all, than to say something hurtful or negative. You must use your mind the way the surgeon uses the scalpel, to cut away error, but not to harm either yourself or others. You can focus on the error, but not the person. You speak with zeal and enthusiasm. You are a better orator and public speaker. You are learning about the tremendous power of the mind.

The Spiritual Perspective. What we say above applies here too. Your new dept and penetration enables you to see mental errors and to correct them. The intellect is getting a major "cosmic detox" now and all the phenomena described above are just side effects. The mind is a wonderful servant, but not a good master, but to be a good servant it needs to be purified of error.

Transiting Pluto Conjunction Venus

A Neutral but very long term transit. This has been going on for many years and will continue for many more. A current love relationship will die and be reborn - or another will be reborn in its place. By the time this transit is over your whole love and social situation (including friendships) will be radically different. It will be in the image and likeness of your ideal. You are suffering the birth pangs of a new love and social life - and birth pangs can be painful. Love feelings are unusually intense. Love passions are so intense that the highs are unusually high. You experience levels of passion you never experienced before. Love passions are so high that you are willing to sacrifice all for it. Lukewarm, tepid, half hearted love is not for you. You want a love that consumes your whole being - that occupies all your faculties. You want to be dominated by love almost to the exclusion of all other interests. This love intensity must not be allowed to go negative. If it does, there will be jealousy, possessiveness, and even the desire to commit crimes of passion in the name of love. It can lead to all kinds of bizarre and pathological behavior. Artists will have the ability to sway (and reach) masses of people these days with their art. Art is a real power as you learn. There is a need now - a very pressing need - to purify your concepts about love. Love itself is never a problem, but the impurities in love are - and these will be revealed very graphically now.

The Spiritual Perspective. Your love and artistic nature is getting a major cosmic detox these days. The end result is to give birth to the love life that you dream of - to the relationships that you dream of. Much of what you are feeling are the "labor pains" that accompany every new birth. Your love energy is so strong now that you will "get whomever you go after" - but you will also experience the consequences of this. There is no other way to give birth to the True Love Life except that way. A few mistakes will teach wisdom. Better choices will be made in the future.

Transiting Pluto Conjunction Mars

A Neutral but very powerful and dynamic aspect. It must be handled "just so". Both of these forces are not things to be trifled with. If this transit is to the Natal Chart it has been going on for many years now and will continue for many more. If this is to the Solar Return Chart it is only in effect for the coming year. The physical energy, the testosterone levels, libido and passions are greatly intensified now. The sexual drive and needs are magnified. And, different people will resolve this in different ways. The temper needs watching these days as you want what you when you want it and are not likely to look kindly at any interference or thwarting of your will. In a woman's chart she will feel this energy from the men in her life. This intense energy gives the drive to achieve almost any objective in life. There is power to penetrate or eliminate any obstacle that stands in one's way. The native will not shirk war or conflict. And, probably there will be many conflicts these days. When things don't happen on schedule or are delayed there are feelings of frustration and anger - and this can lead to conflicts. There is a need to be more tolerant of these things and of other people. Athletes will perform much better these days - there is a one pointed concentration on their athletic prowess and performance. But over intensity - trying too hard - can lead to excess or injury (when the aspects get negative). The native has an uncanny ability to get his or her way either by direct action or through guile. Many are undergoing a transformation of their sexual lives - changing their sexual attitudes and mores. The inner warrior is powerful these days, but needs to be kept in check - in right alignment with what is right. We all fight wars in our lives, but the winners are the ones who fight the "just war" with the right kind of weapons. In many cases there will be a need to confront death - either in a physical way or psychological way. Whether the confrontation with death is physical or psychological depends on many other things in the Horoscope - noone need actually die. The overall energy levels are greatly enhanced and this brings both opportunity and challenge. An accident with a small compact car that can't travel too fast is not pleasant, but survivable. An accident with a jet plane capable of traveling 500 miles an hour, is much more serious. Your extra power can create extra problems for you if it is abused. All of this extra energy must be channeled to constructive and positive causes. If it turns negative this energy is capable of great destruction.

The Spiritual Perspective. Much of what we say above applies here too. The sexual energy, libido, and physical energies are undergoing a cosmic detox. Anyone who has undergone any kind of detox knows that in the process pathologies and impurities are washed out of the system. They are brought up to consciousness, re-experienced, and then flushed out. Since these energies are very dynamic, it is important to understand what is going on.

Transiting Pluto Conjunction Jupiter

A Neutral and long term transit. In the Natal Horoscope these trends have been going on for some years now and will continue for some more years. But now, since the aspect is exact, the energies are most intense. If this transit is to the Solar Return, the trend is only in effect for the current year. Pluto, the transforming power of the cosmos is now working on your financial life, wealth concepts, earning power, religious and philosophical beliefs, and your personal world view. On the financial level, wealth should be increasing. You have access to outside capital, outside resources, outside investors who are supporting your financial goals. The danger here is that you could feel "under pressure" from these forces - feel a need to perform beyond expectations - make decisions based on these pressures that you ordinarily wouldn't make. This financial intensity often leads to a "boom or bust" mentality. If other aspects and transits support, these pressures lead to "large success" - a larger than life manifestation. It brings both personal wealth and wealth to the shareholders and partners. If other aspects are stressful to this transit - it can lead to "bust" and even bankruptcy. But even these need not be feared, for Pluto is the planet of "renewal" and "regeneration". If financial attitudes have been amiss, the mistakes will be revealed - the lumps taken - and the stage set for a "renewal". Death is never the final chapter. After death, comes rebirth and renewal. After the crucifixion comes the resurrection. This is a time for doing in depth analysis of the wealth concepts, the philosophy of wealth, and the actions you take because of these beliefs - such introspection is very much worthwhile as it can spare a person from gratuitous financial shock and suffering. It is a time for getting financially healthier, by cutting costs, eliminating waste and eliminating unnecessary desires and financial addictions. It is time for a "detox" in the financial life and attitudes. This discussion is also valid for your religious and philosophical beliefs as well. Your personal religion and religious beliefs - your personal metaphysics and world view - is getting purified these days. Though this can be painful sometimes, it is a very good thing. In the end nothing has a more profound impact on life and on behavior, than our personal religion - our religious beliefs. So, this is a time for greater interest in religion and philosophy - for pondering these things - for going deeply into them. Often (and we have seen this graphically on September 11, 2001) the difference between heaven and hell, harmony and strife, health or disease, wealth or poverty - is merely a philosophical concept - an interpretation of scripture, or an interpretation of an event. So paying attention to your "invisible metaphysics" will bring great rewards. Many natives under this aspect will have "born again" experiences. They will rediscover their religion. Others will break with their religions and be 'born again" in another path. Others may have the urge to become religious reformers. This is all case by case. This is also a time for pondering the "meaning" of your life and embarking on a life (and financial path) that is meaningful to you. Philosophical conflicts can be very intense during this transit - and, while some of this is natural and unavoidable - it is best to minimize these things. Religious reform - personal or universal - is seldom accomplished by argument or coercion. Interior revelation is the most effective way. This transit will also have many other meanings for you, but these will depend on the specific rulerships of Pluto and Jupiter in your chart. This is something best discussed verbally - with your personal astrologer.

The Spiritual Perspective. What we say above applies here too.

Transiting Pluto Conjunction Saturn

A very difficult and long term transit. You've been feeling the effects of this for many years now, but now it is most intense. Healthwise you need to give more attention to your spine, knees, teeth and skeletal alignment. You feel as if your world is coming apart. The order and reality that you lived with for so many years seems to be crumbling and changing. What will take its place? What you thought of as "Eternal Verities" are neither "eternal" nor "verities". You feel insecure and uncertain about things. If you are centered in Spirit and cling to those kinds of "verities" this transit will be a breeze, for spiritual verities never change. But if you were resting on the verities of materialism or government or corporate culture verities - the earth is shaking and quaking beneath you. Those kinds of verities are only "specifics" for a time and were not meant to be forever. These are being transformed and changed. The pillars of your reality are being challenged. This aspect also has many personal implications. The way you manage, order, control your life is changing. You are changing your management style. You are entering a personal "new order". If you are a parent, teacher, boss - someone in authority - you are experiencing much rebellion to your authority. In many cases, because of your insecurity, you are "over controlling" and this leads to rebellion. This will force you to re-think, re-tool, and re-invent your sense of authority and order. Overcoming insecurity and fear is your major challenge now. In many cases this aspect shows the death of a parent, elder or authority figure in the life - but other things in the Horoscope need to confirm this. In many cases it is also showing career changes too - often uncomfortable.

The Spiritual Perspective. Much of what we say above applies here too. A cosmic detox is going on in your sense of order and reality - on the very foundations upon which you base your life. Your "personal order and routine" is getting detoxed too. So all the phenomena described above is just a side effect of this.

Transiting Pluto Conjunction Uranus

A Neutral and long term transit. On the one hand it creates an almost fanatical - zealous and passionate - desire for personal freedom. Those who have been stuck in routines - in steady, humdrum jobs or humdrum relationships - will certainly chafe under this transit and most likely will do anything to break out of these things. The native is more inclined to rebel, to upset the status quo, under this transit. The good thing here is that this transit will certainly lead to greater personal freedom and a more exciting life. The native will draw on his or her inventiveness, creativity and originality to support this freedom. There are many ways to live life, to earn money, to govern a relationship - and the native wants to explore them all and then make a choice. The down side here, is that the native will desire NO obligations, no personal restrictions whatsoever - the urge for personal freedom can be overdone - and this can be unrealistic both in life and in love. So a fine line has to be drawn. The native should seek maximum personal freedom that is consistent with the rights of others. Revolutionary causes will become very attractive these days - but again, these causes need to be examined on a deeper level. Are they truly superior? Or are they merely arguing for change for the sake of change? There will be more sexual experimentation under this transit than normal - and as long as it is constructive it is wonderful. Often the native will travel for the sake of travel - and not so much because there is any real, organic, need for it. There is great restlessness in the nature these days. Those of scientific bent - high tech people, mathematicians, astrologers and astronomers - will make important breakthroughs under this transit - their understanding of science, of their own fields, will be deepened. Many - no matter the field of their expertise - will feel that being original and unique - is the most important thing these days. Many will overdo this, and just adopt eccentric behaviors, to show their originality. Some, who are truly being original (thinking from the "Origin") will be perceived as "eccentric" by others. But the native is unlikely to care about this.

The Spiritual Perspective. There is a strong spiritual message in this transit. There is a need to examine one's notions of freedom, equality etc - to go deeply into them. To weed out the notions that are untrue (merely platitudes with emotional force behind them) from the true ones. What is real freedom? Is it merely doing what you want to do? Or is it something deeper? Is the indulgence of the lower self real freedom or another form of bondage? Is there any true freedom outside the Will of the Higher Power? These are thoughts to ponder.

Transiting Pluto Conjunction Neptune

A Neutral and long term transit. For those on a spiritual path, this is a time for great spiritual breakthroughs. There is a lust, a passion, a focus on the spirit that guarantees success eventually. Zeal and passion is a prerequisite for spiritual success. The desire for spirit and spirit only, must be one- pointed. And, this is what is happening these days. The lukewarm rarely make it to heaven. The path is arduous, filled with dangers and obstructions, and thus the zealous and passionate ones are the only ones with the "juice" to overcome these things. Interestingly, once the breakthroughs to Higher Consciousness are made, there will be a "death" to previously held spiritual concepts and attitudes. It is like the child who reads books on sex - or hears tales about the wonders of sex. He or she forms concepts about it, which by their nature can never be completely true. But then, at the right time, the child grows up and actually experiences sex. Then he or she truly understands what it is. The notions and concepts are now understood - but discarded. The experience itself transcended the concept. So it is with the spirit. For those not on a spiritual path, there will be a desire to embark on one. Spiritual disciplines such as meditation, mantra, prayer, fasting etc. hold more allure - also there is a greater ability to master these disciplines. So this transit is an opportunity to embark on a serious path. Others will be more inclined to get involved (and in a passionate and zealous way) with idealistic world causes. And though the motives are probably good - a desire to end some form of suffering in the world - the fanaticism can be dangerous - can lead to conflict and even violence. These things only perpetuate more suffering. There is a danger of becoming like a religious fanatic (but in the name of some holy cause) and unconsciously push one's ideals on others in coercive ways. Younger souls can be more prone to addictions such as alcohol and drugs these days. The psychic faculties are enhanced under this transit - basically a wonderful thing - but one must be trained and pure enough to handle one's visions. Psychism without the spirit can be a very painful thing. This is a time for reviewing one's spiritual ideals and separating the wheat from the chaff.

The Spiritual Perspective. Much of what we say above applies here. The spirituality, the spiritual ideals, the intuition, the path, are all getting a detox. Like any power or urge in life, whether it be sex, an appetite, the mental nature etc., the essence is good and holy. But impurities have crept in and so these get detoxed. The wheat get separated from the chaff.

Transiting Pluto Conjunction Pluto

A Neutral transit. In the Natal Chart this aspect doesn't happen in a person's lifetime. Sometimes it happens in early life, but is not significant as it only reinforces the Natal tendencies. This aspect will often happen in the Solar Return but again it is not significant as it will only reinforce the tendencies of the Solar Return.

Transiting Pluto Conjunction Ascendant

A Neutral and long term transit. If this is to the Natal Chart, these trends have been going on for many years now and will continue for many more years. Now, it is at its most intense. If this is to the Solar Return, it is only in effect for the current year. Personal magnetism and personal force is unusually high. The sex appeal is great. You see through others and situations. Psychic abilities are very much increased. You are in a long term period of transformation of the body and personal appearance. Different people will take different routes to this end - some will undertake cosmetic surgery. Others, will transform the body through diet, yoga, exercise and detox regimes. But the central desire is to reform the body and image on a deep level - not just cosmetically. This is a period for giving birth to the "new you" - the "you that you desire to be " - the "ideal you". Of course, none of this can happen if you don't also change your self concept - and redefine your personality. So these re-definitions are also happening. By the time this transit is over with your body and image WILL be radically transformed.

The Spiritual Perspective. Much of what we say above applies here too. A detox of the body, the image and the self concept is happening. You are giving birth to your "ideal self" and there are labor pains involved.

Transiting Pluto Conjunction Midheaven

A Neutral and long term transit if this is to the Natal Horoscope. If this is to the Solar Return these trends are only valid for the current year. If this is to the Natal these trends have been going on for some years now and will continue for some more years - but now the energy is most intense. This transit brings major transformation to the career and the lifework. It will bring a career crisis that will force tough decisions. The native will either stay in the present career, but pursue it in a whole different way, or actually change the career path. But there are many good things that will happen here and many scenarios of how these changes will come about. In some cases the native will attain the career objectives (for this transit amplifies the ambitions, and gives an almost fanatical desire for outer success) and then look for new worlds to conquer. Or, he or she may find, that the so-called success that was lusted for is not all it was cracked up to be, and doesn't satisfy - thus the change. Sometimes the death of an industry or company that one works for changes the career path. Often, this transit shows the death or near death of a parent or parent figure - but many other things in the chart can modify this. The desire for career success under this transit, can be likened to sexual desire. It is lustful, one pointed, and can be obsessive. Though this makes success more likely, if overdone can create karmic conse-quences that are not pleasant. The native will attain to career success as much by guile as by sheer energy. In general, all the things that come under Pluto's dominion - sex, debt, taxes, wills and estates, insurance claims, making money for others, personal reinvention, outside investors, life after death, will become more prominent in the life these days. They become "high priorities".

The Spiritual Perspective. Spiritually, this is a time to purify the ambitions and the life work - to think deeply about one's dharma (mission in life, and reason for the incarnation) and then about how to do it. In truth, as one ponders these things, he or she will be led to the revelation that there is one and only one "business" in life - "the Father's Business" - and we are supposed to be about that and nothing else. Such a revelation will surely cause a "death" to much or our career thinking. In one fell swoop, the egoic mind, with its plots, stratagems, ploys and manipulations is silenced - struck dumb. Not only are its efforts extraneous and beside the point, but they are often actual obstructions to the true business of life. Inner silence will guide us more truly to the True Career than any plans hatched by the mind of a mortal.

Transiting Pluto Square Moon

A difficult and long term transit. If this transit is to the Natal Chart it has been in effect for many years - and will continue to be in effect for some more years. If this is in the Solar Return, it is only in effect for the current year. Often this shows a death in the family - though other factors in the Horoscope can deny this. But even if there isn't a "literal" death, there is major emotional and domestic change. You are engaged in "disengaging" from the family, from a current domestic situation, and from deep emotional and psychological patterns. It is an excellent period for deep psychological therapy, as very deep elements in the subconscious are surfacing now so that you can understand them and remove them. There is a purging going on in the unconscious. The dream life can be very troubled these days. The emotional passions are strong. Tempers can be high. Sexual and financial issues can disturb the domestic tranquillity. Often this transit brings major repairs in the home - or major renovations (not just cosmetic) - and these come as the result of crisis - not in a smooth and planned way. Though you might be separating from family members now, this need not be permanent - it is a separation on one level so that you can relate with them on a higher and better level. Healthwise the stomach and breasts need more attention. It is a period for dealing with the dirty laundry in the subconscious and in your past - and dirty laundry is not a pleasant task. Its something that needs to be done though and the end result will be good.

The Spiritual Perspective. Much of what we say above applies here too. The pain that many of you are experiencing is not punitive - it is the cosmic goad that forces you to change your emotional patterns. Few of us make these kinds of changes unless we are forced to through pain and suffering. But for the spiritual person there need be none of these things. There might be some pain - but not suffering. Pain and suffering are two different things. When one understands what is going on - a complete emotional re-birth and renewal - there is no suffering. The pain is seen as the "pangs of childbirth" - labor pains. We know that the end result will be something beautiful and we endure. Also, we can get a new glimpse of the "underworld" forces in Nature and in the world. On the surface they seem terrible - but they too are instruments of a Cosmic Plan - they do the heavy lifting, the "dirty work".

Transiting Pluto Square Sun

A difficult and long term transit. This transit has been in effect for many years and will be in effect for many more years. The effects of this transit will happen (and have been happening) as a process and not all at once. Your sense of who you are - your true will and life urges - the way that you like to shine - are all undergoing deep - and perhaps painful - transformation. Often this transit produces career changes as you go deeper into what you really want to do in life. Sexuality can be overdone or underdone. If you are not "grown up" this transit will force it. And, if you are old beyond your years this transit will lead you to your inner child. In many cases there is a near death experience - or the native is somehow touched by death - that causes a re-evaluation and change in the life pattern and goals. One feels one's "mortality" these days and thus must come to grips with it. One has many "death and rebirth" experiences. Love affairs now can be tested. The personal creativity will undergo radical - perhaps painful - change. Often this transit produces an intense power struggle or ego conflict which roots out old and effete patterns. One's light and will comes under attack from "underground" or "underworld" forces. There are powerful challenges to one's authority. The true hero will conquer - but with work and difficulty. This struggle can unduly deplete the vitality - and can be overdone. Healthwise more care needs to be given to the heart.

The Spiritual Perspective. Your innate, inborn "star quality" (and everyone has this) is getting detoxed these days. Probably this process is unpleasant now as old memories, old experiences or false ideas are flushed to the surface. The ego and self esteem are challenged as part of the process. Since your true "I Am" can never be challenged, these challenges are happening to your "notions of I Am" - on the conceptual level. A true and better "I Am" is being born and you are experiencing some of the labor pains. By the way this is a good yardstick by which to measure things. If it can be challenged or opposed - if it can die - then it is not who you really are. Personal creativity is also challenged this period - also with the same intent. Your attitude to creativity and to children - your notions about "the joy of life" - are all getting detoxed and new and better attitudes are being born.

Transiting Pluto Square Mercury

A difficult and long term transit. In the Natal Horoscope this aspect has been in effect for many years - and will continue to be in effect for some more years. In the Solar Return Horoscope, these trends are only in effect for the current year. Old ideas, old ways of thinking, old concepts are being transformed, reformed and changed the "hard way" - through conflict, argument and debate. Powerful forces are arrayed against your ideas and logical process. Only what is true and real will remain. Intellectual interests are in conflict with sexual interests. Your ideas are subjected to minute and intense scrutiny - much of it unflattering. Your speech and your writings can arouse deep and underground forces. If you are not careful with your speech you can actually arouse violence. This is a time for deepening the thought process and ideas and for clearing yourself of mental and intellectual debris. Healthwise there is a need to give more attention to the nervous system, the lungs, intestines, arms and shoulders.

The Spiritual Perspective. Your ideas and thought processes have needed transformation for a long time, but this is a difficult process and few undertake it unless they are goaded into it. So now, the Divine supplies the goad - the push - the motivation. What is happening now is "be thou renewed by the renewing power of the mind". Transformation begins in the mind first. Its effects will be felt in the body and in many other areas of life. But we begin in the mind. The mind will die and be reborn under this transit. Pluto knows how to do this. Anything that makes for a lie will be removed. Your intellect and thought process are undergoing a cosmic "detox".

Transiting Pluto Square Venus

A difficult and long term transit. This aspect has been in effect for many years - and will continue to be in effect for some more years. Generally, unless other transits help, this shows the end of an important love relationship, marriage or friendship. Sometimes this shows the actual death of a lover, spouse or friend - but many other things in the Horoscope can deny this. Your love attitudes, your sense of beauty and aesthetics, comes under intense and powerful attack. You begin to see that "taste" is a personal thing and not everyone is going to agree with you. Artistic creations also undergo much criticism and attack. The purpose of this transit is not to cause pain or harm. The cosmos doesn't intend for you to be lonely or friendless, but it is transforming and reforming your love and social attitudes - the "hard way" - through conflict. By the time this transit is over (in a number of years) you will have new love and social attitudes - and probably better ones. Love passions are running high these days and can often turn negative. The impurities in your love life or relationship are graphically seen.

The Spiritual Perspective. Much of what we say above applies here. Your love nature and relationships have long needed a detox - but perhaps you procrastinated as it can often be hard work and sometimes unpleasant. Now the Divine "forces" you into it, through some unpleasant experiences. A death and rebirth experience is happening in your love life and relationships. This whole area of life is going to be so different as to be like a "new thing".

Transiting Pluto Square Mars

A difficult and long term transit if this is to the Natal Chart. If this is to the Solar Return it is only in effect this year. In the Natal Chart these trends and tendencies have been going on for many years and will continue for some more years - now they are at their greatest intensity. You are fighting a war these days and you're not sure who the real enemy is, as he, she or they are hidden. Your courage is being tested under fire. You are coming face to face with survival issues. Libido is expressing in an unbalanced way - either too much or too little. Difficult to keep it in balance. If other things in the chart confirm, there are tendencies to surgeries. Athletes are either trying too hard or not enough and can be more injury prone these days. Tempers are more likely to flare both within yourself and others and there is a great need to cool things down. Passions are intense and prone to get out of hand if you're not careful. The sexuality is getting transformed and changed - the ultimate result is good - but the process is uncomfortable. Violent tendencies need to be kept in check as they will almost certainly invite violence in return - and right quickly too.

The Spiritual Perspective. What we say above applies here too. The challenge is staying in unconditional love and the practice of forgiveness. Vengefulness and spite are great spiritual dangers. If force needs to be used, it must be from a loving and "wise" space and must be used "surgically" - with great measurement.

Transiting Pluto Square Jupiter

A difficult and long term transit. This transit has been going on for many years and will continue for many more years. Short term transits in the interim will either make this transit stronger or modify it. Basically two important areas of life are being effected - finance and personal philosophy and religion. A transformation is going on in your financial life. Wealth attitudes and practices are being severely tested. Your urge to expand meets with powerful and "underground" (difficult to detect) forces. Perhaps there is a financial crisis. Some people teeter on the verge of bankruptcy (though other things in the Horoscope can modify this.) You want to expand your business, but find it difficult to raise outside capital or borrow for this. You could be forced to borrow in unfavorable ways and pay a steep price for these borrowings. Debt is a problem. There could be financial losses. There is an unpleasant need to "downsize", cut back, cut costs and eliminate waste. The whole purpose of this transit is to bring up hidden flaws in your wealth attitudes or practices so that you can recognize them and then eliminate them. So long as they were underground you were helpless - now that they surface you can do something about it. Crisis, though unpleasant, is not the bad thing that many think. It forces necessary change. Often it is the answer to prayer - deeply disguised. It is the doorway to greater wealth. The same kinds of things are happening to your religious and philosophical beliefs. Your deeply held beliefs - your personal view of life and with world - comes under intense attack. There is a danger of religious fanaticism these days. Perhaps your personal fanaticism (which you didn't know existed) brings out the fanaticism of others. There is a crisis of faith. Your religious and philosophical beliefs are being transformed. What is true about them will remain, but the rubbish will be eliminated. Only pure gold can withstand the fires of the furnace. If you personally cooperate with these processes - with a view towards unearthing errors and then eliminating them - the various crises will be less severe. There will be no need for them. If they come you will be well able to handle them.

The Spiritual Perspective. Much of what we say above applies here as well. Financial attitudes, religious and philosophical beliefs are in need of detox and cleansing. You probably would have neglected doing these things unless the cosmos pushed you - in the form of crisis. So now you are doing what has long needed to be done.

Transiting Pluto Square Saturn

A difficult and long term transit. This is so whether it is in the Natal or Solar Return Chart. Your notions of reality, stability, order - your bedrock values - the values upon which you base your life - are being challenged now. Is your sense of reality correct? You will have opportunity to find out now. While this transit is going on there are apt to be feelings of great insecurity. You made plans based on certain assumptions of reality, which assumptions are no longer true - or perhaps only partially true. Your sense of reality is being changed - perhaps the hard way - through the school of hard knocks. Often this transit shows the demise of a parent, authority figure or authority structure in your life - but other things in the chart could deny this. Though this process could be uncomfortable, the end result will be good. Spirit wants to destroy old structures, thought forms, and orders so that something new and better can replace them. If the native is in authority - a parent, executive or government official - there will be rebellion against it - there will be challenges to it. The management style, the way the native sets limits and discipline, will get purified. You are literally creating a "New Order for the Ages". On a health level more attention needs to be given to the spine, knees, teeth and overall skeletal alignment.

The Spiritual Perspective. Much of what we say applies here. Your sense of right order is getting a healthy "detox" and all that makes for a lie will be removed. Perhaps you thought that the right way to order your day (or week) was "such and such". The Divine will reveal a better way. "Such and Such" gets changed by events that you cannot ignore. A good meditation now is "not my order, but thy order, thy process, be done."

Transiting Pluto Square Uranus

A difficult and long term aspect. If this is to the Natal Chart, these energies and trends have been going on for some years now and will continue for some more years. In the Solar Return Chart this transit is only valid for the current year. This is a period where friendships get tested. Many friendships have gone down the tubes these past few years. New friends are coming into the picture, to be sure, but the process could have been painful. There is the actual death of friends, or friends are having near death kinds of experiences - surgeries and the like. The social life is getting transformed. A new "picture" is manifesting in your life and the new picture is a good one - but the process of the manifestation can be difficult. Be patient now. The stage is being set for a whole new set of friends. Your freedom urges are also being obstructed and opposed - perhaps by secret forces -forces unknown to you. You feel an inner sense of obstruction and bondage. You can't fully express your freedom, originality and new ideas. Often, unbeknownst to you, your innovations could be harmful to others - to entrenched financial or political interests - hence the secret opposition. Use this conflict to further refine your innovations, inventions, and freedom urges. Ideas can sound good on paper or in our minds, but we never know how good they really are until they are faced with adverse conditions. Good innovations are able to handle these things. Poorly thought out ones, can't. Perhaps an innovation or invention you had was shot down these past few years. Perhaps the innovation was really unworkable, but more likely it merely needs more refining and retooling. Many, under this transit, are afraid to express their originality or freedom because of sexual fears - their sex life binds them to present conditions. Sexual experimentation is more likely now - but be sure to keep it constructive and non harmful.

The Spiritual Perspective. Much of what we say above applies here too. Your scientific mind - your scientific ideas - are getting a healthy detox. Much of your science will have to be revised - perhaps because of new discoveries or new revelation. Your innovations and inventions are getting detoxed and purified as well. The problems and stress are coming from your resistance to the change and the attachments to old science. Sometimes this manifests as the "death of old equipment", and you are forced to upgrade to new and better equipment. Your friendships are getting a healthy detox as well. Probably this should have been done long ago and you procrastinated, but now you can't - you must deal with these issues.

Transiting Pluto Square Neptune

A difficult and long term transit. This is so whether it is in the Natal or Solar Return Horoscope. (You have had this aspect in past Solar Returns and will undoubtedly have them in future ones too.) Your spirituality, spiritual ideals, intuitive guidance, spiritual regime is under attack by deep and powerful forces. All of these areas are being transformed into something better, higher and finer - but the process can be uncomfortable. There are many scenarios as to what will happen, and because this transit goes for so many years, it is likely that you will experience a little of all the scenarios. Though it is uncomfortable, the end result will be very good. Perhaps your spirituality and spiritual regime is being mocked or undermined. Perhaps it is attacked. Perhaps you are shown how far you are from being able to practice your ideals. But rejoice in these things, for when you are attacked in "My Name" - for "My Name's Sake" - there is great blessing in this. If you are on the correct spiritual path, this is a period for gaining strength in your meditative practice - for deepening it. You are like the athlete in training. The rigors of the practice - especially the unfavorable conditions - build the muscles.

You must persist. If your ideals are amiss, askew, based on false assumptions, or if your understanding is incomplete - you will find out about this now. For the fire of opposition is also a purifying fire - you will see the errors and be able to make corrections. Your intuition will get tested in the fire too. If you have been merely following animal gut instincts and calling it intuition, you will see it now. It is also likely that your taste in the fine arts is coming under attack - what you think is beautiful and inspired - is not considered so by prevailing trends. It is good to see that others can have different opinions and different tastes and that yours is not the end all and be all. Those who are creative artists might find that their creations don't meet with universal favor. And this too is healthy. Mystics and spiritual channels will find more resistance to their channelings at this time. Be not dismayed. If the channelings are true, they will survive the onslaught - which is only temporary. Time will reveal their correctness. On a health level this is a time for taking better care of the feet. This is a time for transforming your notions of spirituality and for deepening your already existing practice.

The Spiritual Perspective. All that we say above applies here too. Your spirituality (your attitudes, beliefs, orientation, and especially the spiritual faculties) is getting a good, healthy cosmic detox. Since, eventually, the spiritual faculties will have to be so good that life and death decisions - both personal and for others - will be based on this - this detox, though unpleasant - is a good thing. Real and true spiritual experience will be the "de-toxifier" now. The child reads books about sex and forms all kinds of concepts. Then the child grows up and actually experiences it - and he or she can dispense with the books and the concepts - none of them can really describe what it is. The concept dies and reality takes its place. A similar process is happening in the spiritual life now.

Transiting Pluto Square Pluto

A difficult and long term transit. This transit can only occur to your

Natal chart and has been going on for many years now. It will continue for some more years - but now it is most intense. Your normal sexuality is out of synch with the sexual styles of the period. The way you transform and regenerate yourself is out of synch with the current styles and methods of transformation. Similarly with your occult or deep psychological interests. Often the native is locked into a psychological struggle of some sort - an underground struggle with opponents that are just as willful and determined as the native.

The Spiritual Perspective. Here we see a curious phenomena - the way you transform yourself and others - your notions of alchemy - are themselves being transformed. Impurities, misunderstandings and errors are revealed so that you can take corrective action. The sexual nature - it urges and attitudes - are also being cleansed and alchemicalized - something that needed to be done for a long time, but now the Divine supplies the goad and the impetus for it.

Transiting Pluto Square Ascendant

A difficult and long term transit if this is to the Natal chart. In the Solar Return this transit is only in effect for the current year. In the Natal chart these trends have been going on for some years now and will continue for some more years. Now, because it is exact, the energies are most intense. Change and transformation are happening in your image, body, personal appearance and relation-ships. Your self concept is changing and this automatically changes your relationships. The body is probably getting "detoxed" these days. Best if you do it voluntarily and in a way that you control. The desire here is to re- invent the image - and this is good. But the path to this can be stormy. Some opt for cosmetic types of surgery under this transit - but more care is needed and more homework. Deep transformation - true renewal - is generally a messy business but the end result is good. So be patient and know that your physical and social trials are leading to a new birth. In order to revamp a house it is often necessary to tear out old wiring and plumbing - sometimes to tear down walls. While it is unsightly and perhaps unpleasant, it is the preliminary to the beautiful end result. So it is with you. Self esteem and self confidence could be better these days too - but other factors in the chart can modify this.

The Spiritual Perspective. Much of what we say above, applies here too. The body and image have needed a "renewal" for a long time, but perhaps you procrastinated. So, now, the Divine supplies the impetus - probably through some unpleasant types of experience. You have no choice. You have to "restore and rebuild" the Holy Temple.

Transiting Pluto Square Midheaven

A difficult and long term transit. If this is to the Natal it has been going on for some years now and will continue for some more years - right now it is most intense though. In the Solar Return this is only in effect for the current year. Your career, job and career aspirations are undergoing major transformation - and perhaps in unpleasant and shocking ways. Perhaps you are too attached to your current career path - perhaps out of fear or insecurity. It could be that you need to be doing something different and much happier for you, but you are afraid to let go. So the Cosmos, through its various instrumentalities, has to pry you loose. You are forced to consider worst case scenarios in the career situation (and perhaps in your relations with elders, authority figures and the government). In many cases there is change of the career path. In many cases, the native pursues the same career but from a different inner place and in a new way. Bosses, elders, and perhaps a parent are removed from the scene - this doesn't have to happen by death, but it could be in another ways - ways that are like a death. A friendly boss or mentor is forced out and now a new one comes in. A parent moves far away and is not as available as before. In general there is a "death and rebirth" experience in the career.

The Spiritual Perspective. Your sense of your "mission in life" has needed a detox for some time and now the Divine "forces the issue". Impurities will be purged from this area of life and generally this is unpleasant. It is often shocking to see what we've been harboring about ourselves in this area. But though the process isn't comfortable, the end result will be very good. You will have a clearer sense of your Dharma, and a clearer path to it.

Transiting Pluto Opposition Moon

A difficult and long term transit - especially if this is to the Natal Horoscope. These trends have been going on for some years now and will continue for some more years - only now, the energies are most intense. If this is to the Solar Return, this transit is only in effect for the current year. Major transformations - deep and radical - are happening in the home, with the family, the domestic pattern and on the emotional level. And these are probably not pleasant, though ultimately it will be good. There is an emotional separation from family members. Sometimes (though other things in the chart can deny this) there is a death in the family. Often there is a move that isn't comfortable. Sometimes there are major repairs and renovations going on in the physical home, and these are not going smoothly either - they interfere with normal living habits and patterns. In a man's chart it often shows a death or near death experience involving the women in his life. In a woman's chart, it can show a near death experience on a personal level - or a need to confront death and death issues on a psychological level. The cosmos will so arrange things that death and death issues will have to be confronted and dealt with. In a woman's chart, it will often show a detox of the body and major changes in the physical image and appearance. She will have a "born again" experience. On a spiritual level, emotional habit patterns, addictions and attachments are being broken and transformed, and the psyche is being "renewed and reborn". As this process continues it leads to profound changes in the home, domestic and family pattern as a matter of course. The new domestic, family and emotional pattern that is being born - perhaps through much labor pains - will be something radically new - more in line with the "true desire of the heart" - almost unrecognizable. Now these things don't happen overnight - but gradually as a process. Pluto works very slowly - but very thoroughly. Rejoice in the labor pains - it means a new baby - a new creation - is being born.

The Spiritual Perspective. Much of what we say above applies here as well. There is a need for transformation and detox of the emotional life - the habitual emotional habits and patterns - the emotional attachments to family that are perhaps pathological. But this can be difficult and demanding work. It can be very time consuming, especially with the deeper patterns. So many people need a push to do the work - a cosmic shove. And, this is what this transit is about. It is a push to get you to do things - the emotional house cleaning - that long needed doing.

Transiting Pluto Opposition Sun

A difficult and long term transit, whether it occurs in the Natal or Solar Return Chart. You have had this transit in past Solar Returns and will likely have them in future ones too. So, these trends have been going on for many years now and will continue for some more years. But now, because the aspect is exact, it is most intense. In general your will, your way, your ego, self esteem and self confidence is being challenged by intense and powerful forces in the environment. Perhaps this comes on the financial level - perhaps it is debt or taxes that prevent you from "doing what you love" and from "shining the way you like to shine". Perhaps it is the investors in your business. Perhaps competitors. Your innate "star quality" is being tested. This is a time for refining and transforming your sense of "I Am". Best if you do this on your own - voluntarily - as the process will be more comfortable. If you don't do this voluntarily, others will force you do it. You need to define who you are or others will do it for you. And this is not pleasant. Libido and overall energy will not be up to its usual standards and sometimes, sexual issues, reduce self esteem. Personal creativity will come under attack, and the challenge is to continue being creative in a hostile environment. Don't give up. Often there will be problems with men or with children - their difficulties impact on you. This is a time for transforming your attitudes towards creativity, men and children. False ideas, attitudes and actions will be revealed now so that you can take corrective actions. It seems harder to experience the "joy of life" these days. Perhaps there has been a death or near death in the family (but many other things in the Horoscope can modify this.) Perhaps the men in your life - or an important male figure - have undergone a surgery. But the joy of life is still there if you are willing to accept it. On a health level the heart needs more attention.

The Spiritual Perspective. Your true and divine I Am never needs adjusting or detoxification, so it is only your "ideas" or "concepts" of your Immortal Nature that are getting detoxed these days. Who you really are far transcends your highest dream or highest concept. So, the end result will be good. Lower ideas (no matter how lofty they seem to you) need to "die" so that a truer and loftier "I Am" can manifest. Often this aspect brings an "ego death" - not a literal one. The ego dies and becomes resurrected on another level. It is an important spiritual initiation that is happening now.

Transiting Pluto Opposition Mercury

A difficult and long term transit. In the Natal this has been going on for many years now. In the Solar Return Chart it is only valid for the current year. Your concepts, thinking and ways of communication are undergoing long term transformation and change. But this is deep transformation. You are shown, perhaps in painful ways, the inadequacies of your current ways of thinking and speaking. The old intellect is going to die and be reborn in a new way. Haphazard, ill researched and unconscious thought, is going to be unearthed and revealed for what it is. On a health level, you need to take better care of your intestines, lungs, arms, shoulders and respiratory system. On a more mundane level, this transit can show problems with your car, computer, modem, faxes and communication equipment. Often there are problems with the mail or the post office. The way to handle this transit is to "agree quickly with thine adversary" - analyze your thought processes from the point of view of the opposition. You may see weaknesses that you didn't know about. On the other hand, you may also find strengths there too. But this practice will help you weed out mental and intellectual debris.

The Spiritual Perspective. Much of what we say above applies here too. Your mind and thought process is being "renewed" and this doesn't happen overnight but as a process. Your are being "born again" on the mental level. It is going to happen one way or another, but you can reduce the unpleasantness (the labor pains) by cooperating with the process rather than obstructing it. Your mind and intellect, which up to now, could have been your spiritual adversary, is now going to become your spiritual friend and ally. If you can assist in this "mental detox" by ridding your mind of error - the major pathology of the mental body - you will speed up the process. Look at your thoughts and ideas from the Higher Spiritual Perspective - are they really true? Sometimes True? Once in a while True? Totally false? Just your conscious attention will reveal these things and they will lose their power over you.

Transiting Pluto Opposition Venus

A difficult and long term transit. If this is to the Natal Horoscope, these trends have been going on for some years and will continue for many more years. In the Solar Return Horoscope, this transit is only in effect for the current year. Pluto's purpose, spiritually, is to transform and renew - to eliminate impurities and give birth to the love life and relationship that you long for, yearn for, and deserve. But this ideal love cannot happen so long as there are negative, destructive, untrue, or impure concepts, thoughts, and behavior patterns in love. Pluto is setting this right and it probably isn't pleasant. Transformation is a messy business in any area. It is not color coordinated, with harmonious music playing in the background - it can get down and dirty and painful - it is more like child birth than anything else. One goes through the unpleasantness of the transformation process, because one knows that (just as in child birth) the end result will be beautiful. Pain and discomfort is the price we pay for this. So your love life, relationships, friendships and love attitudes are all undergoing deep transformation. The end result will be beautiful - a new love life, a new social circle, a new relationship - and it will be better than what you had before. So patience and fortitude while this process is going on. Some of the phenomena we often see is the death of a present love relationship - or a severe testing of a current relationship. Your love attitudes are under attack by either the partner or others. You feel that you are being coerced lovewise and socially (in friendships). Sex and money are often the causes for the inharmony. Perhaps you are in relation-ships that are uncomfortable and you see no way out. You have to change. The correct way to change is to work on the errors in your own mind and heart. When these are eliminated, the love life will straighten right out. Often, friendships are ended and new ones begin. You are having a "born again" experience in the love and social life.

The Spiritual Perspective. Much of what we say above applies here. The love life and love attitudes require transformation and "detox". This is not punitive but for your personal benefit. But few will undertake this hard work, unless there is a goad - and that is the purpose of this transit. You can make things a lot easier by surren-dering your love life to the Divine and letting it have its way. Those who are cooperating with the process will feel a minimum of stress. Those who resist will have major dramas and crises in love.

Transiting Pluto Opposition Mars

A difficult and long term transit that has been in effect for many years and will continue to be in effect for more years to come. You seem involved in a war - a power struggle. Your courage and independence are at stake. Your ability to act independently is under attack. There is strong and determined opposition to your athletic interests. Sexuality can be overdone or underdone. Your courage is being tested. But this is all surface phenomena. What is really going on is a complete transformation of your sexuality, sexual attitudes and your physical and athletic abilities. Athletes will completely change their performances by the time this transit is over. Military people will change their strategy, tactics and approach to these issues. You will have a truer sense of courage by the time this transit is over. Sometimes there are near death experiences under this transit. Healthwise, the sexual organs need more attention.

The Spiritual Perspective. Your sexuality and use of your energy has needed a detox for a long time. Impurities have crept in. Perhaps you have procrastinated in cleansing and clearing this area of life, so now, the Divine forces the issue. It presents you with situations that you cannot ignore - you must do the detox - physically, mentally and emotionally.

Transiting Pluto Opposition Jupiter

A difficult and long term transit. In the Natal Chart these energies have been going on for some years now and will continue for some more years. In the Solar Return, this transit is only valid for the current year. A complete and total transformation is going on in two important areas of your life - your finances and wealth attitudes, and in your religious and philosophical life. Because this transit is a stressful one, this transformation is probably unpleasant. The lessons are coming to you in the form of challenges, rather than in pleasant ways (but other things in your chart can modify this.) Ultimately, the Great Transformer's intention is to renew and rejuvenate both your finances and religious life and beliefs, but before renewal comes there needs to be a death - a change. Impurities in these areas need to be flushed to the surface. Errors, false beliefs, negative patterns and attitudes need to come up and be revealed for what they are - and then dealt with. This is usually not pleasant. The impurities come to you in the form of "challenging situations" or people. But these are really inner states clothed in form and you need to see them for what they are. Often, under this transit, the native will face financial crisis - perhaps a near death experience in finances - a near bankruptcy or other crisis. Much depends on how the native has conducted his or her financial affairs. If financial affairs have been seriously mismanaged, this transit can bring an actual bankruptcy. Often there is a large expense, a tax bite, or insurance expense that puts a dent in the bottom line. There is a need now to balance one's own financial interest with those of others - especially partners or shareholders. One cannot go too far either way. On the surface it would seem that the interest of partners and shareholders are opposite and antithetical to your own - but this is only seeming. Somewhere there is a middle position and you must find it. This transit will also test your religious and philosophical beliefs. Axioms of faith will be tested by real life experiences. These testings are wonderful as they lead to new and higher - more realistic - positions. False beliefs will die and change - and good riddance too. True beliefs will survive.

The Spiritual Perspective. Much of what we say above applies here too. A detox of both the financial life and the "inner religion" has been needed for some time. Perhaps you delayed or procrastinated. Now the Divine forces the issue. What happens - generally unpleasant experiences - should be considered "revelation" rather than punishment. "This is what happens when you hold certain beliefs and attitudes - this is what it leads to". All of this will lead to a renewal, eventually, in your finances and religious life - but on a much healthier and better level.

Transiting Pluto Opposition Saturn

A difficult and long term transit. This has been going for many years now and will continue for some more years - but now the energy is most intense. (This is only so in the Natal chart, if this occurs in your Solar Return, the aspect is only in effect for the duration of your Solar Return - 1 year.) Your sense of order, reality and practicality is under attack and is in process of being transformed. The normal way you organize things - the normal order of your life - is probably not adequate and you will have to make important adjustments - perhaps even completely re-order your life in a whole new way. This is a time for learning where your normal order - your normal sense of reality - is inadequate and thus you will be able to make the improvements. On a health level you need to give more attention to your spine, knees, teeth, bones and overall skeletal alignment. The breakup of your personal order can create feelings of insecurity and fear. But this is temporary. You will create a new and better order. Management decisions are probably under intense attack. There is resistance and even fanatic opposition to your authority. Sometimes this transit brings the death or near death of elders, authorities, a parent, or boss - but other things in the Horoscope can deny this. In many cases, you've lived your life according to an established reality that you accepted - it might not have been your preference - but that is how you lived - now the rules are changing and there is some discomfort about it.

The Spiritual Perspective. Much of what we say above applies here. Your sense of order and organization is being "detoxed" by the Divine. It will probably "die" under this transit and good riddance. Pluto's spiritual message is that "death is unreal" - after death comes resurrection - a new and better and healthier order will emerge from all this.

Transiting Pluto Opposition Uranus

This is a difficult and long term transit, whether it is in the Natal or

Solar Return charts. These trends have been going on for many years and will continue for some more years. Chances are that you have had this aspect in past Solar Returns and will have them again in future ones. Often this shows the death of a friendship or the actual death of a friend - but other things in the chart need to confirm this. Sometimes it shows that a friend, or organization that you are involved with has a "near death experience". An invention or innovation that you are working on either dies or has a near death experience. High tech equipment can "die" under this kind of transit too.

The Spiritual Perspective. Your sense of originality, your desire for freedom, innovation and experimentation in your life is undergoing deep transformation. Sometimes transformation happens harmoniously - through intelligence and understanding. Sometimes it happens through problems, situations and conflict - and this is probably the way it is happening these days. Certain ingrained patterns, beliefs or attitudes cannot be transformed in any other way - it is only the BIG situation that does it - that re-defines things - that clarifies things in your mind and produces change. This a time for reviewing your notions of personal freedom, originality, and innovation - are these real and true? Do you mask anger and blind rebellion behind these basically positive tendencies - are they merely fronts for something much deeper in you that hasn't been looked at? Are your innovations truly superior to the norm? Are they merely personal preference which you have elevated to some "divine status"? Are your innovations hurtful or helpful to others and to the world? Now you will find out. And, if so, these tendencies will be challenged. As this transit goes on, all kinds of phenomena will happen. It might, initially, make you more rebellious (or bring out more of the rebellion in people close to you) than before. And this could perpetuate the sense of conflict going on. But the purpose of this transit is not to take away your freedom or originality - but to cleanse and purify it so that it operates in the correct way - the way it was designed to operate - for your personal good and for the good of all around you and the world at large. There are many ways that this transit can play out (the houses ruled by Uranus and Pluto will play a big role here) - an invention comes under attack by others and perhaps has a "near death experience). Friendships will get tested and perhaps the death of a significant friendship. There will be upheavals in organizations that you belong to - and the organization could have a "near death experience" - a crisis of survival. Your understanding of science, technology, astronomy and astrology gets tested and will probably be revised. Powerful forces oppose your personal freedom and seek to limit it or distract you from it. Powerful forces might challenge your new and original ideas.

Transiting Pluto Opposition Neptune

A difficult and long term transit. This is so whether it occurs in the Natal or Solar Return Horoscopes. These trends have been going on for some years now and will continue for some more years - only now, the energy is most intense. This is an important period in your spiritual life. Great transformation is taking place here - in your attitudes, commitment, modes of practice, teachers and teachings, and ideals. And, this is as it should be. Now is the time when you find out how real your path, or teachings or ideals are. Can they stand the test of fierce opposition? Are they truly spiritual or merely deep psychological needs masking as spirituality? This is a time where you find out why certain ideals are not manifest in the world - as you come face to face with powerful antagonistic forces. These are not necessarily evil, but more concerned with survival. These forces might find your ideals or practices very threatening and you are dealing with the kick back of this. You might find it more difficult to meditate these days - as secret distractions - very subtle - divert your attention. You might find that you ideals are under attack and you are forced to defend them and this too is a distraction. Neptune rules your ability to transcend the mundane world, and you might find that this transcendence is more difficult to achieve these days.

Certain forces want to keep you "tied down" to this world and prevent your access to the spiritual realms. During this transit it would be normal to change teachings and modes of practice. Sexual urges could also pull you away from your spiritual practice and ideals. Your intuitive faculties will get tested too - probably through strong opposition. If the intuitions are real, they will be proven so in spite of the fiercest opposition. And, if they are not - the fallacy will be revealed. Intuition, dreams, and inner phenomena probably need more verification during this transit. But the end result is going to be a purification of the spiritual faculties and of your spiritual ideals and understanding. And this is a wonderful thing. It will lead to a spiritual renewal on a better and loftier plane.

The Spiritual Perspective. Much of what we say above applies here as well. A much needed detox of your spiritual life is happening. When it is over, you will soar to new and higher levels.

Transiting Pluto Opposition Pluto

This transit doesn't happen in one lifetime.

Transiting Pluto Opposition Ascendant

A difficult and long term transit - if this is to the Natal Horoscope. These trends have been going on for many years and will continue for many more years. If this transit is to the Solar Return it is only in effect for the current year. This transit shows great challenges to the self esteem and self confidence. These can come from relationships, the love life (if Pluto opposes from the 7th House) or from health and work issues (if Pluto opposes from the 6th House). If Pluto is opposing from the 7th House it shows that a current relationship or marriage or partnership is in crisis and the ego is under the gun because of it. The relationship can end, or merely have a "near death" experience. Sometimes it is the partner who is undergoing crisis and projecting his or her problems on to you. And, sometimes it is personal character flaw that is causing the crisis in the relationship. There is a need to transform the body, the image and the appearance in deep and dramatic ways. If Pluto is opposing the Ascendant from the 6th House chances are that health issues (often-times a surgery or detox regime) are challenging the ego and bringing changes to the body and image. Though this process is probably not pleasant the end result is good - physical transformation and a transformation of the self concept.

The Spiritual Perspective. Much of what we said above applies here. The body and image require some transformation and detoxing and since we rarely do things unless we are pushed, the cosmos supplies the push. Detox is rarely a pleasant experience, but the end result is good.

Transiting Pluto Opposition Midheaven

A difficult and long term transit - especially if this is to the Natal chart. If this is to the Natal chart these energies have been going on for some years now and will continue for some more years. Now, because the aspect is exact, the energy is most intense. If this is to the Solar Return Horoscope this transit is only in effect for the current year. Deep emotional and family changes - changes in the domestic and family pattern, are challenging your career aspirations - perhaps by distracting you from them. Because the feelings and the domestic life are being transformed, you are perhaps questioning your current career path and in all probability will change it. This doesn't mean that you will change careers per se (though sometimes it does happen) but more likely will change the way you pursue your career - or its current direction. Career attitudes will also get cleansed and purified. Every career is built on a psychological foundation - and these foundations are being revamped and renewed - while the "construction-deconstruction" is going on - career focus is not what it should be.

The Spiritual Perspective. Much of what we say above applies here

too. A detox in the emotional and family life is certainly bringing much needed changes to the career and to your life mission. There is a need to rid your self of "side issues" and distractions when it comes to your life mission. Perhaps these distractions came from the family or from emotional traumas from the past - perhaps they come from siblings or from false ideas. Whatever the cause, these are being removed. When the process is over you will have a new sense of purpose and clarity.

Transiting Pluto Trine Moon

A happy and long term transit that has been going on for many years now - and will continue for many more years. (This is so if this aspect is to your Natal chart, in the Solar Return, the aspect has been in effect only since your most recent birthday.) Psychic and emotional energy is very powerful and very strong. You have occult powers now. You visualize or feel a thing and it happens very quickly. Depth psychology and emotional transformation proceed in harmonious and successful ways. There is much emotional and psychological growth these days. Your psychological insights are penetrating. You see deep into people and understand why they feel as they do. Professional therapists are enjoying much success. The home and domestic situation is being transformed in a positive and harmonious way - into the image of your ideal. You have unusual ability to focus your psychic energy in a specified direction - either in meditation or to achieve some end. It is easy to borrow money for the home or for home improvements. Family type businesses do well - but other things in the Horoscope can deny this.

The Spiritual Perspective. A transformation and detox is happening in your home, emotional life and with the family - but it is happy and harmonious. You are not in resistance. You are giving birth to the ideal home and family situation. Transformation can be a messy business, but for you, these days it is harmonious.

Transiting Pluto Trine Sun

A happy and long term transit that has been going on for many years now and will continue for many more years. Now it is most intense as the aspect is exact. This is a long term phenomenon even if it occurs in the Solar Return Horoscope - for it has been happening for many previous Solar Returns and will happen for a few more. Ego and self esteem - basic self confidence - is unusually strong - especially if nothing else in the chart denies. You have secret and powerful support for your life goals. Sexuality will be stronger now - virility will increase in men. On a financial level you are attracting support - whether it be through loans, increased lines of credit, investors, or the spouse - for your life goals. People are willing to invest in you. Your star quality - in whatever field you're in - tends to prosper others. You are able to focus on your life goals. Your overall energy is stronger. Transformations that are occurring in the world and in your environment - which can be devastating for others - seem to aid you and push you further to your goals. You are very much in synch with the transformations that are occurring all around you. This is a period (its been happening for some years) where your career and life work are being transformed - but in happy and pleasant ways. The negatives are being eliminated - and rather easily at that. Obstacles are being blasted from your path - often without your knowledge. If nothing else denies, this is a healthy and successful period.

The Spiritual Perspective. Much of what we say above applies here too. A positive and healthy transformation is happening with your sense of I Am - obstacles to its true expression are being removed. Your light is shining brighter than ever. There is a greater understanding of death and its offices - dying to certain things leads to more life in other areas.

Transiting Pluto Trine Mercury

A happy and long term transit - especially if this is to the Natal

Horoscope. These energies and trends have been going on for some years now and will continue for some more years. In the Solar Return this transit is only valid for the current year. The mind and the communication abilities are more powerful these days. You have a new found depth and penetration to the mental process. The mind is deepened in positive ways. This is a period of strong intellectual advancement. The speech and writing are more eloquent and powerful and capable of affecting masses of people. Your ideas and thought process receive secret and underground support. Your writing and speech has much "buzz" to it - much "word of mouth" promotion. Your word and thought are more potent these days and the spiritual challenge will be to keep the words and thoughts positive and beneficial to others. Since the mind is more powerful, both the negative and positive thoughts are also more powerful and projected with greater energy. Thus, negative thinking can create more mischief now than usual. Important to stay positive - constructive. This is a wonderful transit for writers, teachers and marketing people - and if nothing else denies - bodes great success in these activities.

The Spiritual Perspective. Much of what we say above applies here. The mind and the thought process is greatly strengthened and so the challenge is to use this power constructively. Mental detoxing - a very important thing - goes much easier under this transit, you have less resistance to it. You cooperate with it.

Transiting Pluto Trine Venus

A happy and long term transit. If this is to the Natal Horoscope these trends have been going on for some years now and will continue for some more years. If this is to the Solar Return, this transit is only in effect for the current year. If nothing else in the Horoscope denies, this is a strong social and romantic period in your life. The social grace is strengthened. Your ability to attract others into your life is stronger than usual. If you like someone you will usually get him or her. Love passions are unusually intense these days but in a positive way. The negatives of too much intensity - jealousy and possessiveness - are generally absent. Sexuality is happier. This is also a period of greater prosperity. Borrowing power is stronger than usual. Others trust you with their money and are willing to back your ideas. Both the love and financial life is being renewed, regenerated and reborn in pleasant ways.

The Spiritual Perspective. Much of what we say above applies here too. A positive and happy transformation is taking place in your love and social life. Marriages are becoming more loving. Singles might marry. Friendships are becoming more harmonious and fulfilling. You are giving birth to your "ideal love life" and it's happy.

Transiting Pluto Trine Mars

A happy and long term transit. If this is to the Natal, this transit has been going on for some years now and will continue for a few more years. Now the energies are most intense as the aspect is exact. In the Solar Return this transit is only valid for the current year. Overall physical, athletic and sexual energies are very much "juiced up" - you are like an athlete on steroids. Sexuality will be very intense. (Whatever your age and stage in life - it will be stronger than usual.) Athletic performance will increase. Transformations happening in the world and in your environment will tend to increase and enhance your courage, sense of adventure and overall physical energy. You will be able to achieve more because you can do more. People who work with their bodies or in the construction or military trades will find it easier to attract investors or credit lines for their projects. If one is on the spiritual path, one becomes a warrior of light - fighting with the weapons of light. Someone not on the spiritual path will become more militaristic, argumentative, self willed, on a more mundane level. If nothing else denies, this is a period where you get your way in life. You are confident, brash, and easily bowl over the competition or opponents.

The Spiritual Perspective. Much of what we say above applies here. You have huge amounts of energy. Personal power is very much enhanced. How will you use it? There are problems that arise from "powerlessness" and there are problems that arise from power. With power comes greater responsibility. Abuse of great power brings great karmic kickbacks. So using what you have lawfully and justly is the challenge now.

Transiting Pluto Trine Jupiter

A happy and long term transit. This transit has been in effect for many years now (in your Natal Chart) and will continue to be in effect for years to come. Now, it is at its most intense. (In the Solar Return Chart this has only been in effect since your most recent birthday.) This is a beautiful transit for wealth. There is much secret support - underground support - for your wealth goals. Powerful and invisible forces are focused on helping you. If nothing else in the Horoscope denies, you will achieve (or have already achieved) large wealth and larger than life success. Your wealth goals support your sexual interests. You have wonderful ability to attract outside capital to your projects - either through borrowing or through outside investors. Debts are easily paid but also easily made. The money people in your life are supporting financial goals. You prosper others and you prosper yourself. Your wealth goals will tend to prosper others. Many people are mystified at your success as the reasons are all covert and not readily discernable. This is also a period of religious and philosophical expansion - intense interest in these things.

The Spiritual Perspective. You are giving birth to your true wealth ideals and the process is happening in a happy way - not through shocks, disappointments or traumas. Some childbirths go easy, some are more complicated - this one seems easy (but other things in the chart could complicate things.) The financial life is getting detoxed (also the religious and spiritual life - they go hand in hand) and it happens harmoniously. This is how transformation SHOULD happen. You seem non-resistant to the changes - you flow with them.

Transiting Pluto Trine Saturn

A happy and long term transit. In the Natal chart these trends have been going on for some years now and will continue e for some more years. In the Solar Return chart these trends are valid for the current year. But you could have this aspect in the next Solar Return too. Your ability to take charge of your life, to order, manage (yourself and others) and organize is greatly strengthened now. Your ability to discipline yourself and others likewise. You have a good sense of reality these days and you know when to push ahead and when to slow down. Your caution, sense of realism, and what some would call "fuddy duddyism" is actually sexy these days. Your management decisions receive secret and powerful support. There is also much underground support for your career aspirations - you might not even be aware of it. Push ahead boldly towards your career goals.

The Spiritual Perspective. The personal order that you set up in life - your daily routine - your sense of priorities - is a very important thing. As your goals change so does your "personal order". This is normal and natural. The change in "personal order" can be disruptive-painful-traumatic or it can flow easily and naturally. This is one of those latter times. You adjust very well to the changes. In fact the order that you are creating is really your own "ideal".

Transiting Pluto Trine Uranus

A happy and long term transit. Whether this transit is to the Natal Chart or Solar Return it has been going on for some years now and will continue for years to come. Basically, your inventiveness and originality is being strengthened. You can expect heightened mathe-matical, scientific, technological and astrological ability. Your urges to freedom, to experiment, to break with tradition in positive ways are supported by secret, underground forces. Society, the world at large, is being transformed in such a way as to support all these urges and powers in you. Your inventions and innovations have a secret underground market. Friendships go better now and you are making friends with people who wield secret power. Your understanding of science, technology, astronomy, astrology is being transformed and changed in a very positive way. Your fondest hopes and wishes are coming to pass in secret ways.

The Spiritual Perspective. You are more original and innovative - but how will you use this great gift? This is the challenge of this transit. Will it be constructively or destructively? Your scientific mind and understanding is being transformed and changed, but the transformation is happening harmoniously. You seem to cooperate with the process.

Transiting Pluto Trine Neptune

A happy and long term transit - whether this occurs in the Natal or Solar Return Horoscope. These trends have been going on for many years and are likely to continue for many more. Your spiritual faculties (ESP, Prophetic abilities, understanding) and ideals are being renewed and regenerated in happy and pleasant ways. The ability to meditate is much stronger. The ability to stay in contact with the Higher Power is much stronger. Your creative inspirations, channelings, and spiritual ideals are receiving secret and powerful support. Your spiritual nature is getting deepened in happy ways. Many obstacles are being cleared from your spiritual path, with little or no effort on your part.

The Spiritual Perspective. Much of what we say above applies here too. You are giving birth to the spirituality that you dreamed of - your own ideal - and the birth process is normal, natural and easy.

Transiting Pluto Trine Pluto

A happy and long term transit. This transit can only happen in the Natal chart. These trends have been going on for many years and will continue for many more years. Your efforts at personal transformation and reinvention are in synch with the times. You have secret help and secret resources. Libido (if nothing else denies) is also enhanced. You have greater ability to attract outside capital to your projects. You have more ability to make money for others and this tends to increase personal prosperity as well. For those on a spiritual path there is more ability to penetrate into the secrets of the cosmos - into past lives, and life after death. The normal fears of death that most people have are greatly assuaged these days - though other things in the Horoscope can deny this.

The Spiritual Perspective. Much of what we say above applies here too. All the natural "Plutonic abilities" are greatly strengthened and the challenge is whether you will put these to constructive or destructive use.

Transiting Pluto Trine Ascendant

A happy and long term transit. If this is in the Solar Return it is only in effect this year. You are in process of transforming your body, image, personal appearance and self concept. This transformation goes well - in harmony and order. Diet and detox regimes go well and are harmonious. You are sexually magnetic to the opposite sex. You exude sex appeal - perhaps unconsciously.

The Spiritual Perspective. Much of what we say above applies here. Detox and personal reinvention can sometimes be a messy business. Much old and effete material needs to come up, be looked at, confronted, digested and then eliminated. But now this process goes smoothly - as it should. You are not resisting the process but flowing with it and this makes it a lot easier. A new body and image - a new you is being born.

Transiting Pluto Trine Midheaven

A happy and long term transit - these trends have been going on for many years (if this is to the Natal Horoscope) and will likely continue for many more years. In the Solar Return chart, this transit only reinforces the essential nature of the chart and is only in effect for the current year. You are in a very strong career period. The ambitions are intense and pursued with one pointed zeal. You are focused on your outer aspirations and life work and purpose. This intense focus will often lead to success in its own right. Your efforts at self transformation (which can often be a messy business) help rather than hinder your career success. Your sexuality and sexual interests also seem to support the career. Also your interest in the deeper things of life - depth psychology, life after death, reincarnation and the like - also seem to further the career.

The Spiritual Perspective. Your career path is getting transformed and detoxed. But the process is happy and harmonious (unless other things in the chart deny). You seem to flow with the changes. A new career path or project is being born.

Transiting Pluto Sextile Moon

A happy and long term transit. In this Natal chart this has been going on for some years now and will continue for many years to come. In the Solar Return it is only valid for the current year. The cosmos is bringing you positive and happy opportunities to cleanse, purify and renew both your emotional and domestic situation. There are also opportunities to renew and resurrect your family relationships - to reform them on a better level. In general there is much psychological progress happening. Your insights into moods, feelings, emotional states, family relationships are deepening - most importantly, if nothing else denies, these insights are happening harmoniously. Probably you will do physical renovations of the home under these transits - at least the opportunity will be there if you want it.

The Spiritual Perspective. Much of what we say above applies here as well. You are being given opportunity and encouragement to detox your emotional life and family relationships. If you take the opportunity you can renew and rejuvenate these areas on a higher level.

Transiting Pluto Sextile Sun

A happy and long term transit whether it be to the Natal or to the Solar Return. You are receiving secret, underground encouragement and support to do what you really love to do. Your self esteem and self confidence is also stronger. In general the libido and creativity will be stronger. You will have more opportunities to do what you love to do and to do things that make you shine. In general this is a good aspect for health and overall vitality.

The Spiritual Perspective. Much of what we say above applies here too. You have opportunities to detox your sense of "I Am" - to rid it of encrustation and side issues. Thus, you can renew and rejuvenate your sense of self and shine all the brighter. The Cosmos makes it easy for you to do this.

Transiting Pluto Sextile Mercury

A happy and long term transit. If this is in the Solar Return it is only in effect this year. This transit deepens the mind and increases the concentration. You have opportunities to delve deeply into your studies - to learn about things in a very deep way. Your ideas, mental process, and style of expression can influence masses of people, excite sexual interest, and attract outside investors.

The Spiritual Perspective. Much of what we say above applies here. You have opportunities to detox the mind and the thought process - to rid the mind of false and irrelevant thoughts and ideas. When this happens the thinking will naturally be better, more powerful, and the judgement will be more sound.

Transiting Pluto Sextile Venus

A happy and long term transit. In the Natal chart this has been going on for some years and will continue for some more years. In the Solar Return it is only valid for the current year. This is a very positive love and social transit. The sex life will tend to be good. There will be good sexual exchange with the beloved. There are opportunities for intense, passionate kinds of love. Unless other things deny, it is the sexual magnetism that promotes the love. The social grace and the love vibrations will tend to be stronger, concentrated and one pointed. This focus and intensity tends to bring social and romantic success.

The Spiritual Perspective. There are opportunities - and happy ones - to detox and transform the love and social life - the love and social attitudes. And these things will tend to be harmonious. You are not resistant to the process - which is usually the cause of most suffering - but flowing with it. You have opportunities to give birth to the ideal love life - whether you are married or single.

Transiting Pluto Sextile Mars

A happy and long term transit. If this is to the Solar Return it will only be in effect for the current year, but if it is to the Natal, these trends have been going on for some years and will continue for some more years. Now, the effect is strongest as the aspect is exact. In general this is a good aspect for libido and athletic performance. You have secret support and encouragement for these kinds of activities. Overall energy is increased, and in general, this is a good health aspect - though other things in the Horoscope can deny this. Your courage and independence is stronger than usual - if nothing else denies. Extra energy gives you the firepower to achieve your goals - or to at least make good progress towards them.

The Spiritual Perspective. You are being given opportunities to detox, rejuvenate and renew you sexual attitudes, sex life and physical body - also your athletic performance and abilities. These are happy opportunities and should be taken.

Transiting Pluto Sextile Jupiter

A happy and long term transit if it is to the Natal Horoscope. In the Solar Return it is only valid for the current year. In general this is a nice prosperity transit. Your financial goals are receiving secret help and encouragement. You will have opportunities to attract outside investors and outside capital. For those in the occult or spiritual field, occultists and occult powers will enhance the wealth. In depth psychology will also help to transform the financial attitudes for the better. This transit also impacts on the religious life - the philosophy of life, the world view, the metaphysical belief systems are deepened and supported. New research supports what you have always believed to be true.

The Spiritual Perspective. The Divine is giving you opportunities and encouragement to detox, purify and renew both your financial and philosophical beliefs - they are both related.

Transiting Pluto Sextile Saturn

A happy and long term transit. Whether this occurs in the Natal or Solar Return chart, this has been going on for some years now and will continue for some more years. You have wonderful opportunities - and encouragement - to change and eliminate rigid routines, irksome barriers and blocks in your life. There are opportunities to update and transform your sense of order and organization in more positive ways. Your overall ability to take charge of your life, to order, organize, administrate things is stronger than usual. Your sense of order and reality gets secret support. Positive, well thought out management decisions will turn out better than you thought - providing nothing else in the Horoscope denies. Your ability to succeed through sheer merit is stronger.

The Spiritual Perspective. The process of transformation is not all "sturm and drang" - there are pleasant and easy periods to this too. You seem non-resistant to the transformation process happening and so the needed changes happen harmoniously. The transformation process is not destroying your ability to manage, order and organize, but actually enhancing it.

Transiting Pluto Sextile Uranus

A long term and happy transit. Your originality, freedom loving urges, experimentalism and urge to break barriers receives powerful and secret support. This is a time where there will be opportunities to raise financing, attract investors, or even borrow to finance new inventions or new ideas, The spouse or partners see financial merit in your originality or new inventions and are willing to back them. In other cases, you find that you have the financial wherewithal to lead a freer type lifestyle.

The Spiritual Perspective. Though the Truth is One, we all come here to express it in our own unique way. Correctly understood, this uniqueness is not "eccentricity" but a great gift which should be expressed correctly. Many don't express it out of fear. Many over express it from other psychological motivations. Now the Divine grants opportunity to purify and renew this aspect of your self, so that you can express it correctly. When correctly expressed these urges are a true service to humanity.

Transiting Pluto Sextile Neptune

A happy and long term transit. This is so whether it occurs in the Natal or Solar Return Chart. The trends have been going on for many years and are likely to continue for many more. This transit strengthens the spirituality and is especially favorable for those on a spiritual path. Those who are not on a spiritual path could embark on one during this transit. The power to focus and meditate is greatly strengthened. There is greater ability to access spiritual

states and to transcend the mortal world. The overall idealism, chari-
tableness and desire to relieve suffering is stronger. Those who are
not on a spiritual path might find themselves more involved with
altruistic (hopefully) causes and mass movements.

The Spiritual Perspective. What we say above applies here too.

Transiting Pluto Sextile Pluto

A happy and long term transit. This can only occur in the Natal
chart. Your sexual, financial, transformation urges are in synch (and
receiving support) from the current sexual, financial and transformation forces. Your ideas and attitudes to these things are in style
and are thus stronger. You have less opposition to overcome (but
other transits could deny this). Thus you have more ability to
reinvent yourself than normal. Your ability to make money for others
is stronger than usual. And there is greater access to outside capital
or outside investors. If nothing else in the chart denies, you have a
good feeling for bonds and the bond market. You are a savvy
shopper for loans and mortgages.

The Spiritual Perspective. The transformational, transfigurational
power of the being is greatly strengthened now. Your ability to take
lemons and make lemonade is greatly enhanced. Sexuality is
enhanced. How will you use this power?

Transiting Pluto Sextile Ascendant

A happy and long term transit - especially if it is in the Natal Chart.
In the Natal Chart, this transit has been going on for some years and
will continue for some more years. In the Solar Return this transit is
only valid for the current year. Basically, you have opportunities
(and encouragement) to transform and reinvent your body, image
and self concept - these are happy opportunities. Some people will
transform their bodies through diet, yoga, Tai Chi, Euryhtmy,
meditation and other spiritual disciplines. Others will do it through

cosmetic surgery or through buying new wardrobes. But there is help in upgrading and transforming the image. Detox regimes are more effective now. You have the opportunity to adopt a new look and a new self concept.

The Spiritual Perspective. The Real Body is created in the image and the likeness of the Divine, but humans have obscured it with false concepts and habits. Now the Divine grants opportunity to purify, detox and renew this present physical body - to make it the way it was designed to be. This is not done by "adding" anything to it, but by removing what doesn't belong there.

Transiting Pluto Sextile Midheaven

A happy and long term transit. If this is in the Solar Return it is only in effect this year. You have the opportunity to enlist the aid of very powerful (and perhaps secret) forces towards your career goals. Reformers and rebels, occultists and psychologists, can aid your career quest these days - each in their own way.

The Spiritual Perspective. Perhaps your life mission has become clouded with side issues and irrelevancies. Now the Divine grants opportunity to purify this area of life. In the purification, renewal will occur.

Footnotes

1. Planets in Transit by Robert Hand

2. The Uranian astrologers use even more aspects than these, but this is a specialized branch of astrology.

3. This is a terrible word, and I can hear my teachers loudly complaining. In truth there is no such thing as metaphysics - it is only physics on a higher, more rarified level that can't be discerned by the five senses. I am using it for lack of a better way of expressing this idea.

4. Happily, the Hindus never fell into this error, and their Astrology was always part of their religion - always spiritual - always seen as a path to the Divine. The modern Western Astrologer would do well to study the Hindu Approach to it - the Kabbalistic approach would also be good.

5. We need not get hung up on words here. This term is used in a generic sense and not in a religious sense. Different religions have different names for this power - the Jews refer to it as "the Messiah Power" - Hindus as Krishna Consciousness. We are referring to a force in consciousness and not to any specific person or personality.

Dodona Books

ASTROLOGY, NUMEROLOGY AND GENERAL DIVINATION

The priestesses and priests received the oracles of the Dodona shrine through the rustling leaves of the sacred oak tree. The oracle was an early form of divination, and divination has existed perhaps as long as humankind itself. We use divination to foresee future possibilities, to answer questions about our lives, to explain the unexplainable, for revealing hidden dynamics in ourselves and others, for personal growth and to guide us onto the right pathway through life. Dodona Books offers a broad spectrum of divination systems to suit all, including Astrology, Tarot, Runes, Ogham, Palmistry, Dream Interpretation, Scrying, Dowsing, I Ching, Numerology, Angels and Faeries, Tasseomancy and Introspection.

If you have enjoyed this book, why not tell other readers by posting a review on your preferred book site. Recent bestsellers from Dodona Books are:

Palmistry: From Apprentice to Pro in 24 Hours
The Easiest Palmistry Course Ever Written
Johnny Fincham
Now anyone who wishes to can learn the secrets of Palmistry in this no-nonsense guide.
Paperback: 978-1-84694-047-7 ebook: 978-1-84694-644-8

Numerology Made Easy
Hilary H. Carter

2012. 666. Sometimes a number speaks a thousand words. This user-friendly guide to numerology teaches you to decode the language of numbers.

Paperback: 978-1-84694-717-9 ebook: 978-1-84694-718-6

Let the Numbers Guide You
The Spiritual Science of Numerology

Shiv Charan Singh

One of the oldest arts of Divination, Numerology can be found at the core of many religions. This book helps to rediscover the spiritual importance of using numbers.

Paperback: 978-1-90381-664-6

How to Survive a Pisces
Mary English

From the successful series on the signs of the Zodiac, *How to Survive a Pisces* helps you avoid common mishaps associated with relationships with a Pisces.

Paperback: 978-1-84694-252-5 ebook: 978-1-84694-658-5

The Syzygy Oracle
Transformational Tarot and The Tree of Life, The Ego, Essence and the Evolution of Consciousness

Heather Mendel

In image and word, this primer on Kabbalah, Tarot and conscious evolution offers daily spiritual practices for developing trust in our intuitive wisdom.

Paperback: 978-1-78279-160-7 ebook: 978-1-78279-159-1